POPULATION, ENVIRONMENT AND PEOPLE

EDITED BY

Noël Hinrichs

For the Council on Population and Environment

Foreword by René Dubos

McGraw-Hill Book Company
NEW YORK   ST. LOUIS
SAN FRANCISCO   DÜSSELDORF
JOHANNESBURG   KUALA LUMPUR
LONDON   MEXICO   MONTREAL
NEW DELHI   PANAMA   RIO DE JANEIRO
SINGAPORE   SYDNEY   TORONTO

POPULATION, ENVIRONMENT, AND PEOPLE

This book was set in Univers
by Allen-Wayne,
and printed and bound by Murray Printing Co.
The designer was Allen-Wayne.
The cover was designed by J. E. O'Connor.
The editor was James R. Young.
Sally Ellyson supervised production.

To the delegates
to the First National Congress
on Optimum Population
and Environment

The Council on Population and Environment, sponsors
of the First National Congress on Optimum Population and
Environment, is a national organization established to
promote public awareness of the nature of the population-
environment situation and to bring together people and
groups who are now dealing with particular aspects of that
situation, in order to achieve the general consensus and unity
of effort necessary to reverse the twin trends of overpopulation and the destructive use of the environment. The
Council is a non-profit corporation with headquarters at
100 East Ohio Street, Chicago, Illinois.

CONTENTS

FOREWORD

I was raised in a small farming village of France, with a population of 450 persons. Despite my early experiences of uncrowded country life, or perhaps because of them, I love crowds and cities. Furthermore I still find it difficult to believe, even though I know it to be a fact, that the world is now overcrowded. The immense majority of human beings, I suspect, are just as confused and ambivalent as I am in their attitude toward the population problem. All over the world the largest and most polluted cities are also the ones with the greatest appeal even though their inhabitants uniformly complain of congestion and pollution. Most educated people want at least three children, even though they know that families of this size inevitably spell a population crisis in the near future. Judging from contemporary behavior of all social classes in all countries, it seems unlikely that the population problem can be solved by a purely intellectual, analytical approach.

I have come to believe, in fact, that the very word overpopulation is so abstract that it cannot generate the kind of emotional response needed to motivate action. Academic studies of overpopulation usually deal with numbers and graphs, which do not relate to daily life and therefore do not convey a sense of urgency. Few are those among us who can convert mathematical formulations into a living experience. In contrast, population problems acquire emotional value when they are considered from the point of view of their effects on the life of people. And this is precisely the point of view taken by the contributors to *Population, Environment and People*. They deal with overpopulation, not as numbers of people, but rather with regard to its effects on the quality of the physical and human environment.

Consider, for example, the impact of a moderate increase in the U.S. population on the National Parks System. Between 1930 and 1970, the use of the National Parks increased fifty fold, from 3 million to 150 million visitors-days per annum. This spectacular increase has naturally resulted in much damage to the lands, waters, plants and animals of the Parks. The damage is not caused by gross mis-behavior on the part of the tourists but simply by the impact on nature of automobile traffic and camping practices. The U.S. popu-lation is of course larger now than it was in 1930, but the fifty fold increase in Parks use between 1930 and 1970 reflects primarily technological expansion and greater economic affluence.

The present book illustrates by many examples how human and environmental health are suffering from the synergistic effects of in-creased population size and technological insults. It describes also how the present destructive trends could be interrupted or even reversed by certain technical, social, and political measures. But it also properly emphasizes that what is most needed is a reformulation of our attitudes toward property, family, and ways of life in general. This does not imply a radical change in political institutions, but rather the acceptance of the self-evident truth that, in a finite world, growth cannot continue forever.

The wisdom of the ages has taught us, furthermore, that the optimum level is always much below the maximum possible level — whether in the size of the population or in the utilization of resources. Almost in-variably, the attainment of the maximum level is followed by some form of collapse. In most natural processes, an optimum much below the maximum is achieved through spontaneous checks and balances. In human life, the rejection of the maximum for the sake of the optimum requires conscious and purposeful self-control — based on factual information and on value judgments. Fortunately, the contributors to *Population, Environment and People* are as much concerned with value judgments as with factual information.

René Dubos
The Rockefeller University

INTRODUCTION

THIS IS A BOOK for the reader who already knows that population growth and the degradation of the environment have to be checked before they destroy the world — his world — as a habitation for human beings. He has heard this often enough, and he wants more than another reminder of impending calamity; in short, he wants to do something about it. But he is mature enough to recognize the complexity of the situation and to see that its resolution, however urgent, entails changes at least as great as those that accompanied the Industrial Revolution. He is suspicious of simplistic and utopian proposals for reversing the course of history, and at the same time he resents bland reassurances from government and industry that the situation can be remedied without radical changes. To this reader we offer no ready-made solutions, but we do say, with some reason, that there is a way of finding solutions, and we invite him to explore it with us.

The exploration should begin with a new look at the problem. Just what is the population-environment situation?

The answer, if we leave out a good many complicating factors, is that population is increasing toward a point beyond which the environment will not be able to sustain it, and at the same time the environment is being destroyed by wasteful and short-sighted economic practices.

This is true, but incomplete, simply because it does leave out the complicating factors. These become apparent as soon as we ask *how* the twin trends of population growth and environmental destruction are to be reversed, for we are dealing with human beings, and that means we have to take ethics and customs, politics and economic interests into account. They, too, are part of the situation; and it is not enough to say that we must revise our ethical beliefs and alter our social and economic behavior to fit the situation; we must also explain how this

1

is to be done, and done in ways that do not create more problems than they solve. Obviously an industrial system that provides us with secondary goods such as mass transportation only at the cost of such primary goods as fresh air and pure water needs to be overhauled, but it is an industrial system on which all of us depend, whether we like it or not. How can we reconstruct this system without throwing millions of people out of work? This is not to deny that it can be reconstructed; it is simply to recognize that the ecological revolution will take time, as did the Industrial Revolution.

Time, and something more. This "something more" is what should concern us at this stage of the ecological revolution. Call it consensus, meaning a sufficiently general agreement as to the nature of the situation and how we propose to deal with it.

As of now, this agreement is lacking. The situation is complicated by economic, political, ethical, and sociological factors that significantly increase the difficulty of resolving it, and even the experts disagree as to what relative weights should be assigned to these factors. And if we are candid, those of us who recognize the urgency of the situation and are committed to fight for the necessary changes will admit that we disagree about our particular ends. What is an optimum population? How much wilderness do we want? What kinds of cities? And what are our priorities? It is easy enough to say what we are against, but what we are for is another matter, and without sufficient agreement on the part of experts and leaders, what hope is there of engaging the still uncommitted majority in the necessary struggle?

These remarks are not intended to discourage the reader; on the contrary, it is by recognizing the existence of these disagreements as part of the situation that we begin to discern a way out. The way out lies through dialogue.

Perhaps the word has a tired sound; it has been used so often to denote mere talk or word-fighting or to cover up compromises to which no one gives more than a half-hearted assent, but there is no substitute for it, or for what it connotes.

Dialogue is communication undertaken for the sake of consensus. Thus it is not a means of promoting this or that opinion, however correct the opinion may be; any opinion advanced in true dialogue is subject to scrutiny; it is neither to be accepted unquestioningly nor rejected out of hand, but rather to be considered and developed as an hypothesis. The question is not whether the opinion is in itself true or false, but what its implications are. Dialogue implies listening as well as talking and a willingness to follow the argument wherever it leads.

It is not always easy to engage in dialogue. An expert, annoyed by the confident ignorance of a layman, may find it hard to take, and the layman, in turn, may resent the expert's reluctance to give simple answers to complex questions. But if dialogue is difficult, it is also rewarding, sometimes far beyond the expectations of the participants, for out of it come insights no one man, however brilliant, could have attained by himself.

Moreover, dialogue not only produces new insights and new ways of action; it also educes practical consents to those new ways. Our American Revolution is an example of what dialogue can produce in the area of politics, and it illustrates the mysterious power of dialogue to go beyond the anticipations of the people who engage in it. The Continental Congress of 1774 met to discuss reconciliation with Great Britain; its eventual result was the Declaration of Independence.

To be sure, dialogue is slow, and initially it is discouraging, for it begins by bringing out disagreements instead of the unanimity we are looking for. Merely practical men are apt to become impatient with it — and to go off to repeat their old mistakes. Dogmatists turn against it and denounce its evolving opinions as heresy. It can be exploited by propagandists and self-seekers, and it tends to wander from the issues and to bog down in irrelevance; for these reasons it needs a good moderator and informed participants.

Most of all it needs perseverance in the search for consensus; but if we do persevere we sometimes discover that the dialogue has suddenly taken a great leap forward and that we have arrived at a degree of consensus that would have seemed impossible a little while ago.

At this stage in the development of the population-environment movement dialogue is not entirely lacking, but by and large it has been neglected. There has been a great deal of talk and some action taken with regard to this or that aspect of environmental degradation and population growth — and we should remember that dialogue degenerates into stale theorizing unless it is accompanied by action — but as of now there is not enough communication between activist groups to prevent overlapping and even conflict of efforts.

More seriously, there is far too little dialogue between the experts, whose advice we all need, and between these experts and the general public. Most laymen who have become aware of the population-environment situation and have tried to inform themselves about it have been surprised — perhaps shocked is not too strong a word — to discover the apparent unwillingness of the experts to engage in dialogue with one another. We are all familiar with the sort of meeting or conference at which Dr. A delivers himself of a well-organized and even stirring speech and then departs to address another conference while Dr. B delivers himself of an equally good speech in direct contradiction to most of what Dr. A has told us. As laymen we are left with the job of reconciling the two conflicting arguments, a job both doctors would agree laymen are not capable of performing adequately. But this is almost the only point on which they do agree.

If we visit the universities, traditionally the *locus* for dialogue between experts, we discover a similar refusal to attempt the cross-fertilization of opinions. It is not C. P. Snow's "two cultures" that we find, but a proliferation of sub-cultures, all compartmentalized and each with its own peculiar language, a language usually not intelligible to the layman.

It is conceivable that the necessity, imposed by dialogue, of having to express oneself clearly would itself contribute to the progress of science; but that is not for the layman to say. Our concern here is to remind the reader of his need to engage in dialogue and of his right to demand of the experts who advise him that they, too, join in the dialogue. We need them and we suspect that they need us. As Talleyrand remarked, "There is only one person who is wiser than anybody, and that is everybody." The population-environment situation calls for all the wisdom we can muster.

THIS BOOK is the product of a dialogue that began in Chicago, one January day a couple of years ago, when four men and women were moved to discuss with each other the population-environment situation. All four — a minister, a doctor, a housewife, and a lawyer — had been active in working both for population limitation and for conservation causes; however, on that day in 1969 something new happened, in the form of a common recognition that the situation whose aspects they had been working to ameliorate was unitary and that unless it was treated as such, specific attempts to reform could have limited success at best. The catalytic agent in this case was Paul Ehrlich, whose book, *The Population Bomb,* had recently appeared, but the discussion that ensued was not confined to Ehrlich's arguments; it took into account various opinions, some of which conflicted with his. Presently the discussion was joined by other men and women with a diversity of backgrounds and interests but a common impulse to develop the dialogue they were engaged in to a point at which it could become public, open to anyone who was honestly concerned about population trends and the destruction of the environment. Under the leadership of Canon Don Shaw, its chief instigator, the discussion evolved into the First National Congress on Optimum Population and Environment, held in Chicago in June, 1970.

The Congress was unique — perhaps even historic — in that its delegates were representative of the broad spectrum of American interests and organizations. This was not a conference confined to experts nor a partisan group of the already-committed. It included many people who were suspicious of the ecological movement because they supposed it to be a gigantic distraction from immediate social problems. Their testimony was an invaluable corrective to any easy assumption that the population-environment situation could be rectified by the simplistic means of propaganda and good advice, however well-intentioned these might be.

The Congress did not attempt to gloss over the deep differences between groups; rather it brought them out into the open, on the grounds we have mentioned: the belief that the existence of these differences is part of the situation. But it did more than bring out disagreements; its great achievement was the creation of a climate of opinion in which the dialogue could develop and become effective. No one who attended the Congress will forget the sense of possibility it generated. For the first time there was a feeling that however difficult the ecological problem might be there were human resources for solving it. The courage to face the situation was rewarded as courage always is, by hope.

Obviously the Congress did not arrive at final conclusions. The dialogue is open-ended and must be so for a long time to come, but people who are impatient for concrete results may be sure that these will occur as the dialogue continues.

THIS BOOK is drawn from the expert testimony given to the delegates to the First National Congress by its resource persons and key speakers. Like the Congress it does not attempt to provide a neat set of final answers; on the other hand neither is it a haphazard collection of essays on ecological topics. It is a source book for the reader who wants to become an effective participant in the dialogue by discovering the scope of its subject-matter and the nature of the arguments that have been advanced so far.

This purpose explains the arrangement of the book and the selection of its contents. Part I is concerned with the nature of the situation as a whole. The contributions to Part II deal with the specifically human limiting factors involved in the situation, with the ethical, political, economic, and social realities that advocates of change must take into account. Part III considers practical ways of dealing with the situation as the dialogue develops. It can be read as a discussion of possible strategies and tactics for transforming general concern with the situation into effective action to resolve it. Finally, Part IV gives philosophic significance to the dialogue by placing the situation in its larger context and in so doing provides us with a better motivation than fear of calamity for engaging in the struggle that lies ahead.

We have tried to present the leading arguments of our contributors not only in an orderly fashion but also at sufficient length, so that they can be read as arguments rather than as abbreviated and disjunct statements of opinion. This has necessitated omitting from the book some of the papers that were presented at the Congress, not for lack of merit but because of the limitations of length imposed on any book intended to be useful to the general public. In no case has a contribution been omitted or altered to suit the editor's predilections. His function, as he saw it, was to be the impartial conveyer of the ideas that informed the dialogue at the Chicago Congress and which he believes will help it to continue.

THE BASIC PROBLEM

PART ONE

What is the crux of the population-environment situation? It would seem that this is the first issue we have to settle, but here at the very outset we find three widely divergent opinions.

For Paul Ehrlich what is crucial is unrestricted human reproduction. For him, this is the principal cause of the destruction of the environment. This being so, we should concentrate our efforts on reversing the world's population growth rate. Moreover, Dr. Ehrlich adds, the time is short.

Philip Hauser disagrees sharply. In his view, the problem to tackle is the maldistribution of our present population and the social maladies that arise from it. While he believes that the growth rate must eventually be reversed, he does not feel that overpopulation, in a purely numerical sense, is an immediate danger. If we treat it as such, we run the risk of seeing concern for our real problems replaced by general apathy and cynicism.

But there are more than two sides to the question. Raymond Dasmann sees the crux of the situation in the misuse of the ecosystems on whose functioning the human population depends. To his argument, for which he has adduced evidence dealing largely with land use — or misuse — we have added the testimony of Joel Hedgpeth, who deals with the misuse of the seas and coastal waters.

So we have a three-sided disagreement to reconcile, and the task will not be easy, for the arguments for each case are powerful; furthermore, each is representative of a considerable body of public opinion.

THE POPULATION CRISIS: WHERE WE STAND

Paul Ehrlich

With the publication of The Population Bomb *in 1968, Paul Ehrlich did more than any man since Malthus to produce a general public awareness of the population crisis. It is unlikely that anybody who reads this book has not also read that one — or remained unmoved by it. In the essay that follows, Dr. Ehrlich makes a persuasive restatement of the argument that underlies his most popular book. Here it is presented in juxtaposition with some conflicting arguments, not with the idea of confronting the reader with a choice of sides to take but to enable him to grasp some of the dimensions of the total problem.*

Paul Ehrlich is a Professor of Biology at Stanford University and a member of the Advisory Board of the Council on Population and Environment.

We are in grave, grave trouble. There are 3.6 billion human beings on the face of the Earth. According to our best estimates, there are somewhere between three and seven times more people than this planet can possibly maintain over a long period of time. We are able to sustain so large a population (mostly living in misery) at the moment only because we are burning our capital, a process that does not seem to appeal to industrialists in conducting their businesses but seems perfectly acceptable on a global scale. Non-renewable resources are being exhausted at a horrendous rate, and we are destroying the capability of the planetary ecosystem to renew the supply of renewable resources. One would hope that the human species could survive at least a few thousand years into the future, since it has survived for some four million years in the past. Today the prospects look dim.

The human population is not only too large, it is growing at a mind-boggling rate — about two percent per year. At this rate the population doubles every 35–40 years. Every year 70 million people are currently being added to this planet — every three years an equivalent of the United States to feed, clothe and house. In all the wars the United States has ever fought, from the Revolution through Cambodia, we have suffered about 600,000 battle deaths. World population growth now grows by twice that number every week.

Georg Borgstrom has described the world today as a vast network of slums in which there remain a few oases. Roughly 15 percent of the people in the world live in affluence. About 60 percent live in utter misery, and the remainder are on the border-line. Somewhere between one and two billion people are undernourished or malnourished today. Undernourished people receive too few calories; malnourished people lack some essential nutrients in their diets, most often high-quality protein. People sometimes ask when the food-population crisis is going to arrive. It has arrived. Last year it struck ten to twenty million people who died of starvation, some of them in the United States.

Hunger and malnutrition are most prevalent in the underdeveloped world, where birth rates are high and the majority of people live in poverty. Most vulnerable to both hunger and malnutrition are young children and mothers. Protein malnutrition in pregnancy, infancy and early childhood can result in permanent stunting of growth and damage to the brain, if the child survives. High infant and child mortality rates in part reflect the high incidence of malnutrition in underdeveloped areas.

If all the food produced was equitably distributed, and a minimum was lost between the fields and the consumers to pests and spoilage, there would probably be enough calories — just barely — to go around. But there would still be a shortage of high quality protein.

Propaganda often appears in the news media claiming that the world's greatest problem during the next decade will be "food surpluses." In fact these "surpluses" already exist in many places. The catch is that they are economic surpluses which have nothing to do with who is and who is not being fed. People are starving because they have no money to buy food. *Demand* for food is not the same as *need* for it.

In 1968 I attended a World Congress on Freedom from Hunger and heard a Filipino representative assert that new miracle rices would make the Philippines rice self-sufficient in 1970. Shortly after, the Filipinos put high price supports under rice and lower price supports under corn. This effectively priced rice out of the diets of many

Filipinos, and those people had to switch to eating corn. The result was that a great quantity of low quality rice was dumped on the world market at prices well below the domestic supported prices. The Philippines announced that they were now self-sufficient in rice. Simultaneously they pleaded with the United States for more loans because they were going bankrupt trying to maintain the price supports.

What about the Green Revolution? Even its most optimistic promoters assert that it can at best provide sufficient food increases for the next twenty years to keep up with population growth during that time. If no headway has been made in population control by then, we will only have succeeded in postponing the inevitable. Success for the Green Revolution is, however, by no means a sure thing; there are numerous complex social, economic and environmental obstacles to its success.

Overlying the submarginal food situation, and much more serious in many ways, is the problem of environmental deterioration. Human activities may so completely destroy the life support systems of our planet that its carrying capacity for humanity may be reduced to zero. There is some chance that we may already have gone beyond the point of no return.

One example of environmental deterioration is the situation regarding chlorinated hydrocarbons: synthetic molecules that are manufactured for various purposes, largely as pesticides, but also as industrial solvents. The best known chlorinated hydrocarbon is DDT, the original synthetic insecticide.

Chlorinated hydrocarbons have four important characteristics:

1. They are deadly poisons. They are biologically active to a high degree and in various ways, which is why they are such successful pesticides. They kill pests; they can kill you.

2. They are highly mobile. They vaporize into the atmosphere, cling to dust particles, and move all over the planet. DDT is found in the Arctic, the Antarctic, the oceans, everywhere.

3. They are very stable; not easily degraded into harmless materials. Because of their high mobility it is not known exactly how long DDT and its biologically active breakdown products will remain in ecological systems. If ten pounds of DDT are sprayed in your back yard, and ten years later five pounds are still there, that does not mean that the other five pounds have broken down into something harmless. Rather, it means that at least part of it has moved on.

4. They are highly fat-soluble. All living organisms contain fat. Consequently DDT and its chemical relatives are continually removed from the nonliving environment and absorbed by organisms. DDT can be found in the environment, not in rock or water, but in organisms.

Because of this unique combination of traits, DDT has contaminated all organisms, with no exceptions. Moreover, it is concentrated by food chains — that is, predators usually contain more DDT than herbivores, and herbivores have more than green plants. As a result, animals such as pelicans, eagles, and fishes that feed near the tops of food chains have begun to suffer reproductive failure from DDT poisoning.

Long-term exposure to DDT and similar compounds is undoubtedly a direct health threat to people as well. It may already have reduced the life expectancy of everybody born since 1945 by many years. Nobody knows, but there is enough evidence of serious effects to make biologists extremely nervous. That is not as dangerous, however, as turning off the earth's entire life-support system. Mankind has existed for millions of years with a lower life expectancy that we have been enjoying in this century; we can survive as a species with that. But we cannot survive without the ecological systems on which all life, including mankind, depends.

An ecological system depends, at least in part, on its complexity for stability. As the system becomes simpler, it also becomes more and more unstable. Many human activities besides the use of chlorinated hydrocarbons have the effect of destablizing the ecological system. Agriculture is a major one. When someone says, "why should I care about birds or tuna becoming extinct?" the answer is that this is not merely a symptom of damage to the system, it also simplifies the system. The removal of each species removes one more element of stability. Fundamentally, we are attacking a system that provides us with every bit of food we eat, that provides and maintains all the oxygen in the atmosphere, and that takes care of all the waste disposal. The dispersal of chlorinated hydrocarbons is only one kind of generalized assault we are making on the ecological system of the planet.

Another example of serious environmental destruction involves the subtle effects of air pollution. It shows similarity to the DDT story; most people are worried about the direct result of poisoning. This, of course, is something to worry about, but the subtle effects are probably even more important. One of these effects of air pollution is to alter the climate of the planet. Nobody can predict exactly what changes will occur, but historical events indicate how serious these could be. For instance, a single volcanic explosion similar to that of Tambora in Sumatra in 1815 might well produce the worst disaster mankind has ever seen. When the 1815 volcano exploded, it put roughly 150 cubic kilometers of dust into the atmosphere, enough to cool the earth to the point that there was no summer in much of the Northern Hemisphere in the year 1816. Enough pollutants have already accumulated in the atmosphere to cool the earth significantly since 1940, so that a modern Tambora would have a good head start. Imagine what cancelling one summer in the Northern Hemisphere would mean to the world today! There would be a great escalation of hunger even in the United States, because there is less than one year's reserve of food. Even ignoring the possibility of disaster, we are unquestionably accelerating climatic change, which inevitably reduces agricultural productivity.

Agriculture itself, particularly as practised in developed countries, contributes greatly to environmental deterioration in various ways. Besides pesticides, synthetic fertilizers pollute our fresh water systems and may ultimately destroy the soil's fertility. Agricultural activity also adds to air pollution, especially to dust in the atmosphere. In our frantic efforts to meet today's demands we may be jeopardizing our future ability to produce food.

The oceans, which today provide 20 percent of man's animal protein, are also threatened by pollution. DDT not only kills organisms at the top of the food chains, it has been shown to have serious effects on phytoplankton, which is the basic source of all the food from the sea. In addition, we are overexploiting many oceanic fisheries today. Some kinds of whales have nearly been driven to extinction. Some of the fisheries may soon follow unless some way can be found to control fishing policies.

Overexploitation is, of course, not limited to food resources. We are supporting ourselves by depleting resources such as fresh water, minerals, and fossil fuels. Water tables are being lowered in many parts of the world. We are consuming fresh water faster than it can be restored underground. Demand for water in the U.S. for agriculture and industry as well as domestic use is rising at such a rate that the country faces serious water shortages in the near future. Northern and southern California are already squabbling over the limited supply. Many vital mineral supplies will run out by the end of the century, or shortly after, if present trends of consumption continue.

The problems of environmental deterioration and resource depletion are largely caused by affluent, white Americans and their equivalents in Europe, the Soviet Union, and Japan. The fact that population growth in developed areas is slower than that in other parts of the world is insignificant in this context. The birth of every American baby is roughly fifty times the stress on the environment of this planet as the birth of every Indian baby. This estimate is based on power consumption figures, which are an excellent measure of the degree of pollution. The birth of every American baby puts roughly three hundred times the demand on the nonrenewable materials of the planet as the birth of every Indonesian baby (based on per capita steel consumption figures).

In a world where protein starvation is the most serious problem, the overdeveloped countries take seven units of protein from the protein-starved peoples of the world for every five units we return to them. In fact, the overdeveloped countries take one-sixth of the world's fisheries production from the Peruvians, many of whom are protein starved, and feed it to our dogs, cats, pigs, and cattle. In short, we are both the looters and polluters of the globe.

An array of potent possibilities for future disaster exists besides the obvious massive famines. For example, the human population today is the largest and densest the world has ever seen. It is also the weakest, since there are more *hungry* people today than there were people in 1875. With jet airplanes that take people from continent to continent in a matter of hours, this is a perfect set-up for a world-wide plague — most likely a virus plague. We came close in 1967 when a virus never before seen in man transferred from monkeys to laboratory workers in Marburg, Germany. In that medically sophisticated environment it was, fortunately, contained. The disease was extremely contagious, and before it was stopped 30 people contracted it; seven died. Imagine what would have happened if that lethal disease had escaped into the world, which as a whole is not well fed and lacks medical care. We came close — the infected monkeys were in the *London Airport* on their way to Marburg two weeks before the disease broke out.

Another very real possibility is thermonuclear war. One of the fundamental causes of wars is competition for resources, competition which is in part a function of population growth. Every time a person is added to the planet that competition is intensified. The ecological effects of such a war would almost certainly guarantee the end of civilization.

The world resource situation is the fundamental reason why American soldiers are in Southeast Asia. In one form or another there will most likely be an American presence there as long as we have a "cowboy" economy. Resources also underlie our policies in Latin American and our Middle East foreign policy. We are a resource-poor nation, which, with one-fifteenth of the world's people, uses some 30 percent of the natural resources consumed every year. We do not have those natural resources on our lands, so we must import virtually every resource we need.

This makes a very grim picture of the future. The human population is growing at a ridiculous rate, has far outstripped the resources of the planet, and the whole situation is compounded by environmental deterioration. What is being done about it?

So far, remarkably little has been done, despite a tremendous increase in rhetoric during the last few months. A first important step does seem to have been accomplished in the U.S.; public recognition of the crisis has reached a high level. Perhaps the man in the street does not understand the dimensions of the problems and the solutions they demand. But he knows we are in trouble. If the crisis is to be met, this is essential.

On the international front, the only visible positive action consists of the family planning programs established in some underdeveloped countries and the attempt to start a Green Revolution. Family planning is demonstrably ineffective as a method of population control in the absence of some effective way of persuading individuals to have an absolute maximum of two children. The Green Revolution may be very helpful in the food situation, but it cannot solve the fundamental problem. Much more effort should be put into both sorts of programs. Rather than engaging in futile wars and arms races, developed countries might usefully put their resources into helping their fellow passengers on our little spaceship.

But before Americans can begin to influence the population policies of other nations, we will have to control our own population growth and our environmental problems. President Nixon is extending family planning services to the poor; commendable, but unlikely to have a significant effect on population growth. The poor contribute but a small fraction of the total number of births. Nor are the poor, the Blacks, and the Chicanos the primary producers of pollution; they are the victims of it. Blacks and Chicanos have higher DDT levels in their tissues than the average U.S. citizen. Migrant farm workers in California are being killed directly by pesticides in the fields today.

The President has also established an Environmental Quality Council. Whether this can be effective in solving our environmental problems remains to be seen. So far the tendency of administration effort seems to be toward stop-gap efforts (such as secondary sewage treatment plants) which "solve" one pollution problem only to aggravate another.

Solution of the population-resource-environment crisis within the U.S. will require nothing less than profound changes in our way of life. First we need a firm commitment to population control. We need a presidential statement to the effect that we can no longer afford population growth; that no patriotic American couple should, from now on, have more than two children. Probably the U.S. birth rate can be reduced to a replacement level with a changed social climate, complete access to all forms of birth control, including abortion for everyone, and a few mild governmental measures to discourage reproduction.

There will be necessary adjustments to the resultant change in age structure. The average age of the population will rise from the late twenties to the late thirties. There will be fewer children and many adults will have to derive satisfaction from contact with other people's children. The situation for school systems would be much improved of course. There would be an opportunity to raise their quality rather than continually struggling to accommodate huge masses of children. They might also be able to expand and improve programs for adult education, which could be part of a solution for problems raised by the larger proportion of older people.

Today, largely because of the growing labor pool (the result of population growth), old people are often forced to retire long before their potentially active years are over. These old people are put into retirement ghettoes, neglected and isolated from society. Americans consider them a "problem" because they are not self-supporting and are so far out of touch with younger people. In a stabilized population, where forced retirement might become unnecessary and education could be a continuous process throughout life, there could be "swinging" old folks integrated into the society, rather than conservative old people put out to pasture.

There will also be some important economic changes. No one today can deny that the United States has the grossest national product in the world. Instead of predicting five hundred billion dollars more of it in the next fifty years, our President could have said that we already have too much product, that we can no longer afford an economy that focuses not on the *quality* of products or of capital, but on quantity and waste. We must abandon our obsolete "cowboy" economy, based on the idea that we can always foul our nest and move on. We need a transition to what Kenneth Boulding calls a "spaceman" economy, where goods are of high quality, where the recycling of materials is emphasized, where power companies will not simultaneously try to increase demand and then persuade us that they must destroy the country to meet that demand. We must minimize our demands on power and on the resources of the world.

Economics must come to encompass the real values of materials and energy sources which exist in finite supplies. It must also include the real costs to society of pollution from all sources. Other more accurate indexes of the national economic state than gross national product should be devised.

Together with people of other nations, Americans must now decide whether there will be a future for mankind. The choice is just that simple. We must unite to solve the crises of overpopulation and pollution, abolish war, try to create a decent life for all people. If we try, perhaps there can be a very exciting, challenging and rewarding future in the next century and beyond. But if we fail, at the very least, we can look forward to a new dark age.

ON POPULATION AND ENVIRONMENTAL POLICY AND PROBLEMS

Philip M. Hauser

Dr. Hauser, Professor of Sociology and Director of the Population Research Center at the University of Chicago, disagrees so sharply with Paul Ehrlich that the impatient reader may fail to note that in some areas they do agree; moreover, their major disagreements are not on whether this or that factor is contributing to the problem but rather on the relative weights to be assigned to each factor. For Dr. Hauser the population implosion and displosion — concepts he explains and develops in this essay —are more important and more in need of immediate attention than the population explosion. Both men are deeply concerned with the population crisis and committed to the task of resolving it, and to read Dr. Hauser's essay merely as an attempt to refute Dr. Ehrlich's argument is to miss the point.

Nevertheless, the disagreements between these two experts are wide enough to point up the need for further dialogue.

I have three objectives in mind in this essay. One, as a demographer who first taught a course in population over forty years ago I wish at the very outset to identify myself completely with the objectives of the First National Congress on Optimum Population and Environment. There is no question but that population is among the more serious problems which confront mankind, many aspects of population, as I shall try to indicate. Moreover, there is no question that the time is long overdue when men must deal with the problems of environmental pollution. This I should like to stress at the very outset because of some of the critical observations that I shall make.

Second, I should like to place the problem of dealing with excessive fertility and excessive rates of population growth in perspective, in a perspective which calls attention to other problems being generated by population phenomena of at least equal significance, which in the main have not yet attracted either national or world consciousness in a way that the problem of excessive fertility and growth rates has. In my judgment these other problems may be creating more human misery during the remainder of this century than excessive fertility and growth rates.

Third, I should like to call attention to some of the statements that have been made with respect to population problems and environmental problems which, in my judgment, although they perhaps have justification in having alerted the nation to the problems, may raise questions of credibility and may, if disillusionment should come, result in a short run aroused public becoming a long run apathetic one. This may be particularly true of the predictions for the 1970's — predictions that are not likely to be confirmed by the course of events.

Let us turn to a consideration of the framework within which the current discussion of population and environment should be cast.

THREE POPULATION DEVELOPMENTS
Man or some close relative of man has been on this planet for some four million years. During his occupation of the earth, man, as the only complex culture-building animal on the globe, has generated four developments which have more profoundly affected his values, his thoughts, his behaviorisms, his social institutions and his environment than anything else to which you might refer. These four developments, perhaps in dramatic language, may be termed the population explosion, the population implosion, the population displosion and the accelerated tempo of technological change.

These developments are interrelated. The population explosion has fed the population implosion. Both have fed the population displosion. Technological change has generally preceded social change and has been both antecedent and consequent to the other developments.

Most people now understand what is meant by the population explosion. But this understanding is a relatively recent achievement. It refers, of course, to the remarkable acceleration in the rate of population growth during the three centuries of the modern era in the present economically advanced nations; and during the post-World War-II period for the two-thirds of mankind in the developing nations in Asia, Latin America and Africa. We have, in effect, had two population explosions, and it is the latter one, of very recent origin, which is now gaining momentum and which harbors grave portent for the future not only of the peoples in the developing nations but also for the entire population of the globe.

By the population implosion I refer to the increasing concentration of the peoples of the world on relatively small portions of the earth's surface, a phenomenon better known as urbanization or metropolitanization.

In using the term population displosion I have taken an archaic word from the dictionary to refer to the increasing heterogeneity of peoples who share not only the same geographic locale but, increasingly, the same life space, social, political and economic activities. By heterogeneity I refer to the diversity of peoples by culture, by language, by religion, by value systems, by ethnicity and by race.

All three of these developments are of relatively recent origin. All three have generated unprecedented problems which plague this nation as well as the entire world.

Although we cannot relax in our efforts to decrease growth rates, it is necessary to recognize that there are other population problems of at least equal importance which must be dealt with simultaneously.

Man is the only culture building animal who has created a social world, a 20th Century demographic and technological world in which he is still trying to learn how to live. We are experiencing great difficulty in dealing with the problems that the new man-made deomgraphic and technological world has precipitated.

We have yet to develop in the United States or anywhere in this world a mechanism in government that is as responsible to our new collective needs for goods and services, as is the market mechanism responsive to private needs for goods and services. In the private sector the medium for effecting response by market mechanism is afforded by purchasing power, effective demand. For goods and services for which money is available the private sector is very responsive in the production of goods and services. On the collective front, which has been transformed by reason of the four developments to which I have referred, new needs have emerged, including the needs for an unpolluted environment, and for population control. But there is no mechanism very responsive to these needs.

Whereas money is the medium in producing response in the private sector, the medium for affecting response from government to meet collective needs, in this nation and throughout the world, seems to be demonstration, protest, violence, riots, and guerrilla warfare.

The problem areas of population control and of environmental pollution are, then, just two of the many other areas of collective needs that are not now being adequately met in the United States, or for that matter, in the world as a whole.

Let us next set forth the facts about all three of these population developments in the world and in the United States.

The World

For the world as a whole let me point out that it took most of the four million years that man has been on this earth to generate a population of one billion persons. That number was not achieved until about 1850. It required but 80 years to produce a second billion. Two billion was the world population in 1930. It took only 30 years to generate a third billion. Three billion was the world population in 1960.

Should present levels of fertility and the mortality trend continue, the world would have 7.5 billion persons by the end of this century, little more than one human generation away. Even with allowance for fertility reduction of the type assumed in the "high projection" of the United Nations, it is almost certain the world, short of the catastrophic, would have seven billion by the year 2000. That means in the next 30 years man will be adding to the population of this earth as many people as are now on the earth, the product of mankind from the beginning of time on this planet.

The world population implosion is also a relatively recent phenomenon. Mankind did not achieve permanent human settlement until as recently as the Neolithic Age, some 10,000 years ago. Man did not achieve enough in the way of technological development, on the one hand, and social organizational development, on the other, to permit cities the size of a hundred thousand or more until as recently as Greco-Roman civilization. Mankind did not achieve enough in the way of technological and social organizational development to permit the proliferation of cities of a million or more until as recently as the beginning of the 19th Century, only 170 years ago.

The prospect is that with present trends the proportion of the world population that is urban, using the definition of the United Nations of a population of 20,000 or more persons, will have increased from around a little more than 2 percent in 1800 to about 20 percent by mid-century,

1950, to perhaps between 40 and 50 percent, by the end of this century. That is a dramatically rapid transformation in population distribution and in the nature of man's life activities on this globe.

Next let us consider the global population displosion. This is a little harder to quantify for the world as a whole. We have always had diverse peoples on the globe as far back as we have had any data. But diverse peoples sharing the same life space — social, political, economic activities — as well as the same geographic area, and sharing them in a pluralistic society on an egalitarian basis is an even more recent phenomenon than the population explosion or the population implosion. Problems generated by the population displosion are manifest in the frictions of people still trying to learn how to live together. Witness the conflict between Protestants and Catholics in Northern Ireland, between the Arabs and Israeli in Western Asia, between the Chinese and Malays in Malasia, between Muslim and Hindu in India and Pakistan, among the various linguistic groups of Hindus within India, between white and black in the United States of America.

The United States

The three population developments are evident also in the history of the U.S.A. When our first census was taken in 1790 we were a nation of fewer than four million people. When our 18th decennial census was taken in 1960 we were a nation of 180 million. When the results of the 1970 census are announced as required by law in December of this year, we shall have become a nation of 205 million. Short of catastrophe we are almost certain to become a nation of 300 million by the end of the century. Thus, another 100 million Americans will be added within little more than a human generation — 30 years. This anticipated increment is in part attributable to the second Post-World War II baby boom now underway. Beginning in October, 1968, for the first time since 1957, the number of births each month has exceeded the births in the same month for the preceding year. We are now experiencing the echo effect of the first post-World War II baby boom as the issue of the first baby boom is entering reproductive age.

Moreover, for a number of reasons age at marriage, for the first time in several decades, has turned upward, as has also age of birth of the first child.

We may have countervailing forces to the new upsurge in births. The recession in which we now find ourselves tends to decrease marriage rates and birth rates, but the impact of the recession is almost certain not completely to offset this basic fact: that the women 20 to 29 years of age, those who are the most prolific reproducers, are increasing by 35 percent in the period between 1968 and 1975. In consequence even if birth rates do turn down some, we are still likely to have a second post-war baby boom. The population explosion in the United States is still under way.

Does this mean we require compulsory forms of family limitation? In my judgment, no. This is one of the current overstatements that I am afraid may produce boomerang effects.

Consider this important perspective. In 1800 the average number of children per completed family in this country was six. At the present time the average number of children per completed family is about three. On a purely voluntaristic basis we have diminished the number of children born during the reproductive life of couples by 50 percent. Moreover, if age specific birth rates at the present time were to continue to hold, the average number of children born per completed family would be about 2.5. Since, with present mortality, it requires 2.11 children per couple to produce a zero rate of growth, the United States at the present time is not much more than half to one child per couple away from a zero rate of growth. I am convinced, therefore, that we can achieve zero growth without sanctions and penalties of the type being advocated in some quarters.

Now let us turn to the population implosion in the United States. Understanding of the population implosion is a prerequisite to understanding the urban crisis with which we are afflicted and which is another example of collective needs not being met by reason of the insensitivity of governmental response.

When our first census was taken in 1790, 95 percent of the American people lived in rural places, on farms and places having fewer than 2500 persons. By our 18th decennial census in 1960, 70 percent of the population was urban and 63 percent metropolitan, as defined by the federal government, those living in central cities of 50,000 or more, and the counties in which they were located.

This nation did not become an urban nation in the sense that more than half of our people lived in urban places until as recently as 1920, when 51 percent resided in urban areas. Not until 1970 did this nation complete her first half century as an urban nation — a period less than one lifetime. Small wonder we have an urban crisis. We are still trying to learn how to live in this new demographic and technological world.

It is a virtual certainty that the hundred million persons we may add to our population in the next 30 years will go into urban places. In fact, more than all of them may go into urban areas because in the decade from 1950 to 1960, for the first time in the history of this nation, urban places recorded a greater increase than the total population increase of the United States. This is not a mistake in arithmetic on my part. What it means is that for the first time rural population actually decreased in absolute numbers between 1950 and 1960. Between now and the end of the century perhaps 70 to 80 percent of the population increment will go into our metropolitan areas. The population implosion is also still under way in the United States.

Finally, let us consider the U.S. population displosion. Without great elaboration let us recall that as recently as 1900 a little more than half of the American people, 51 percent, were native white of native parentage. The other 49 percent were either foreign born; second generation foreign born, the children of immigrants or mixed parentage; blacks; or members of other races. As recently as 1960, still our most recently published census, 30 percent of the American people, almost a third, were either foreign born, second generation immigrants, blacks or members of other races.

The consequences of the population displosion have become highlighted in this country during and since World War II because of the large internal migratory movement of blacks. The ongoing revolt of the blacks is the largest element of what euphemistically is called "the urban crisis" in the United States.

As recently as 1910 about 89 percent of all non-whites lived in the South. That proportion, incidentally, was only two or three percentage points below the concentration of blacks in the South in 1860, as recorded in the last census taken before the Civil War. By 1960, 40 percent of non-whites resided in the North. During this decade, we may pass the 50-50 point in the distribution of blacks between the North and the South.

What is even more significant for understanding the revolt of the blacks is the fact that in 1910, 73 percent of all blacks in this nation were rural, residing on farms and places of fewer than 2500 — largely in the rural slum South. By 1960, in 50 years, less than one lifetime, blacks have been transformed from 73 percent rural to 73 percent urban, and have become more urbanized than the white population of this nation. And with what preparation? Drawing again on the 1960 census results, 23 percent of all adult blacks, those 25 years of age and over, were functionally illiterate, had not gone beyond fifth grade, could not read a metropolitan newspaper with ease. This was their share of the American heritage. The population displosion is also still under way in the United States.

PROBLEMS GENERATED

The population explosion has generated some of the problems which account for the convening of the First National Congress on Optimum Population and Environment. There is little need to list all of the problems which affect the world and the nation by reason of excessively high fertility and population growth rates. In the developing nations in Asia, Africa and Latin America the major problem is to be found in the way in which explosive population growth obstructs economic development and therefore precludes the achievement of national aspirations for higher levels of living. Moreover, the peoples in the developing nations may be faced with problems of actual survival. In consequence, for at least the remainder of this century, it may be anticipated that there will be more not less social unrest, more not less political instability, and more not less threats to world peace.

In the economically advanced nations, including this nation, the population explosion does not raise questions of actual survival — certainly not in the short run — say to the end of this century. But it does raise serious questions about the quality of life, already seriously impaired. A few examples may be cited to document this assertion. Deleterious effects on the quality of life in the United States are certainly in evidence as a result of our first Post-World War II baby boom. The tidal wave of post war babies inundated the schools — primary, secondary, and higher — in turn with visibly adverse impact on the quality of education. The baby boom has produced drastic changes in our age structure with serious consequences throughout the American society and economy. At the present time the United States is experiencing a labor force explosion as another echo effect of the baby boom, with the economy unable to absorb bulging new entrants to the labor force — especially the youngsters of disadvantaged minority groups.

Another consequence of the baby boom is evident in rising rates of delinquency and crime. Most of us are aware of statements made by police authorities that delinquency and crime are increasing much more rapidly than the population. To a demographer this is a naive statement, because delinquency is not the product of the total population but rather of specific age groups. Moreover, crime is also disproportionately the product of relatively young age groups. What is significant to understand increasing delinquency is the fact that during the 1960's youngsters 15 to 19 years of age, by whom definition delinquency is committed, increased by 42 percent. Even if delinquency rates remained the same there would be a 42 percent increase in delinquency during the 1960's by reason of the increase in the size of the age group. We did not, however, provide for a 42 percent increase in police, or in reformatories, or in other agencies which deal with the problems of delinquency.

Consider still another example of the impact of the changing age structure. Persons 10 to 25 years of age increased by 55 percent during the 1960's, after a decrease, incidentally, of about three percent during the 1950's. During the 1950's persons of this age group actually decreased in absolute number because they were the product of the low birth rate of the depression decade, when the bottom fell out of the marriage and baby markets as well as the stock market. This is why automotive insurance companies have discovered what reserves are for. In our society there is virtually nothing more dangerous than a young male under 25 years of age behind the wheel of an automobile. We are now slaughtering 55,000 people a year with automobiles.

There are many other examples of diminished quality of life in the United States by reason of excessive population growth. Consider the drastic changes which have occurred since 1950 in persons per square mile of national parks and forests, inland waters, coastline and other recreational facilities. Consider "the commuter's crises", parking problems, and increasing harassments of everyday living as queues get longer and longer. Consider the longer run consequences of the exhaustion of non-renewable resources and the ultimate limit to be imposed by the limitations of space. We are faced with rapidly increasing numbers of people but with finite, limited space.

The First National Congress on Optimum Population and Environment is concerned primarily with the problem of excessive fertility and high growth rates. In the United States, we may add 100 million people in the next 30 years. There is definite need further to diminish the birth rate even though we are perhaps not more than half to one child per couple away from a zero rate of growth. There are two specific things to be done to dampen our fertility.

First, the problem of higher national growth cannot be attributed to the disadvantaged, the poor, the undereducated, the minority groups who have large families. Their contribution to total growth is relatively minor.

The major contribution to the high national growth rate is to be traced to the dominant, white, middle-class people having third and fourth children. It is the third and fourth children of middle class America that spells the difference between the explosive growth during the remainder of this century and a lower zero rate of growth.

What about the disadvantaged minority groups? How can they be induced to decrease their birth rates? On this subject we are faced with the same problem that the whole world is faced with in respect to the diminution of fertility in the developing regions of the world. I have just returned from three months of population study in Asia and Africa. We do not know yet whether present family planning methods are going to achieve their objectives. We do know this: There has never been a people on the face of this earth that having acquired education and a higher level of living did not decrease their birth rates. We have yet to discover whether it is possible for a people mired in illiteracy and poverty, isolated as a subcultural group, and living in a traditional type of society, to decrease their birth rate.

Within the United States I am convinced of this: There will be no problem about decreasing the birth rate of the poor and the uneducated when they get the opportunity fully to participate in the American society and economy. It is doubtful that the proliferation of birth control clinics and the distribution of contraceptives alone will be enough. The problem is one of changing the social milieu of these people and admitting them to full citizenship in the United States.

Let us next turn to other kinds of population problems, which I insist are at least as important as the problems of excessive population growth and environmental pollution.

Consider the problems being generated by the population implosion, the problems of "the urban crisis." The population implosion has generated many physical problems of which air, water, and general environmental pollution are just examples. What about surface and air congestion, what about inadequate recreational space, what about the inadequate supply and quality of housing, what about, above all, the urban slum, the ghettos? These are physical problems, problems of manmade or adapted environment which, in my judgment, are at least as important as environmental pollution. In my judgment it is at least as important to eliminate the slums of Chicago and the slums throughout the United States as it is to save Lake Michigan. It may well be that the solution of these types of problems is more important than saving Lake Michigan in determining whether the United States during the rest of this century remains a viable nation.

In addition to the physical problems precipitated by the population implosion, consider the personal and social problems. These include the problems of crime and delinquency; of alcoholism and drug addiction; of the revolt of youth, characterized at one extreme by youngsters who cannot cope and therefore seek forms of retreatism as the hippie and, at the other extreme, by youngsters who cannot cope and therefore become activists who in their frenzy, unhappily or happily, are now blowing themselves us with bombs intended to destroy "the establishment".

The population implosion has also exacerbated the problems, manifest in the revolt of women, because it is urbanization that is transforming the role of women, may I say dramatically, from that of female to that of human being. This is what the feminist movement is all about, again a manifestation of the transition from what Redfield calls "the little community" to what Mannheim calls the "mass society".

Consider also the economic problems generated or exacerbated by the population implosion. These include the problems of unemployment, of underemployment, of poverty, of the exploitation of the consumer. There are, in addition, governmental problems associated with urbanization. Included are the relationship in this country of the federal, state, and local governments; of the relation between government and the social and economic order; of fragmented political entities in metropolitan areas. We in this nation are still afflicted with the 18th century form of local English governments. England has long since gotten rid of its impact but we are still stuck with it, as a result of which it is almost impossible to deal with the problems arising from the new form of collective living we have created — metropolitanism as a way of life.

Our contemporary society is filled with examples of "cultural lag", a concept introduced by one of my professors, a gentleman from Georgia, William F. Ogburn, who pointed out that different elements of our culture change at different rates — some things lagging behind others. One concrete instance of cultural lag that helps account for our inability to deal with many of our problems, including pollution, follows. As recently as 1960, there were 39 states in this union in which the urban population constituted the majority of the people but not a single state in the union in which the urban population controlled the state legislature. As a result of our rapid urbanization and the failure of state governments to reapportion as required by their constitutions, the federal government is in such spheres as urban renewal, public housing, civil rights, mass transportation and education. The state legislatures in this country have given us one of the finest examples of civil disobedience by deliberately refusing to reapportion during the first 60 years of this century; and because the malapportioned legislatures have callously ignored urban problems, the urban population of this nation, 70 percent in 1960, was forced to turn to the federal government for the resolution of their problems. It is not that the federal government has usurped "state rights"; it is, rather, that state legislatures have been committing suicide and have made themselves the fifth wheel in the government of these United States.

Finally let us consider the problems of the population displosion. Our racist society is now undergoing a black revolt still gaining momentum; and a white backlash is still under way as represented by the recent political victory of the racist gubernatorial candidate in Alabama. Racism and reaction to it, a product of the population displosion, may tear this country apart.

ENVIRONMENTAL POLLUTION

Let us turn next to my final objective — dealing with the overstatements and misstatements appearing in some of the population and environmental discussions. I deal with this subject in an effort to prevent the emergence of a credibility gap that could transform public anger and zeal into public disillusionment and apathy. I think we have got such a good case for managing excessive population growth and environmental pollution that it is unnecessary to engage in a hard sell; it is unnecessary to utter partial truths; it is unnecessary to distort.

While population and environment hucksterism must be given credit for creating awareness and stimulating public reaction and pressure for the resolution of the problems, it may in overstating anticipated dire consequences, especially in the short run during the 1970's, produce large boomerang effects leading to public disillusionment and relaxation. The resolution of population and environmental problems cannot be achieved by annual catharsis of the type manifest on Earth Day. It requires rather first the achievement of consensus on population and environmental goals; and then persistent, continuous, uninterrupted inputs for the achievement of the goals.

Among the distortions which have been promulgated on population and environmental problems are the following:

1. "The population explosion is responsible for environmental pollution."

2. "Zero population growth must be achieved as rapidly as possible even through negative population growth; i.e., through a drastic decrease in the birth rate so that it falls below the death rate."

3. "Technology is to be blamed for environmental pollution."

4. "Environmental pollution is to be attributed to the free enterprise capitalist system."

5. "Consumption levels of the American people must be diminished; for example, electric toothbrushes should be abandoned to decrease pollution levels."

6. "Tens of millions of people will starve to death during the 1970's."

7. "Tens of millions of people will die of poisoning because of polluted air and water during the 1970's."

8. "It may already be too late to prevent ecological disaster."

All of these statements, each of which may contain grains of truth, are false and misleading. Let us consider each of them in turn.

1. "The population explosion is responsible for environmental pollution." This statement is true only in the sense that if there were no people or if population did not grow as rapidly, there would be no, or less, pollution. It fails to recognize that pollution in the U.S. and in the world as a whole could continue to increase significantly even if there were no further population growth. Pollution could continue to increase because of increased levels of consumption and production without further population growth or through even decreased efforts to eliminate pollution. It fails also to recognize that continued population growth, even excessive growth, need not necessarily result in increased pollution or ravages of the environment.

2. "Zero population growth must be achieved as rapidly as possible, even through negative population growth, i.e., through a drastic decrease in the birth rate so that it falls below the death rate." To "believe" in the slogan "Zero Population Growth" is similar to believing in the law of gravitation — it is inevitable. Given the finite dimensions of this planet any rate of population growth will, in the long run, produce saturation. Space is the limiting factor to population growth. The question is not should there be zero population growth, but at what rate and by what means is it to be achieved? To achieve zero growth in the U.S., it is only necessary, as has been indicated above, for the population to do a little bit more of what they are already doing in fertility control. It is quite unnecessary for this nation to impose sanctions that would penalize families with large numbers of children — penalties that would fall disporportionately on the poor and disadvantaged minority groups. What is needed rather is increased education and increased levels of living for the poor and positive incentives for fertility reduction; and increased education and public pressure, which is already mounting, against third and fourth children in middle-class families, the preponderant proportion of families.

Moreover, there is nothing in prospect in this nation that should require couples under pressure to have only one child to achieve a negative growth rate. The price of achieving zero population growth as soon as possible, meaning almost immediately, would be a high price that would not and should not be paid by the American people.

It should be mentioned that much of the youth now sloganeering for zero population growth is unaware of the fact that a zero growth rate would undoubtedly solve the "youth problem" as viewed by their elders. For a zero growth rate in the U.S. could lead to a population with an average age of 40 years instead of the present 27 years. Immediate zero population growth would cause drastic changes in the nation's age structure which would force drastic readjustments in almost every sector of the American society — labor, business, education, recreation, and probably politics and government as well.

3. "Technology is to be blamed for environmental pollution." Technology, even as science, is not an evil but a neutral agent which can be used for good or evil. In the U.S. technology has been permitted to produce pollution, but it can also be used to eliminate pollution. It is not technology which is responsible for pollution then, but rather the failure of this nation to use technology to eliminate it.

4. "Environmental pollution is to be attributed to the free enterprise capitalist system." This statement fails to recognize the fact that socialist systems are as polluted as capitalist systems. In both capitalist and socialist societies consumption is privatized, but pollution has been socialized and the payment of much of its cost deferred. The U.S.S.R., even as the U.S., is now becoming concerned about the pollution of its waters, its air and its general environment. One interesting recent evidence of this fact is the Russian worriment about the decreased production of caviar by reason of pollution of the Caspian Sea.

5. "Consumption levels of the American people must be diminished; for example, electric toothbrushes should be abandoned to decrease pollution levels." This is among the more absurd distortions which are being broadcast to the American people. It is not our high level of consumption which is producing pollution. It is unwillingness up to this point to pay the cost for the elimination of pollution. The economic muscle of the U.S., with the adjustment of priorities, could certainly eliminate pollution without decreasing living levels.

6. "Tens of millions of people will starve to death during the 1970's." This distortion undoubtedly rests on projections of food supply and population made before the "green revolution" which is resulting in substantial increases in food production in the developing areas and in the world as a whole. Although there are still uncertainties about whether increased levels of food production can be sustained, the prospect is that mankind has achieved at least three or four decades of grace before widespread famine faces the people in the developing areas. To be sure in the longer run, mankind must achieve control of rates of population increase, but the alarmist predictions that millions and millions of people may starve to death during the 70's may raise serious questions of credibility when famine does not occur. The situation is bad enough without Cassandra-like predictions that may on the one hand unnecessarily alarm the public in the short run and unhappily relax the public in the longer run.

7. "Tens of millions of people will die of poisoning because of polluted air and water during the 1970's." This is also an alarmist projection not likely to be realized during the 70's, with the same possible consequences as the alarmist projections about famine and starvation.

8. "It may already be too late to prevent ecological disaster." This statement happily is presented as a conditional prediction, but it could unjustifiably create panic and hysteria. It may be defended as good propaganda, but it cannot be proved. Steps already being taken suggest that mankind, made aware of the problem, can formulate the necessary policies and programs so that it will not be "too late." This statement could also produce boomerang effects. If it is "too late," why bother? Perhaps all that is necessary is to follow the injunction of the wise man who said "if treed by a bear, you may as well relax and enjoy the view."

CONCLUDING OBSERVATIONS

Since the first census taken in 1790, U.S. population doubled five times up to 1950, and may complete a sixth doubling by the end of this century. By the year 2000, short of the catastrophic, the U.S. is likely to have a population of some 300 million persons — 100 million more than will be reported by the 1970 census, 205 million. The anticipated increment is being fed by the second post-World War II baby boom, the echo effect of the first post-war baby boom, which has been under way now since October, 1968, and which is likely to gather momentum.

There is need to dampen the birth rate and growth rate of the population of the United States. This can undoubtedly be achieved by voluntarism of the type which has already characterized the reproductive habits of the American people. The poor and uneducated in the U.S. should be afforded the necessary education and increased levels of living which will result in their fertility reduction; the middle class of the U.S. should be increasingly made aware of the fact that it is their third and fourth children who contribute to the undesirable high growth of the nation.

To eliminate pollution the American people must be prepared to pay the cost of the required action both through increased costs of goods and services and increased taxation. No amount of railing against technology, the capitalist system, or the population explosion will decrease pollution. What is required are measures that will make it mandatory for producers to include non-pollution measures as cost items, and the creation of public agencies with sufficient funds and power to protect the common property resources of the nation — air, water, and public lands.

Population and environmental problems are both chronic and acute. But it will avail us little to be misled by distorted versions of either the problems or their interrelationships, and it may harm us to relax in our efforts to deal with these problems after present doomsday predictions fail to materialize. What is needed is not a repetition of cathartic Earth Days but a great effort to arrive at consensus on desirable goals in respect of population and environment, and then persistent, uninterrupted inputs to accomplish these goals. The achievement of such goals need not be depended on distortions of the facts, half-truths, and alarmist predictions.

It has taken over a half century on the part of demographers to alert the nation and the world to the necessity to deal with the population explosion — excessively high birth and growth rates. It is well that energies are now being devoted to this subject, but there are other population problems which merit as much if not more attention, problems produced by the population implosion; i.e., urbanization, and the population displosion; i.e., the sharing of not only the geographic area but also the same life space — social, economic, and political activities — by persons differing by culture, language, religion, ethnicity, and race. Problems arising from the population implosion and displosion may create more human misery during the remainder of this century than the problems produced by the population explosion.

Among the problems deserving at least equal priority as the problems of the population explosion and environmental pollution are:

a.   the other physical problems created by the population implosion — not only air, water, and environmental pollution, but also surface and air traffic congestion, slum housing, inadequate recreational facilities, etc. The pollution represented by urban slums is no less important than keeping Lake Michigan alive; and failure to remedy it may be fraught with consequences at least as serious to the U.S. as the death of Lake Michigan.

b. the personal and social problems exacerbated by the population implosion — delinquency and crime, alcoholism and drug addiction, the revolt of youth, the revolt of consumers, the revolt of women.

c. problems produced by the population displosion — the revolt of the blacks and the white backlash. Polarization on the race issue may tear this nation apart.

The problems of the population explosion and environmental pollution are serious and must be faced. But they should not be used as a smoke screen to obscure problems also caused or worsened by population factors which are at least as important and which between now and the end of the century may threaten the viability of American society.

POPULATION GROWTH AND THE NATURAL ENVIRONMENT

Raymond F. Dasmann

Dr. Dasmann was formerly Director of International Programs at the Conservation Foundation and is now a Senior Ecologist at the International Union for Conservation of Nature and Natural Resources, in Switzerland. He is the author of many books on conservation and biology, notably The Destruction of California *and* A Different Kind of Country. No Further Retreat *will be published shortly, and* Man and the Biosphere *is now in preparation for UNESCO.*

With Dr. Dasmann's essay the focus shifts from population control to the reciprocal effects of population growth and environmental degradation. Together with these he considers the idea of quality as applied to environment. Using Florida and California as examples, he argues against the unplanned use of ecosystems, especially for short-term economic gains.

Like Paul Ehrlich he accepts the necessity for restricting human reproduction and like Philip Hauser he is concerned with the effects of urban overcrowding; nevertheless he differs from both men in arguing that "the crisis of the environment . . . is not a crisis of population as such," and in positing conditions in which, he believes, some degree of population increase would be ecologically acceptable.

A state of nature, in the absence of man, is not some ideal state from which I intend in this discussion to measure our departure. It may well be that the earth, before man evolved, was more optimum for some other species — the giant ground sloth comes to mind. However, these species are not holding a congress in Chicago. We are considering the earth as occupied by man and modified by man's activities. It is the optimum environment for man that is being sought. It makes little difference how beautiful the world might have been before there were poets and artists on earth, or before the perception and understanding that gives rise to poetry and art were present in the human species. Food and shelter, a place in the sun, and the opportunity to reproduce — these are all that most species require. Only mankind, or some vocal segment of the human species, demands more.

FACTORS IN ENVIRONMENTAL QUALITY

Being a member of the vocal segment that demands more, I propose initially to explore a definition of quality of the environment. In a previous paper I defined it as resulting from three factors: environmental health, productivity, and diversity. When these are in reasonable balance, a fourth factor, environmental beauty, may be derived from them. A high quality environment therefore is one that is healthy, not only in the sense of being free from injurious pollutants, but in a positive sense of having a proper balance of those elements required for life. It is a productive environment, meaning that those species adapted to it can grow and reproduce at rates approaching an optimum controlled by the nature of the site and the extent of biological competition. Finally it is a diverse environment, one supporting the greatest number and variety of species and natural communities that are adapted to its physical characteristics. Generally speaking, an environment with these qualities will appear beautiful to man.

Since writing this definition, however, I have become aware of its shortcomings. It applies particularly to those areas inhabited directly by man. However, a contribution to quality in the environment may be made by areas not well suited to human habitation, but attractive to human exploration: high barren mountains, ice sheets, deserts, the open ocean, and other habitats that are not particularly healthy, productive or biologically diverse. Furthermore, a high quality environment must provide the opportunity to avoid contact with other species that are generally considered unacceptable to people — I refer to aggressive carnivores, hosts of productive mosquitoes and biting flies, thickets of healthy poison oak or other diverse assortments of poisonous creatures. These all may have positive contributions to make to environmental quality. Eden can quickly become Hell if it is inhabited by even one human being who is in close proximity or frequent social contact with you and whose presence is psychologically unacceptable to you. Consequently, another factor in environmental quality becomes essential — space. A suitable environment must provide the opportunity for spatial isolation from unacceptable companions. This can be isolation provided by distance, or isolation provided by physical or social barriers to contact between individuals who do not desire such contact. In other words, the environment must provide spearate socio-ecological niches for different kinds of people.

POPULATION SCARCITY AND ENVIRONMENTAL DETERIORATION

I would propose that human population growth, as such, does not necessarily have adverse effects upon environmental quality, at least up to some point of crowding that may differ with the physical and biological characteristics of the natural environment and with the cultural characteristics of the people involved. It is impossible, however, to separate man from his technology, and it is the combined impact of population and technology that we must first consider. Population increase in the United States has been accompanied by change and growth in technology. Whether or not population would continue to grow in the United States in the absence of technological change and growth is a question that this conference should perhaps consider, but it seems likely that the two will continue to be linked. It is more easy to foresee a stable population with continued technological growth. The consequences of this are also important to any consideration of an optimum population.

Recognizing these things, one is forced to conclude that deterioration of the quality of the human environment began early in the history of the United States. In many areas of the country, environmental quality was severely impaired at a time when population was relatively sparse and technology was relatively primitive. Thus the Forest Service, in its review document on *The Western Range* has described the deterioration of the environment in the American West. This took place primarily in the years from 1870 to 1935, at a time when the average population density in much of the West was less than one person per square mile. The deterioration was brought about by uncontrolled grazing of rangelands causing a loss in productivity, health, and diversity of vegetation, serious soil erosion and drastic interference with future productivity. The degradation in some areas was so severe that a point of no return was reached, and only the slow processes of primary biological succession, operating over centuries, can bring repair. Over most of the western range the deterioration of productivity and carrying capacity is still felt by those who seek to earn a livelihood and to produce food and fiber from what are now inferior grasslands or man-made deserts. With a much higher population and a sophisticated modern technology it has been possible to restore some of the less badly damaged lands to a state where they can again be considered high in environmental quality. This process of degradation of range lands by pastoral use, misplaced agricultural effort, removal of fuel or misuse of fire goes on all over the world, but seems most extreme in sparsely populated lands.

The greatest damage to the long-term productivity of America's forested lands also took place in most parts of the country during periods when populations were sparse and technology little advanced. Forests have come back to the eastern United States during recent decades when populations have been approaching their present density and the impact of modern technology on the environment has been considered most severe.

The most widespread decimation of America's wildlife, at least until very recently, took place at a time when our population was sparse and the need for protection of wild species had not become apparent to more than a few naturalists. Since the 1930's wildlife in many areas of America has more than regained its primitive abundance, if not its early diversity.

The process of urbanization, particularly in the past few decades, has released large areas of land that once supported rural populations, and has permitted recovery of their natural vegetation and animal life. The intensification of agricultural productivity on our better farm lands has released still other areas of land for the use of wild species.

I believe that the greatest damage to quality of the environment may well be taking place today, throughout the world, not in the areas of high population density and high technology, but in areas such as the edges of the Sahara and of the Asian deserts where primitive methods of pasture management provide scant support for sparse populations at an enormous cost in land deterioration; areas in the tropical forests of the Americas, Africa, and Asia, where primitive slash-and-burn methods of agriculture provide the support for populations which may be sparse in any comparative sense, but are still excessively high for the carrying capacity of the land as worked by primitive technology; and areas in the savannas of Africa, Latin America and Asia, where low density human populations on marginal lands deplete once diverse and abundant animal populations in order to obtain a subsistence existence. I have been told, although I cannot verify it, that the greatest contribution to particulate pollution of the atmosphere — now a matter of great concern in industrialized countries — comes from the widespread use of fire to clear wooded areas for shifting agriculture or to increase the yield from marginal pastures in sparsely populated areas of the world.

By selecting examples, one could make a strong case for the hypothesis that improvement of the quality of the environment comes with increasing populations and modernization of technology. Indeed Nigel Calder in the book *Eden Was No Garden* does build such a case. But, there is another side to the story. To present this, I wish to focus first on just one of the 50 United States, the state of Florida, and move from there to consider other areas.

THE FLORIDA PATTERN

The rate of population growth and environmental change in Florida is encouraging only to those who seek profit from growth and have little concern for the natural environment. The Florida environment is unique in the United States and thus is in many ways the cause for the difficulties in which the state finds itself. Climatically and biologically it is a blend of tropical, sub-tropical, and warm temperate characteristics that people from other, cooler regions often find attractive. These attractions were not obvious to Americans until relatively recently in our history. Before 1920 much of the state was wilderness and underdeveloped. In the fifty years, from 1850 to 1900, the population of Florida increased six fold, but this increase occurred in a state that had been nearly empty of people. In 1900, only 530,000 people lived there. From 1900 to the early 1950's, the population again increased six fold, and reached slightly over 3 million people. In the succeeding fifteen years, however, it doubled again, and in 1969 was estimated to exceed 6 million permanent residents. These were not distributed evenly around the state. Except in the north-central area, the interior of the state has not proved attractive to people or amenable to settlement. In consequence the population clusters around the coasts. In 1960, 74 percent of the population was urban and only 2.3 percent actually lived on farms. The largest concentration of people was in the Miami-Fort Lauderdale metropolitan area, estimated in 1962 to contain 1,330,000 people. Since this is part of a Gold Coast strip city that extends northward to Palm Beach, a population of 1,500,000 for this metropolitan region in 1962 is a better estimate.

Ranking second in the state is the Tampa-St. Petersburg metropolitan area of the Gulf Coast, with a population in 1962 estimated at approximately 760,000. Next is the Jacksonville metropolitan area with nearly a half million, and in fourth place the Orlando metropolitan area with approximately 300,000. Such figures are not impressive to a New Yorker, but they represent a great pressure of population upon a fragile environment. Furthermore, it is not the numbers but the rate of growth, the rate of urban sprawl, that is discouraging. Thus the town of Naples, far to the south on the Gulf Coast, was in 1960 a neat, orderly, well-contained area with less than 5,000 inhabitants. It is now merely a center for an urbanizing area spreading out in all directions from the Gulf of Mexico. I have observed it from the air periodically during the past four years, and these have been discouraging years for anyone concerned with preservation of natural environments.

Ten miles south of Naples, by air, is Marco Island, which was noted in 1960 for two historic fishing villages, a remarkable long white stretch of beach famous for shelling, and a well-known complex of upland tropical vegetation. In the early 1960's a decision was made to develop the island as a residential area. This process is now well under way and the island has been carved up into what some call the "lace doily" real-estate development pattern of the Florida coast, a complex of boat canals, roads and residential lots. In the near future the same company will move out from Marco to begin development of Cape Romano island, the most northerly of the 10,000 islands, and also to take in all of the adjoining mainland and mangrove coast. Other developers are operating north of Marco, and except for the Audubon sanctuary at Rookery Bay, the prospect is for continuous development from Cape Romano to Naples. Northward, development is moving rapidly up the coast and there now seems no prospect for halting it before a continuous strip city extends from south of Marco to Fort Myers. North of Fort Myers development continues also, with the prospect of a coastal strip city, interrupted only by bays and harbors on up past Tampa–St. Petersburg at least to Tarpon Springs, and probably beyond.

Inland from Naples to the east are a series of uninspired developments including ugly trailer courts and the usual American roadside junk architecture. The Gulf American Corporation, one of the largest and most ruthless developers in the United States, has already carved up much of the palm and pine covered wild country into a rectangular pattern dominated . . . by roads and drainage ditches. Gullible northerners are being sold lots, which in some cases have been under water, and in most or all cases lack adequate provision for sewage disposal or urban amenities. Separating this massive Gulf Coast sprawl from the westward-moving Miami sprawl is the wilderness barrier of the Everglades and Big Cypress country. This, however, has recently been threatened by plans for the construction of a supersonic jetport midway between the coasts. This would in turn provide a new center for urban development that would blot out much of the Big Cypress region and bring urbanization to the edge of the Everglades on both the east and the west.

The government of Collier County, Florida, might have been expected to exercise a greater degree of control over development west of the Everglades. In fact, however, the county lacks an adequate master plan (although it has something that passes for one), lacks a county planning department, lacks planning expertise and has generally shown in the past little concern for environmental values. Rezoning has been a mere formality. Development and growth have been the only goals for such planning as does exist. No limits to growth have been considered.

On the east coast in Dade County, metropolitan Miami is a great sprawling mess which has suffered badly from lack of planning and realistic control over expansion. Although planning expertise is now available, planning is still oriented to additional growth, with the spread of urbanization along the south shore of Biscayne Bay now being organized. This is the only direction left in which the city can expand.

The Florida environment, which provided the original attraction drawing people to Florida, is being destroyed. In the Florida Keys, which were noted for their unusual tropical vegetation and animal life, it is believed by F. C. Craighead that none of the primeval upland hardwood hammock forest remains. There is some excellent old second-growth, particularly on Lignum Vitae Key and north Key Largo, but efforts to have this spared from development have thus far been unsuccessful. Animal life which was once abundant has been much depleted. The crocodile is now near extinction in Florida waters, with a small remnant population on the Upper Keys. The manatee and alligator are considered endangered. The flamingo has disappeared as a breeding bird on the Keys. Most of the marsh and water birds, the herons, egrets, spoonbills, ibises, storks, and the like were pushed to near extinction in the mid-1930's. Under protection from federal and state agencies, notably in Everglades National Park, those species dependent on estuarine environments have recovered in numbers, but those dependent upon fresh-water environments are not doing well. All, however, are now faced with a new threat, as DDT and other persistent pesticides used on agricultural lands and in urban pest control, drift by air or are carried by water into the national park and the surrounding marine environment. All birds that occupy terminal positions on long food chains can now be considered in danger.

Although a great area of the south Florida environment was supposedly set aside for all time in Everglades National Park, Congress has been half-hearted in its support of the park. A large area inside the park boundaries is used for agriculture or is being developed in various ways for agricultural or recreational use. Monroe County, which has jurisdiction over much of this land, does nothing to prevent this development. However, even if all of the land within the park were in federal control, the park would not be secure, since it is dependent upon outside for its water supply. The long argument over water for the Everglades has been discussed in many places and I will not repeat it here. The mismanagement, however, is exemplified by the fact that even in 1970, after several years of high rainfall, the vegetation in the upland areas of the park (meaning areas a few feet above sea level) suffers from drought. In the lowland areas, where excessive water has been allowed to accumulate, marsh vegetation and animal life is being replaced by a pond and lake biota. Everglades National Park, with its unusual vegetation and spectacular animal life can still be saved, but not if population and technology continue to expand unchecked in southern Florida.

Virtually all of the estuarine environments in the developed or developing areas of the Florida coast have been seriously damaged by dredging and land fill and by excessive pollution. Since Florida's fisheries, the richest in the nation, are dependent upon this estuarine environment, their future looks highly insecure.

If quality of the environment in Florida includes access to beaches and unpolluted water, if it involves the presence of a diversity of tropical vegetation and animal life, access to wild land and wild water, the ability to escape from conditions of crowding, then it has already been seriously impaired, and will, with continued growth and development, be lost. Federal, state, and local governments in Florida have shown themselves up to now to be incapable of coping adequately with the problem of growth. The task of repairing the damage that has already been done, particularly through pollution, could require the full efforts of government at all levels for perhaps a decade, if all growth were halted now. With continued growth, I seriously doubt that the damage will be repaired or further damage prevented.

It should be noted that in addition to its six-plus million residents, Florida plays host to an estimated 20 million visitors. Tourism is the state's largest source of primary income. Two-thirds of these tourists reportedly come to enjoy the state's dwindling supply of beaches (beach erosion resulting from interference with drainage patterns is a major problem). These beaches are becoming increasingly crowded and polluted. More than a quarter of the tourists come for fishing, fishing that depends to a large degree upon the continued productivity of estuaries that are being polluted, dredged and filled at an accelerating rate. Nearly 40 percent say that they are attracted by the scenery, which is being battered into a state of ugliness. Admittedly, some come for the purpose of reclining by hotel swimming pools, staring at one another, night clubbing and drinking in pseudo-tropical atmosphere, and these can be kept satisfied for longer.

Obviously Florida has contributed to the total quality of environment for a high percentage of America's population. If the Florida environment continues to be damaged or destroyed the sum total of environmental quality in the United States will be seriously reduced.

THE CALIFORNIA PROBLEM

To move to the other side of the United States, is not to find any improvement in the total picture. California, like Florida, suffers from exceedingly rapid population growth. This has already blotted out great areas of the original natural landscape. The wild scenes of the once vast interior valley of the state are not longer to be found. The elk, the antelope, the great clouds of water birds, and all of the varied animal life of this rich region, exist mostly in historical records. The basins and shorelines of southern California grow ever more crowded and millions live under conditions of air pollution that have made Los Angeles seem like a sick joke to people all over the world. The famous scenery of the Los Angeles region and San Francisco Bay is now rarely discernible. Pollutants from the city threaten the continued existence of pine forests in distant mountains. California's national parks are referred to internationally as examples of how crowding can lead to destruction of those values for the protection of which the parks were originally set aside.

Although the mountains, deserts, dense forests and chaparral of California have been more resistant to the impact of population and technology than the fragile Florida environment, nobody who has known the state for very long can doubt that the quality of environment, measured in terms of freedom from pollution, ability to escape from crowding, and the presence of wild and diverse landscapes and animal life, has declined. California has long since passed any level of population that could be considered optimum in terms of such environmental quality. Like Florida, a moratorium on growth for a decade and a full scale effort on the part of local, state and federal government, would permit some degree of repair of past environmental damage. In the presence of continued, rapid growth, it is only foreseeable that things will grow worse. However, I have discussed California's problems in detail elsewhere and will not belabor them here.

THE POPULATION-TECHNOLOGY-LAND USE CONCEPT

Looking at Florida and California one is tempted to see a direct relationship between population increase and the decline of environmental quality. However, if we analyze the components of the problem, this inverse ratio between numbers of people and quality of the environment disappears, since the increase in numbers has been accompanied by the virtually uncontrolled use of land, and the absence of controls over technological processes. These factors, rather than numbers of people alone, are most directly related to environmental degradation.

Thus, in Collier County, Florida, where existing growth presents a frightening dilemma, the number of people are relatively few despite their accelerating rate of growth. All of those present, and a considerable increase could be accommodated in a relatively small coastal city which could, with proper planning, have very little impact on the total environment. It would be necessary only to provide for full, tertiary sewage treatment with recycling of nutrient materials, to avoid excessive use of those forms of coastal and estuarine land development that involve dredge and fill operations; to minimize the use of polluting forms of transportation and plan transportation corridors to minimize detrimental effects upon the environment — in other words to exercise strict control over land use and over processes that contribute to pollution. The control over recreational land use would also require careful zoning, with virtual exclusion of such use from those areas protected as ecological reserves, and development of facilities to encourage more optimal use of those areas intended to meet mass recreational needs. With such controls, and the rational management of natural vegetation and animal life, a high quality in the natural environment could be provided. However, the empirical evidence suggests that rather than accept these controls, those who profit from the sale or development of land, those who profit from industries or devices that cause pollution, or those who feel that they benefit from the absence of the higher taxes needed to provide pollution control, and finally those who wish to run highways, water developments, or locate power stations and power lines where they please, would rather destroy the natural environment than submit to such controls. If this empirical evidence reflects the true state of human aspiration, then it is fruitless to talk about quality of the environment and only worthwhile discussing the extreme conditions under which the human race can continue to survive. In Florida we are rapidly approaching these extremes.

Nationwide, it is apparent to me that the decrease in environmental quality is to be attributed far more to lack of control over technology, lack of control over land use, and in particular lack of control over pollution than it is to population growth as such. However, since the growth of population exacerbates all of these other failures, and the control of population growth would give us time to bring the other problems under some degree of control, one cannot help but recommend control over human population growth. One should recognize, however, that such control need not be considered permanent, that the opportunities for future population growth need not be inhibited, once the other negative aspects of the growth-technology-land use complex are contained.

The crisis of the environment, now evident in America, particularly as it affects the natural environment, is not a crisis of population as such, nor can we derive from it statements about optimal human population levels. If we look at the population-technology-land use complex, however, it is apparent that we have exceeded any optimum level of pressure on the environment. Reduction in population growth, to the extent that it permits control over technology and land use is thus highly to be recommended. Only with control over technology and land use, would further increase in human populations become tolerable. The extent to which such increase should be permitted to continue cannot be determined solely in terms of preservation of quality of the natural environment in the United States. It is probably more clearly related to problems of availability of fuels, raw materials, and natural resources over the entire world, and to the degree to which these should be provided for the support of United States populations. This is a fascinating and complex problem but not one into which I have been asked by this Congress to delve.

THE SEA: CONTROLLING INTERFACE
OF OUR BIOSPHERE

Joel W. Hedgpeth

Dr. Hedgpeth, Professor of Oceanography and Director of the Marine Science Center at Oregon State University, is the author of many articles on marine conservation. Here he extends Raymond Dasmann's discussion of the effects of uncontrolled technology on the land with a consideration of the ways in which we are misusing the sea; he reminds us of the sea's importance as a major part of our environment and points out that it can no longer be regarded as a convenient dumping ground for the waste products of a wasteful technology.

Less controversial than our first three contributions, Dr. Hedgpeth's essay does not discuss population control as such; but in demonstrating that the resources of the sea are not infinite he is indicating one of the greatest natural limiting factors to unrestricted population growth.

Man's thoughtless opinion of the sea is characteristically expressed in the following letter by the president of Offshore/Sea Development Corporation, which appeared in *Science News* in 1969 (Vol. 96, p. 294):

> As a polluter of the oceans, nature is still ahead of man. For example, during the International Indian Ocean Expedition, Russian and British oceanographers spotted a patch of dead fish in the Indian Ocean twice the size of Portugal, with over 30 million metric tons of protein. Humans could hardly be blamed for this . . . . The devastating poisonous red tides mentioned in your article, "Rumblings From the Deep" (SN: 9/13, p. 213), are more a function of sea temperature than man's tampering with nature.
>
> The ocean, in our opinion can absorb, and purify the wastes generated by man if these wastes are properly diluted. There are more than 10 billion cubic feet of ocean water available for each individual on earth. Unfortunately, a puddle like Lake Erie does not have enough water for proper dilution of the effluents presently flowing into it. A dilution factor of 200 to 1 is usually considered adequate to allow natural chemical and

biological processes to purify sewage. Offshore/Sea Development Corp. is developing large diameter subaqueous pipe systems that could take sewage and heated effluents far enough out into the ocean where, rather than harm marine life, the effluents could actually contribute to the growth of beneficial species.

This gentleman, and others like him, may oot find an appropriate warning in Moby Dick, nevertheless, Melville's great allegory can be read in terms of what man tries to do with, or take from, a nature that seems essentially malevolent because it is not part of what man believes to be his own purpose. When man tries to use nature and profit from it to his own unthinking purposes it will turn upon him and destroy him with a force that is malevolent to the men of the Pequod, but merely another small incident on the vast waste of the ocean. The meaning of the allegory is, of course, that tampering with our ecosystem will bring us the same blind malevolence that is personified by the white whale.

I. THE SHORE

Man, as a terrestrial animal, has never been at ease upon the surface of the sea and has never quite understood its ways. He has reached a certain understanding with the shore and utilizes it to exploit the sea as a means of conveying goods, extracting food, and as esthetic and hygienic amelioration. His most recent utilization of the sea is as his last best hope for a universal septic tank, and he views the shore as an excellent site for sewer pipes, heat producing power plants, and oil docks. It is here, at the shore and in the shallow sea, that the ill effects, the "negative benefits," as one sanitary engineer calls them, may be minimized. But all these uses are not compatible, and they are becoming less so as population increases. It is estimated that at this time "nearly half of all Americans live within a hundred miles of the ocean or the Great Lakes; this proportion will probably increase in future decades. By the end of the century, some 150 to 200 million people may be struggling for places on the beaches and in the narrow coastal waters. Even if the country's entire coastal strip were converted into public beaches, this would mean about two people per foot." (R. Revelle, *Daedalus,* Fall 1967).

Some years ago Carl Sauer wrote a charming paper, "Seashore, Primitive Home of Man?" in which he pointed out that it was curious that no other primates appear to have taken to living on seashores and that man very early if not almost at the beginning settled along the seashore. Here is an ideal place for stones of all sorts and sizes to be used as tools, and abundant food for the restricted populations of a food gathering culture. In any event, the "discovery of the sea, whenever it happened, afforded a living beyond that at any inland location." There is much truth in the idea that we do have a feeling of returning home when we go down to the shore: "We still like to go beachcombing, returning to primitive act and mood. When all the lands will be filled with people and machines, perhaps the last need and observance of man will be, as it was at his beginning, to come down and experience the sea."

This feeling for the shore as a renewable, ever unchanging environment is expressed in crasser terms by the developer who advertises a new seaside subdivision: "POLLUTION FREE!! Give your lungs a break — take a deep breath of clean-clear-healthful salt air at SURFSIDE ESTATES." It seems to be the same feeling that the sanitary engineer has when he sees the crud and corruption disappearing from his ocean outfall into the sea, the same feeling that the sailor has as he leaves the land, and so on. But obviously all this cannot go on together in one place or even scattered along most of the coast, if we are to preserve one of the most important aspects of the shore to many people, the feeling of being, if not alone, at least reasonably by oneself to experience the sea and its ever renewing fresh air. I realize that what is optimum for me, say a spacing of conspicuous houses at least a half-mile apart, may be distressing to those who like to be able to reach through their medicine cabinets into their neighbor's bathroom, but there is also the practical aspect to consider. This is the function served by this interface (in terms of the shore line, without specific reference to the problem of estuaries and marshes) and how excessive development may interfere with it. It modifies the climate and is a valuable food-producing region. A little pollution may or may not be a good thing, depending on the point of view, but the steady increase of oil spillage, warming waters, and corrupted stream discharges certainly cannot improve this environment. Most seriously from the human standpoint is the steady loss of shore lines to development projects, the denial of access and inappropriate use by vehicles of sandy beaches. All of these matters are becoming subjects of concern all over the world.

On February 12, 1970 a conference on conservation of European coasts was held in Strasbourg, France. The British have been concerned for several years about the future of their coastline and have produced a series of reports by the National Parks Commission on the coasts of England and Wales. One of these, interestingly enough, is an analysis of the coast as an educational and scientific resource. The concern for seashores may engender considerable controversy; for the last several years Oregon has been concerned about the ownership of its seashores and has attempted to define the limits of public and private ownership. Unfortunately our legal system so far does not adequately understand what tides really are, or that mean sea level and mean high water have somewhat different meanings depending on the kind of tidal regime. These are quite different on the Atlantic and Pacific coasts of North America.

The State of California is now engaged in conducting a comprehensive survey of its coastal zone, with a view towards eventual zoning and control. One of the critical problems in achieving any sort of wise use or rational zoning of seashores (or any other environment, for that matter) is the often misguided, ill-informed, and opportunistic attitude of local political entities that have the immediate control over the environment and grant the initial use permits. As long as our property tax system is arranged to benefit local government entities, we will have unwise, short-sighted decisions on land use problems.

People will fight for seashores and for bays, as demonstrated by the uprising of citizens in the San Francisco Bay area that persuaded the California State Legislature to pass the act establishing the Bay Conservation and Development Commission. This is a step toward the necessary regional government to offset conflicting, parochial entities.

II. ESTUARIES AND MARSHLANDS

The best recent statement on the "tidal-marsh ecosystem" is that of William A. Niering in "The Environmental Crisis" (Yale, 1970). It is this complex of bays, river mouths and tidal marshes that receives the greatest impact cf our activities. The force of ocean waves may at least prevent certain sorts of environmental degradation, but there is no such control in sheltered areas, which may be obliterated by filling and docks and housing developments, scarified by freeways, and used as sewer farms. The odors from uncontrolled dumping may in time become so offensive that something has to be done, as with the famous case of Halitosis Flats along the east shore of San Francisco Bay. The filling of San Francisco Bay promised to alter the climate of the area. Even the

42,000 acres of estuaries in Oregon are in danger of being nibbled to death by the short-sighted activities of highwaymen, filling engineers, and paper manufacturing companies, and the Governor has declared a moratorium on public projects there. In Chile the Dow chemical people would convert an estuary to a large waste processing pond by damming if off at the mouth.

Although estuaries are a minor part of our environment (Niering states that the estuaries and marshes comprise about .00003 percent of the entire acreage of the United States, for example), they are even more than the open seashore the cradle of man's use of the sea and the beginning of his expansion over the world. Man's first use of bays and estuaries, as demonstrated by aboriginal cultures, was as a source of food. He caught fish and gathered shellfish. We do not know when man learned to put the small oysters back and let them grow to larger oysters, but oyster culture was a thriving industry in Roman times. Probably second in man's use of bays and estuaries came shelter for faring out into greater waters, first as fishermen in rafts and boats, then as merchants trading with other men. For a long period in history the uses of estuaries by fishermen, oyster culturers, and merchants were reasonably compatible. Since the Industrial Revolution, however, we have invented a new use for estuaries, as the end terminal interface of our technological culture. We use them as dumping grounds and sewers. Then we fill them up; and now we look toward the hopefully vast sea itself. We have reversed our historical priorities by placing the natural use of estuaries and tidal marshes last. Yet the significance of these areas for production of food (many fishes caught at sea started out as youngsters in an estuary, and without bearable conditions in estuaries and river mouths our stocks of salmon will perish) has not decreased. They are our prime hope for developing aquaculture for the representative areas that may be more adequately controlled than the larger system of the sea. We need to reassert our original priorities.

In the case of the San Francisco Bay system, our planners and engineers seem to have forgotten the ecological system entirely. In their concern to irrigate marginal lands on the western side of the Central Valley of California and to provide more water for Los Angeles (where most of it will reach the sea through its sewers), they plan to turn the delta area into an artificial system that would function primarily as a vast by-pass valve for the waters of the rivers of all of northern California. At the same time existing agriculture is heavily subsidized for not farming (including the Southern Pacific Railroad!) and Los Angeles is beginning to have serious qualms about perpetual expansion.

We lack at this time a national policy for treating our estuaries and marshlands as an essential part of our environment, a necessary aspect of the diversity that Raymond Dasmann speaks of.

III. THE INEXHAUSTIBLE SEA

The first writer on fisheries was Oppian, who expressed, in his *Halieutica*, about two centuries B.C., an opinion still held by many today: "Infinite beyond ken are the tribes that move and swim in the depths of the sea." Even as late as 1883, after steam trawling had been developed, we find Thomas Henry Huxley, chairman of the first commission to investigate fisheries, declaring at the First International Fisheries Exposition in London: "I believe . . . that the cod fishery, the herring fishery, the pilchard fishery, the mackerel fishery, and probably all the great sea fisheries, are inexhaustible: that is to say that nothing we do seriously affects the number of fish." At that time experienced fishermen were beginning to suspect otherwise and openly disagreed with Huxley. Unfortunately we still have among us these Pollyannas of productivity; probably the most fatuous discussion in print is that of the future of the whale fishery in a book titled "The Inexhaustible Sea" (Daniel and Minot, Collier Books, 1961) because by the 1950's it was already apparent that whales were being killed beyond the minimum necessary for maintenance of the stock. An international committee could not save the whales from this dangerous brinkmanship with extinction. This was already predicted in 1899 by W. C. McIntosh, who conceded it was possible to deplete marine birds and mammals — but not fishes.

Now we believe that we can deplete our fisheries stocks anywhere on the seas by overfishing. The Soviet Union has set unrealizably high quotas for its open seas fisheries fleets, and we have levied upon the anchovies of Peru beyond previous estimates of permissible catch, because the fraction allocated to guano birds has not been utilized during a low period in guano bird population. What now if the guano birds come back? The answer is they cannot, and the Peruvian fertilizer industry is endangered.

A very small percentage of man's total world needs for protein is supplied from the sea — something slightly over two percent. This amounts to a catch of over 50 million metric tons of fish per year

(60.5 in 1967). It is estimated that the krill, Euphausia superba, upon which the blue whales fed, could be harvested now that we have cut the whales down to an insignificant remnant, as the estimated stock of this crustacean is greater than or equivalent to the present entire world fishery. However, the krill is a small shrimp about two inches long, and the processing problems are still to be solved. At best it would be a shrimp paste or more likely reduced to meal for livestock food, like the Peruvian anchovies. (It needs to be emphasized that 45% of the U.S. fish production from the sea goes to feed chickens, not people, which may of course be the most efficient way to convert the protein to usable food.) It is estimated that we may be able to increase the yield of fisheries from the sea by four or possibly five times, but this is nothing like the orders of magnitude suggested for an ever expanding human population. The sea may indeed be vast, but its life is dispersed and most of the biological activity that provides for production of fishes and other edible organisms depends on the events of the upper layers of the sea.

Here is where the sea is vulnerable to the activities of man. Pesticides, detergents, lead from gasoline, and radioactive materials rise into the atmosphere and fall out over the surface of the sea, often in the areas where productivity is greatest. Our sanitary engineers talk of disposing of vast amounts of waste by dispersing them from "deep water" outfalls, but these outfalls are still within the shallow depths of greatest biological and chemical activity in the sea. We know that some pesticides may inhibit reproduction of some kinds of minute marine algae of the phytoplankton, and though the effect could be severe upon some plant not immediately a part of the food chains, it may be a part of the progression of changes within the phytoplankton system that ensures full development of usable species. There is great danger that the shallow waters of the sea may be polluted beyond usability for mankind if we persist in combining waste disposal at the sea's edge with accretion from the atmosphere. The rapidity with which this system works is demonstrated by the decline in fish-eating bird populations (pelicans especially) and the appearance of DDT and its derivatives in Antarctic penguins. It has also been demonstrated that the bottom of the sea is not invulnerable to pollution; the disposal of tons of sludge and solid gunk in the New York Bight has produced a considerable area without life. From this area lenses of water without oxygen may drift for miles, destroying bottom life in areas not directly affected by the solid wastes.

These are early warning signs that we can indeed pollute the oceans, that they are not the inexhaustible, ever-renewing septic tank that some public officials have declared them to be. The most serious aspect that requires consideration is that of the role of the ocean as the mediator of terrestrial climate, source of the hydrologic system that supplies us with water and interface through which the balance of oxygen and carbon dioxide is maintained. Massive pollution and changing of this surface over any considerable area, as by the growing menace of vast oil spills from monster tankers, could affect these basic processes that support life on this planet. The depletion of fisheries, conversion of our entire coast to residential subdivisions, and obliteration of all our estuaries would be minor problems compared to interference with the orderly working of this interface system. For that matter, should we succeed in upsetting the carbon dioxide balance, as some have predicted, the ice caps will melt and we will have a new system of shores, marshes, and estuaries to develop according to some utopian optimum plan.

SUMMARY: WHAT SHOULD BE DONE?

There have been numerous conferences about the uses of the coastal zones, the resources of the sea, and the fate of our estuaries. All seem to agree that the essential prerequisite is a more comprehensive, orderly way of treating these environments if we are to keep them in a reasonably useful state for mankind (to say nothing of maintaining esthetic amenities). Broad regional and national, and eventually international, controls are needed over the use of lands. There should, for example, be an international limit to the size of oil tankers. (Some nations may attempt to ensure this by restricting the size of their docks; the answer proposed to that is a complex of offshore loading and unloading facilities. This sort of thing would increase the danger of spillage.) Extensive reaches of all kinds of shores in the world should be dedicated as interfaces for the maintenance of our environment and of human health. And so on. To do these things requires more awareness of ecological problems than we now have, and a clear declaration of what constitutes an optimum environment. We must also realize that if we are to increase our yield from the sea we must recognize the part that we should contribute to the ecological system. At present in much of the world we do not do this; we propose to draw increasing amounts of biological material from the sea and return to it only our wastes and noxious unusable substances. We should give ourselves to the sea and find other ways to process our anti-biological by-products than diffusing them into what may be in a very few years, in terms of human span, a non-renewable sink.

THE HUMAN FACTORS

PART TWO

In Part I we considered the underlying causes of the population-environment situation. These appeared to be unrestricted population growth, social maladjustments arising from the population implosion and displosion, and destructive misuse of the environment. Without denying the importance of any of these trends, our contributors disagreed as to which we should concentrate on reversing.

Whichever alternative we choose, and perhaps there are other alternatives still to be evolved — one fact stands out. What confronts us is a human situation. "Population" here means people, not a collection of lower organisms whose survival we might ensure by imposing a purely technical solution, as we do when we reduce the number of deer on a given range for the good of the herd. In other words, the situation is complicated by human factors, and these limit our options. Obviously, however desirable population control may be, genocide is not an acceptable means of achieving it. Furthermore, while our industrial system is destructive of the environment it also provides a means of livelihood for millions of people, and any proposal for a drastic reform of the system that failed to anticipate the economic dislocations that would accompany such a reform would have little chance of success.

In addition, there are other, less obvious factors we must reckon with, and these too are topics for the necessary dialogue.

In Part II our contributors discuss some of the more important limitations on the ways in which we can attack and resolve the population-environment problem. Among these are "the tragedy of the commons," a concept that Garrett Hardin explains in the essay that begins this section, genetic laws, ethics, the American political ideology, the changing role of women, the interests of minority groups, our economic institutions, and modern technology.

It is worth noting that not all of these factors are merely restrictive. They represent not only practical difficulties but also human resources for dealing with them.

POPULATION, POLLUTION, AND POLITICAL SYSTEMS

Garrett Hardin

Dr. Hardin, Professor of Biology at the University of California at Santa Barbara, is the author of many books and articles, notably Nature and Man's Fate *and, most recently,* Population, Evolution, and Birth Control. *He is also a director of the Council on Population and Environment.*

Trained as a biologist, he has broadened his interest to include problems of population and the protection of the environment and originated a course in "human ecology" to deal with these and kindred subjects. He has also taken an active part in the struggle for abortion law reform. He writes as a scientist who is a humanist as well, being at home in both of C. P. Snow's two cultures. In what is probably the most controversial article in this book, Dr. Hardin argues that population control and an end to pollution cannot be achieved by purely voluntary means: irresponsible exploitation of "the commons" by some people forces all of us to behave destructively. The only alternative is restricting both the freedom to reproduce and the use of the environment, or what Dr. Hardin has elsewhere called "mutual coercion, mutually agreed on."

To most of us "coercion" has frightening implications. It conjures up visions of a prying, despotic superstate supervising every detail of our lives. To be sure, we accept governmental inference in a good many matters and expect police protection from the irresponsible members of society; but the prospect of interference with anything so intimate as our reproductive behavior is dismaying. Perhaps this is because we forget that the state always has interfered with it in one way or another, hedging it about, for example, with marriage and divorce laws and laws of inheritance. Few people object to compulsory health certificates for couples about to marry. And perhaps the idea of government coercion is less shocking when we reflect that there may exist other forms of coercion than those imposed by government. A climate of opinion in which certain things are "not done" can be at least as powerful as any legislative enactment.

Whether or not he is in agreement with Dr. Hardin's argument, any serious advocate of population control and the restoration of the environment must give serious consideration to the ideas it presents.

As we attempt to bring population growth to an end our best course of action for the immediate future is clear: we must make all forms of birth control, including abortion and sterilization, freely available to everyone. So great is society's interest in preventing the birth of unwanted children that it is economic good sense to furnish all birth control services cost-free to all citizens.

If there are no impediments to birth control the birth rate will drop; but demographic studies indicate that it will still be higher than the death rate, because procreative norms that were functional in a less healthy world still persist. To alter these we need public campaigns of persuasion; we need also to rewrite textual materials for elementary and secondary schools to emphasize that there is more than one kind of good life. Growing up to be a parent is a good thing — for some people. Growing up and *not* becoming a parent is also a good thing — for other people. Those for whom parenthood is truly not a vocation need to feel free to follow their calling.

Women who are deprived of most of the good things of our society frequently cling to multiple motherhood because it is the only career open to them. Impoverished families are an economic drain on society. Taxpayers complain. They do not generally recognize that much of this burden could be lifted if a concerted effort were made to see to it that every woman, whatever her economic level and skills, had open to her the possibility of a meaningful occupation outside the home. The human species is a social animal. Most women, given the choice, prefer useful work in the company of other adults to lonely drudgery in a home with a passel of kids perpetually under foot. A society that offers meaningful work for all automatically diminishes the problem of overpopulation.

All these proposals presuppose only completely voluntary control of births. If realized, will they be enough to solve the population problem? In the long run, probably not. The reasons for making this disturbing statement are several.

First, there is the empirical fact that in every nation a substantial fraction of the citizens are living below the poverty line. This is true even where birth control is fairly effective. Poor people become parents because most young people tend to be overly optimistic about their own futures, to overestimate their ability to provide for a family. Optimism is admirable, in some respects, but it certainly tends to produce overpopulation.

The unjustifiably optimistic tend to have more children than do the realists. Their more numerous children will tend to continue this pattern. Such differential reproduction diminishes the efficacy of volunteerism in population control.

Group differences in reproduction are an even more disturbing threat than individual differences. Consider the Mormons. In the past they have been committed to producing very large families, even under monogamy. At the present time there are about two million Mormons. If they cling indefinitely to their past commitment — and they may not — they will be waging a breeding war against the rest of the United States, whether it is conscious or not. That they constitute only about one percent of the U.S. population at present is no cause for complacency; at the present rate, soon it will be two percent, then four, then 8, 16, 32 . . . — Malthus' geometric series in a competitive setting. The Mormons, or indeed any other group, that can indefinitely maintain a policy of overbreeding will cause even the most ardent "liberal" to question the wisdom of continuing to support the freedom to breed.

The issue of population control needs to be put into a larger framework. What we are all worried about is *freedom.* Now "freedom" is a complex idea, with many facets. Freedom is a function that necessarily diminishes with population size, a point that Aldous Huxley made over and over again. To understand why freedom diminishes with increased population we need to look at the effect of the major political systems on the environment, on pollution, and on population. At the most fundamental level all of these problems can be brought under the umbrella of a unitary theory.

For the exploitation of the environment there are four possible political systems. (Each of these has myriads of variants, but these need not be considered in a first orientation.) These systems and their characteristics are displayed in Table 1, which needs to be gone over in some detail. One of the four possible systems ("Case IV") seems to be a class without any real members and has no name. It is included in the table only for logical completeness and will not be discussed further.

Let's see how the other three systems operate in the exploitation of the environment. As a way of visualizing the problem let us imagine that we are concerned with raising cattle in a pasture, and that we want to so adjust the number of animals that we obtain the maximum sustainable yield, year after year, indefinitely. Every pasture land has its inherent "carrying capacity." We will assume that the number of cattle

Table 1 Political Systems of Environmental Exploitation

| | Rules of the Game | | | | Results of the Game | | | | |
| | Exploitation of Environment by: | | Profits Go to: | | | Gain from Stressing the System: | | | |
Case	Individual (1a)	Group (1b)	Individual (2a)	Group (2b)	Overall Gain (3)	Gain to the Decision-Maker (4)	Intrinsic Responsibility (5)	Temptation to Sabotage Information (6)	Name of the Game
I	✓		✓		−	−	+	0	Private Enterprise
II		✓		✓	−	0	0	+	Socialism
III		✓	✓		−	+	-	(0)	Tragedy of the Commons
IV	✓			✓	−	0	0	+	?

DEFINITIONS

Intrinsic responsibility: Adaptive responsiveness of the decision-maker brought about solely by his acting in his own self-interest.

Jawbone responsibility: The call for non-adaptive responsiveness by an outside party who asks the decision-maker to act contrary to his self-interest; a veiled threat is usually involved.

Contrived responsibility: Adaptive responsiveness involving adventitious rewards and penalties engineered into the system to remedy its lack of intrinsic responsibility.

SOURCES

William Foster Lloyd, 1833. *Two Lectures on the Checks to Population.* Oxford.

Garrett Hardin, 1968. The Tragedy of the Commons. *Science,* 162:1243-1248.

(Both of the above are reprinted in POPULATION, EVOLUTION AND BIRTH CONTROL, 2nd ed., by Garrett Hardin, editor, San Francisco: Freeman & Co., 1969.)

is initially exactly at this carrying capacity. To add one more animal would be to damage the pasture and produce less profit, year after year. We indicate this fact by a negative gain in the whole of column 3.

The pasture (environment) may be managed under a system we call "private enterprise" (Case I). Each man fences in his own portion of the pasture, on which he runs all of his cattle, and only his cattle. The owner is the decision-maker. Under these conditions, the overall gain from his decision accrues entirely to him; in this case, the signs are identical in columns 3 and 4. We may say that the owner is fully *responsible* for his decisions (column 5). If he makes a wrong decision he is not tempted to cover up this information, for if he does he will suffer (column 6). The system works admirably *for those who are in it;* those who are left out of the system of private enterprise may seek to destroy it, a fact that should never be forgotten by the "in-group."

A substitution commonly sought by the "out-group" is "socialism" (Case II). It is believed by many to be more just. Perhaps it is; but it has some significant operational disadvantages. Someone has to make the decisions. What happens to the decision-maker when he makes a bad decision? Not much, intrinsically; the negative gain resulting from a bad decision is shared by all of society, and the portion devolving upon the decision-maker is, practically speaking, zero (column 4). Intrinsically, he is not motivated to sweat very hard to reach the right decision. He is in danger of becoming a time-server, a "bureaucrat" — in the invidious sense. To motivate him, society may embroider the system with adventitous rewards for good performance — prizes and the like; or with penal sentences for bad performance. Facing adventitious rewards and penalties, the decision-maker who makes an error will be strongly motivated to sabotage the information system. He will try to see to it that unfavorable reports are classified as national defense secrets or repressed as a matter of "executive privilege" . . . I'm sure this all sounds dreadfully familiar to you.

No great nation today is operating wholly under one system or another. Russia is a mixed economy; so is the United States. Each basic system is subject to myriads of modifications in the various areas of management. This is well known. What is not so well known — and what we must thoroughly understand if we are to make sense of environment and population problems — is that *there is a third system.*

This third system was first described in 1833 by William Forster Lloyd. His analysis of its characteristics was more implicit than explicit. I will try to reverse the balance.

Suppose that each herdsman brands his cattle, which are then all run together on a common pasture, without fences. When it comes time to sell the cattle, each man obtains all the proceeds from all the cattle bearing his brand. Under this system (Case III), when a man adds one animal too many to his herd he actually benefits at sale time (column 4). It is actually to his interest to overload the environment. The herdsman who does not do so is at a competitive disadvantage vis-à-vis the others. Each man's intrinsic responsibility is less than zero: it is, in fact, negative (column 5). Consequently, each one adds more and more animals to his herd, even though the end result is ruin for all. They are trapped by the system. *Inevitable* ruin is the very essence of what we call tragedy. This is why I call this political system the "tragedy of the commons."

Private enterprise has its disadvantages but it can be made to work, more or less. Socialism has *its* disadvantages, but it also can be made to work, more or less. But, in a crowded world — and we will know no other for our entire lifetime — the tragedy of the commons should be regarded as intolerable.

I am confident that it will be so regarded *when we recognize it.* But men are very clever at hiding the truth with distorting verbiage. What are we to say, for example, of an advertisement that speaks of the glories of American technology in the following terms? Beneath a painting of fantastic new fishing boats it says: "The hungry of the world are being fed, by the ingenuity of American free enterprise harvesting the inexhaustible wealth of the seas." There are three falsehoods in this statement, and the worst of them is the implication that the oceans are being exploited by a free enterprise system. This is tragically not true. The oceans of the world are being treated as a commons, and maritime nations are exploiting them to ruination. No pretty words, no nice intentions, no shiny technology can alter this brutal truth. Only by changing the political system of exploitation can we hope to save any of the "inexhaustible" wealth of the unfenced seas for our grandchildren.

This political analysis also throws light on pollution problems. The steel mills at Gary, Indiana, belch tons of industrial garbage into the air every day, because we unthinkingly allow the air to be used as a commons. In a competitive market, the manufacturer has not enough to gain from the commons to pay for the financial loss incurred by installing expensive control equipment. Every decision-maker is caught in the same bind. Consequently the pollution continues indefinitely.

Decision-makers in Russia behave in the same way. Managers of Russia's pulp-mills are now ruining Lake Baikal with their wastes in the name of "socialism." American managers of metal works on the shores of the Great Lakes dump mercury in the water, making the fish too poisonous to eat, and call their work "private enterprise."

What should be done? A system of private enterprise enforces intrinsic responsibility on the decision-maker. Can such a system solve our major pollution problems? It is doubtful. How would we fence the air? Or the oceans? We could achieve much the same effect if (for example) we forced all steel mill executives to live near their mills and then piped the flue-gases into their homes, without treatment. Under such a responsible system, the pollution would soon be brought to an end!

Everywhere in the world the environment is polluted because we are trapped in the tragedy of the commons. It is an intrinsically irresponsible system. We will not get rid of pollution until we get rid of this iniquitous third political system. In a crowded world we must not allow any man to pollute the common media of air, water, and the "ether" of radio and light waves, beyond the bare necessities of personal survival. We must recognize the existence of the third system of environmental exploitation; we must point out its errors; and we must get rid of it.

Pollution problems cannot be completely solved, however, if we do not stop the growth of population. Pollution is made worse by our attempt to support a large population. Attempting to wring the last bushel of grain from the land, we pollute the media with DDT; with a smaller population we should not have to begrudge the bugs their tax on our crops. As we go to ever more impoverished mineral ores we create ever larger slag-heaps. While our population doubles once in seventy years, our energy requirements double every ten, increasing the per capita production of pollution from electric power plants. The population of American people increases at one percent per year. The population of American automobiles increases at five percent per year; gasoline smog increases in parallel fashion. Surveying cities of various sizes we discover that the number of crimes increases faster than the size of the city; and this in spite of the fact that big cities also spend proportionately more on crime control. Mental illness also is disproportionately greater in large cities.

In matters of pollution and the costs of congestion we are not operating in that realm (so dearly beloved of the apostles of Progress) where we can enjoy "economies of scale." Quite the contrary. Our population is clearly over the hump and going downhill. Every increase in population decreases the quality of life.

Of course we can (and must) develop ever better technological devices to control pollution and related ills. But all such controllers cost money and decrease our real income.

The facts of the case can be usefully summarized in a simple verbal formula:

$$(\text{Population}) \times (\text{Prosperity}) = (\text{Pollution})$$

where the word "pollution" stands for congestion and other spirit-abrading phenomena as well.

At a given level of population an increase in the number of automobiles (prosperity) will decrease the amount of pollution; put smog-control devices on the cars and pollution is diminished, but at the expense of personal prosperity. Electric power plants can be equipped with pollution control equipment — but at a higher cost per kilowatt-hour to the consumer.

Population and prosperity are "trade-offs." If we adhere to fixed standards for pollution, any increase in one will require a corresponding decrease in the other.

Faced with this choice, which do we want — a greater population or greater prosperity? We can't have both (unless we are willing to put up with ever higher levels of pollution and congestion). The interconnection of population and pollution has led Fred Singer to speak of "Popollution" problems.

Most people would, I think, elect for personal prosperity rather than national populousness. But as we think about the problem of controlling population size we discover that we must once more consider the effect of the three great classes of political systems.

A few centuries ago family size was determined largely by a private enterprise system. Parents who were so unwise or so unlucky as to produce too many children had to suffer for it: the stress of too many weakened the whole family and often some of the members starved to death. The outside world did little to interfere with the intrinsic responsibility of this cruel system.

The last two centuries have seen a great increase in the philanthropic activities of the state. More and more of the costs of education are assumed by the community. It is regarded as a disgrace to the community when a child starves to death. Few will argue against the desirability of this change, but we should notice its political significance.

As we approach ever closer to the "welfare state" we produce an ever-purer example of the tragedy of the commons in population matters. The Marxian ideal ". . . to each according to his needs" in fact defines a commons. If parents are free to have as many children as they want because they know that all can dip into the commons then population control becomes difficult if not impossible. Even if the great majority are sensitive to the larger needs of the community, the few who are not will cause the system to break down. Freedom to breed will, in the long run, produce ruin for all.

There is a cliché that says "freedom is indivisible." Properly interpreted, this saying has some wisdom in it; but there is also a sense in which it is false. *Freedom is divisible* — and we must find how to divide it if we are to survive in dignity.

There are many identifiable freedoms; among them are freedom of speech, freedom of assembly, freedom of association, freedom in the choice of residence, freedom in work, and freedom to travel. You can make the list as long as you like.

Ask yourself this question: Is there one freedom on the list that would *increase* if our population became twice as great as it is now? I challenge you to name a single freedom that is likely to become greater with a further increase in population.

By contrast, most of our freedoms would be greater and more secure if the population were only a half, or even a tenth, its present size. With a small enough size we could even enjoy the freedom to pollute again! The residents of a village can still enjoy the convenience (as well as the fragrance) of burning the autumn leaves, an illegal activity in large cities. This is a small matter, perhaps, but it is symbolic.

We have already lost much of our freedom because of population growth, and we will continuously lose more with further growth.

Freedom *is* divisible. If we want to keep the rest of our freedoms we must restrict the freedom to breed. How we can accomplish this is not at this moment clear, but it is surely subject to rational study. A century ago we deprived ourselves of the right to have many wives, and the nation survived. Is losing the freedom to have multiple children so much worse?

It is undoubtedly too soon to pass laws that will definitely restrict the freedom to breed. Such a loss will not be accepted until all men understand that the freedom to breed must be circumscribed in order to retain other, and more precious, freedoms.

Let us begin now on that educational campaign.

THE GENETIC IMPLICATIONS OF AMERICAN LIFE STYLES IN REPRODUCTION AND POPULATION CONTROL

Carl J. Bajema

Supposing we accept coercion in the matter of human reproduction, for the sake of controlling population size, should we stop there? Dr. Bajema argues that we cannot afford to neglect the matter of population quality as well. Without genetic control there will be an increase in the proportion of individuals unfit for life in a complex technological society. And why should the right to reproduce rest on a basis of simple numerical equality or "two children per couple"? Dr. Bajema goes beyond Dr. Hardin's argument in advocating eugenics.

It may be noted that unlike population limitation, eugenics calls for qualitative judgments; and some people will ask, who shall make those judgments? To members of minority groups the question will seem especially pertinent — a reminder that the situation we have to deal with includes ethical and political as well as scientific issues.

Dr. Bajema is a geneticist and a professor of biology at Grand Valley State College in Michigan. He is also Secretary of the American Eugenics Society and editor of Natural Selection in Human Populations, *a study of genetic and social factors in the contemporary world.*

Each generation of mankind is faced with the awesome responsibility of having to make decisions concerning the quantity and quality (both genetic and cultural) of future generations. Because of its concern for its increasing population in relation to natural resources and quality of life America appears to be on the verge of discarding its policy favoring continued population growth and adopting a policy aimed at achieving a zero rate of population growth by voluntary means. The policy that a society adopts with respect to population size will have genetic as well as environmental consequences.

Human populations adapt to their environments genetically as well as culturally. These environments have been and are changing very rapidly with most of the changes being brought about by man himself. Mankind, has, by creating a highly technological society, produced a society in which a large proportion of its citizens cannot contribute to its growth or maintenance because of the limitations (both genetic and environmental) of their intellect. The modern technological societies of democratic nations offer their citizens a wide variety of opportunities for self-fulfillment but find that many of their citizens are incapable of taking advantage of the opportunities open to them.

American society, if it takes its responsibility to future generations seriously, will have to do more than control the size of its population in relation to the environment. American society will have to take steps to insure that individuals yet unborn will have the best genetic and environmental heritage possible to enable them to meet the challenges of the environment and to be able to take advantage of the opportunities for self-fulfillment made available by society.

The question of genetic quality cannot be ignored for very long by American society because it, like all other human societies, has to cope with two perpetual problems as it attempts to adapt to its environment. First, American society has to cope with a continual input of harmful genes into its population via mutation (it has been estimated that approximately one out of every five newly fertilized human eggs is carrying a newly mutated gene that was not present in either of the two parents). The genetic status quo can be maintained in a human population only if the carriers of these mutant genes do not reproduce. Otherwise the proportion of harmful genes in the population will increase. Secondly, American society has to adapt to a rapidly changing environment. For instance, the technologically based, computer age sociocultural environment being created by American society has placed a premium on the possession of high intelligence and creativity. Our society requires individuals with high intelligence and creativity to help it make the appropriate social and technological adjustments in order to culturally adapt to its rapidly changing environment. On the other hand individuals require high intelligence and creativity in order that they, as individuals, can cope with the challenges of the environment and take advantage of the opportunities for self-fulfillment present in our society.

The proportion of the American population that already is genetically handicapped — that suffers a restriction of liberty or competence because of the genes they are carrying — is not small. Therefore the genetic component of the human population-environment equation must be taken into account as we attempt to establish an environment that has a high degree of ecological stability and that maximizes the number of opportunities for self-fulfillment available to each individual human being.

American life styles with respect to sex and reproduction are currently in a tremendous state of flux and are changing rapidly. This makes it very difficult to accurately predict the genetic consequences of these life styles. Yet, because these life styles determine the genetic make-up of future generations of Americans it is necessary that we evaluate the genetic consequences of past and present trends and speculate concerning the probable genetic consequences of projecting these trends into the future. Only then will we be able to determine the severity of the problem and to determine what steps, if any, need to be taken to maintain and improve the genetic heritage of future generations.

American society has developed modern medical techniques which enable many individuals with severe genetic defects to survive to adulthood. Many of these individuals can and do reproduce, thereby passing their harmful genes on to the next generation and increasing the frequency of these genes in the population. At present there is no indication that heredity counseling decreases the probability that these individuals will have children. The life styles of these individuals with respect to reproduction is creating a larger genetic burden for future generations of Americans to bear.

The effect of American life styles in sex and reproduction on such behavioral patterns as intelligence and personality is much less clear. For instance, during most of man's evolution natural selection has favored the genes for intelligence. The genes for higher mental ability conferred an advantage to their carriers in the competition for survival and reproduction both within and between populations. Thus the more intelligent members of the human species passed more genes on to the next generation than did the less intelligent members, with the result that the genes for higher intelligence increased in frequency. As western societies shifted from high birth and death rates toward low birth and death rates, however, a breakdown in the relation of natural selection to achievement or "success" took place.

The practice of family planning spread more rapidly among the better educated strata of society, resulting in negative fertility differentials. At the period of extreme differences which in the United States came during the Great Depression, the couples who were poorly educated were having about twice as many children as the more educated couples. The continued observation of a negative relationship between fertility and such characteristics as education, occupation, and income during the first part of this century led many scientists to believe that this pattern of births was a concomitant of the industrial welfare state society and must make for the genetic deterioration of the human race. This situation was, in part, temporary. The fertility differentials have declined dramatically since World War II. A number of recent studies of American life styles in reproduction, when taken collectively, seem to indicate that, as the proportion of the urban population raised in a farm environment decreases, as the educational attainment of the population increases, and as women gain complete control over childbearing (via contraception and induced abortion) differences of income, occupation, educational attainment, and intelligence (I.Q.) will not be reflected in the number of offspring.

The overall net effect of current American life styles in reproduction appears to be slightly dysgenic — to be favoring an increase in harmful genes which will handicap a larger proportion of the next generation of Americans. American life styles in reproduction are, in part, a function of the population policy of the United States.

What will be the long range genetic implications of controlling or not controlling population size in an industrialized welfare state democracy such as America?

Most contemporary human societies are organized in such a way that they encourage population growth. How is the genetic make-up of future generations affected by the size of the population? What will be the ultimate genetic consequences, given a society that is growing in numbers in relation to its environment? One possible consequence is military aggression coupled with genocide to attain additional living space. This would result in genetic change insofar as the population eradicated or displaced differs genetically from the population that is aggressively expanding the size of its environment. The displacement of the American Indians by Western Europeans is an example of this approach to the problem of population size in relation to the environment. Throughout man's evolution such competition between different populations of human beings has led to an increase in the cultural and genetic supports for aggressive behavior in the human species. Violence as a form of aggressive behavior to solve disagreements among populations appears to have become maladaptive in the nuclear age. It will probably take a nuclear war to prove this contention.

If one assumes that military aggression plus genocide to attain additional living space is not an option open to a society with a population policy encouraging growth in numbers, then a different type of genetic change will probably take place. Most of the scientists who have attempted to ascertain the probable effect that overcrowding in a welfare state will have on man's genetic make-up have concluded that natural selection would favor those behavior patterns that most people consider least desirable. For instance, René Dubos, in discussing the effect of man's future environment on the direction and intensity of natural selection in relation to human personality patterns states that:

> Most disturbing perhaps are the behavioral consequences likely to ensue from overpopulation. The ever-increasing complexity of the social structure will make some form of regimentation unavoidable; freedom and privacy may come to constitute antisocial luxuries and their attainment to involve real hardships. In consequence, there may emerge by selection a stock of human beings suited to accept as a matter of course a regimented and sheltered way of life in a teeming and polluted world, from which all wilderness and fantasy of nature will have disappeared. The domesticated farm animal and the laboratory rodent in a controlled environment will then become true models for the study of man.

The genetic and cultural undesirability of either of these two alternatives outcomes for mankind makes it imperative that societies move quickly to adopt policies aimed at achieving and maintaining an optimum population size that maximizes the dignity and individual worth of a human being rather than maximizing the number of human beings in relation to the environment.

There is strong evidence that contemporary societies can achieve control of their population size by voluntary means, at least in the short run.

What will be the distribution of births in societies that have achieved a zero population growth rate? In a society where population size is constant — where each generation produces only enough offspring to replace itself — there will still be variation among couples with respect to the number of children they will have. Some individuals will be childless or have only one child for a variety of reasons — biological (genetically or environmentally caused sterility), psychological (inability to attract a mate, desire to remain childless), etc. Some individuals will have to have at least three children to compensate for those individuals who have less than two. The resulting differential fertility — variation in the number of children couples have — provides an opportunity for natural selection to operate and would bring about genetic change if the differences in fertility among individuals are correlated with differences (physical, physiological, or behavioral) among individuals.

The United States is developing into a social welfare state democracy, This should result in an environment that will evoke the optimal response from the variety of genotypes (specific combinations of genes that individuals carry) present in the population. It is questionable, however, as to whether a social welfare state democracy creates the type of environment that will automatically bring about an eugenic distribution of births resulting in the maintenance or enhancement of man's genetic heritage. It is also questionable as to whether a social welfare state democracy (or any society for that matter) will be able to achieve and maintain a zero population growth rate — a constant population size — by voluntary means.

Both Charles Darwin and Garrett Hardin have argued that universal compulsion will be necessary to achieve and maintain zero population growth. They argue that appeals to individual conscience as the means by which couples are to restrain themselves from having more than two children won't work, because those individuals or groups who refused to restrain themselves would increase their numbers in relation to the rest, with the result that these individuals or groups with their cultural and/or biological supports for high fertility would constitute a larger and larger proportion of the population of future generations and *Homo contracipiens* would be replaced by *Homo progenetivis.*

Hardin raises this problem in his classic paper, "The Tragedy of the Commons," when he states:

> "If each human family were dependent only on its own resources; if the children of improvident parents starved to death; if, thus, overbreeding brought its own "punishment to the germ line — then there would be no public interest in controlling the breeding of families. But our society is deeply committed to the welfare state, and hence confronted with another aspect of the tragedy of the commons.
>
> In a welfare state, how shall we deal with the family, the religion, the race, or the class (or indeed any distinguishable and cohesive group) that adopts overbreeding as a policy to secure its own aggradizement? To couple the

concept of freedom to breed with the belief that everyone born has an equal right to the commons is to lock the world into a tragic course of action."

The only way out of this dilemma according to Hardin is for society to create reproductive responsibility via social arrangements that produce coercion of some sort. The kind of coercion Hardin talks about is mutual coercion, mutually agreed upon by the majority of the people affected. Compulsory taxes are an example of mutual coercion. Democratic societies frequently have to resort to mutual coercion to escape destruction of the society by the irresponsible. Mutual coercion appears to be the only solution to the problem of pollution. If Hardin is right it may also be the only solution for any society that is attempting to control the size and/or the genetic make-up of its population.

It is impossible for a society to maintain a constant population size if no couple in the population has more than two children. Some couples must have more than two children if society is to maintain a constant population size. Should not the primary consideration in the determination as to who shall have more than two children be the genetic make-up of future generations?

POPULATION AND ECOLOGY:
DUAL THREAT AND RESPONSE

Roger L. Shinn

Dr. Shinn discusses the ethical and religious dimensions of the population-environment situation. In response to Garrett Hardin's and Carl Bajema's arguments for coercion he maintains that neither total freedom nor total coercion is a valid option. "Society has always involved both voluntary and compulsory qualities." Moreover, the acceptance of any method of population limitation we adopt will depend on religious and ethical sanctions. Dr. Shinn urges a re-orientation of religious and ethical thinking with respect to our earth and its inhabitants.

Dr. Shinn is Professor of Social Ethics at Union Theological Seminary in New York, and Adjunct Professor of Religion at Columbia University. Of the dozen books he has published, Man: The New Humanism *is the most recent.*

The basic assumption of my argument is simple — and disturbing. Mankind today is taking risks more loaded with disaster for the whole human race and the planet Earth than ever before in history. The message is loud and clear. Prophets of doom are so common and repetitious today that they must become strident or violent to gain attention. Numerous scientists estimate a life expectancy for humanity of 20-40 years. But the familiarity of prophecy takes nothing from its truth. The human race is, in fact, in deep trouble.

The problem comes from the confluence of three interrelated but distinguishable movements: the population explosion, the plundering of the environment, and the escalation of weapons. Any one of the three is portentous. The combination of them all brings closer the time of probable disaster. This essay will consider the first two movements, not because weaponry is less important than the others, but because it requires a somewhat different style of inquiry.

I

There are still a few people who would debate my basic assumption. Although I have no desire to shut off discussion, part of the problem is that mankind cannot afford the time for leisurely debate. Hence I shall state only briefly the reasoning involved in my assumptions, then get on to their further implications.

First, mankind must stop its growth of population. The evidence leads to a virtually absolute argument. Whereas the human race took something more than a million years to grow to a billion people by about 1850, now it adds a billion in less than 15 years. The doubling of population in about 35 years, if continued, means a geometric progression that cannot by any possibility maintain itself. No ingenuity of productivity or social organization can match an arithmetic that leads straight to infinity. Rather early in that process, if it were to continue unchecked, men would be crowded elbow to elbow; then after a while they would outweigh the earth. Without waiting for such an absurdity, the multiplication leads to starvation and social turmoil. Obviously something – preferably some measures better than war, pestilence, and famine — will stop the explosive growth. There are good reasons for thinking that the halt had best come soon.

Second, mankind must revise radically its exploitation of the natural environment. The human race must learn quickly (1) to get more out of its environment and (2) to despoil it less. Men must exploit nature more skillfully because already 10,000 people die each day from starvation or consequences of malnutrition. Furthermore, as Ivan Bennett shows, the squeeze is getting tighter for the simple reason that babies, as they grow up, eat more. "To maintain the Indian population *at its present level* of nutrition would require 20 percent more food in 1975 than in 1965 *if no new children were added during this ten year period.* To elevate the diet to the minimal standard, recommended by the United Nations Food and Agricultural Organization, a 30 percent increase would be required." Obviously some new children will be born, so the need will be greater. Avoidance of catastrophic starvation requires increased food and better distribution of food. Both depend upon economic development. But such development, in the familiar styles of the past, intensifies the ecological crisis that besets the planet and all its people. Hence man must undertake the paradoxically difficult task of luring more productivity from nature while destroying its resources less.

I have pointed to two necessities, both of which will strain the resolution and skill of species man: the regulation of population and the revision of man's relation to nature. It is urgent to realize that neither will be much help without the other. Any tunnel-vision that concentrates on one objective alone is absurd and immoral. Regulation of population is necessary because of the sheer threat of the geometric progression, no matter how successfully man may learn to live with his environment. Likewise, answers to the economic-ecological crisis are necessary, no matter how successfully man may learn to moderate or even halt his growth in numbers.

II

The confrontation with the double crisis requires a revision, at some points even a reversal, of some traditional ethical convictions. It requires also immense technical and political achievements. But technique and politics usually work in the service of deep human aspirations, fears, and moral attitudes. Some inherited values today need criticism, even displacement, by values more sensitively oriented to human need. Other traditional values, long neglected by arrogant man, need recovery. Four cases of value-revision deserve attention here.

1. The Ethic of Reproduction

The zero-growth rate in population has become a clearly desirable goal. If a few argue that it is not necessary yet, plain arithmetic (as I have shown) dictates that it must come some time; and the overwhelming judgment of those who study the issue is that it should come quickly. A zero-growth rate means that the two-child family becomes normative. Since not all people beget children, the actual rate of reproduction can be fractionally higher, but two children per family is necessarily the general rule. Given the present composition of the human race with its preponderance of young people, the immediate adoption of a two-child-per-family-rule (if that were somehow possible) would still mean a great expansion of population before long-range stabilization could set in.

Any such proposal means change in some deeply-felt folk-ways and beliefs. In some societies social security for the aged depends upon male offspring who live to maturity. A change in the ethic of reproduction in these societies will require a reconstruction of the whole social system and *Gestalt* of values. In other societies the parents of a large family (provided they could support the family) have been considered ethically responsible because they subordinated their own "greed" for the sake of the children. Such families may soon be considered dangerous aggressors against the society.

The "contraception adoption explosion" (Donald Bogue's phrase) is one example of the way in which technical change and ethical change interact. To be sure, France, Switzerland, and Ireland reduced their growth rates dramatically prior to the development of modern contraceptives. But contraception facilitates the adoption of a profound ethical value — the expression of conjugal love combined with responsible parenthood. It has other moral effects. To the extent that the traditional ideal of sexual fidelity within a monogamous relationship depedds upon fear of unwanted offspring, that value becomes obsolete; to the extent that it has other roots, it is unthreatened by contraception. The ethical inhibition against contraception is fast fading. The formal teaching authority of Roman Catholicism remains opposed to contraception; but most Catholic theologians and laymen have accepted contraception, and there is little evidence to support the common opinion that Catholics reproduce more prolifically than other people.

2. The Responsibility of the Affluent

In popular mythology the threat of population is the fault of the poor — of poor societies (like the Indian and Latin American) and of poor classes in other societies. One consequence of the mythology is an ideological conflict. Affluent peoples give moralistic lectures to poor people, whether across the seas or in neighboring ghettoes. The poor resent the condemnation and reply that the wealthy are using population as an evasion of their own responsibility to do something about poverty and advocating genocide or ethnic suicide for the poor.

The ideological conflict is largely unnecessary because its premises are mistaken. True, there is *some* correlation between low education, low income, and high reproduction. But if it is true that high reproduction is a cause of poverty, it is also true that social injustice, causing poverty and low education, is a cause of high reproduction. The rich and powerful have no moral right to preach to the poor about population until they have committed their wealth and power to the cause of justice.

Furthermore, it is the affluent societies and classes that do most ecological damage. Paul Ehrlich has said, "Each American child is fifty times more of a burden on the environment than each Indian child." We who eat quantities of meat, who drive cars and travel in airplanes, who consume the products of industries that plunder the earth and pollute the air — we are the predators of the environment that thus far has sustained our human race.

3. An Ethic of Conservation

The economic-ecological problem has momentous ramifications that have only recently dawned on western, technological man, who has been demonstrating how to wreck the environment without really trying. The common answer, even of the most enlightened, to social problems — to unemployment, to the gap between rich and poor, to the degradation of the cities — has usually been to increase production, with some share of the increase assigned to redress of wrongs. But now, it appears, increased production is the villain in the story. There is no foreseeable rise in productivity that can bring the impoverished majority of the world up to the rate of consumption practiced by the affluent minority.

There are three aspects to the process of increasing production. The first is the consumption of raw materials. The usual estimateiis that the United States, with about 6 percent of the world's population, consumes 40-50 percent of its resources. It is inconceivable that the "underdeveloped" economies of the world should "develop" to the stage of comparable consumption. Detailed analysis of the availability of specific raw materials only intensifies the problem.

The second aspect is pollution of the environment. Industries and individual citizens pour poisons into the water and air. The average person in the United States produces 5.3 lbs. of solid waste per day, or almost a ton a year, with the rate steadily rising. No large city in the country knows how it will dispose of its wastes ten years hence.

The third aspect is the destruction of the general ecological balance. Carbon dioxide is not usually reckoned a poison, but a balance between oxygen and carbon dioxide is a necessity. Animal life and industry turn oxygen into carbon dioxide; plant life reverses the process. No one — quite literally, no one — knows at what point the increase of population and of industry can wreck the ecological balance, leading to melting of polar icecaps and inundation of vast coastal areas.

Conceivably technology, which is presently an ecological threat, can develop processes of recycling chemical materials that will be a blessing. Any such development will require a form of social cost accounting. It may be individually less costly to buy a new alarm clock than to repair an old one, to use disposable rather than returnable containers, to abandon an old car than to turn it in; but social accounting uses a different balance sheet. Society cannot go far in the direction of social accounting without accepting the context of an ethic of conservation.

4. The Urban Atrocity

Increasingly the large city looks like an experiment that failed. Increasingly it is hard to see the relation between urban and urbane. The city, by bringing into proximity a great variety of persons and skills, has the possibility of educational, artistic, economic, and social creativity. But the structure of the American city — its hemmed-in ghettoes, its industrial parks, its fortress-like surburbs, its inept educational systems, its filth, its reliance upon destructive forms of transportation — is an atrocity.

There is a relation between technique and ethic in reconstructing urban life. Technique may develop new forms of living less dependent upon moving people long distances between work and home. But only ethical sensitivity can move people closer to equality in the sharing of burdens and opportunities.

A combined ethical awareness and technology might do something to lessen the gap between urban civilization and nature, between work and leisure. The sharp contrast, often marked by hours each week of cramped travel between work and home destroys a holistic appreciation of life. And leisure, when it must be pursued frantically and expensively in week-ends wedged between weeks of work, almost ceases to be leisure. Conceivably affluent man, straining his resources and spending his income to gain some relief from pressure, may learn something from less wealthy societies for whom relaxation is a more normal part of life.

III

A profound ethic can never isolate ends and means. Nor can it concentrate on single issues in abstraction from the entire meaning and mystery of life. Any one-sided approach to issues of either population or ecology will distort the very human values that are at stake in the crisis. Modern systems analysis has made us aware that even in the realm of technical problems there is urgent need to see the implications of any one issue for other issues. If we increase our purview to include ethical values, the need for wide awareness and sensitivity is even more evident.

There are many ways by which population might be checked. Malaria could be allowed to resume its age-old work. Infanticide, castration to produce eunuchs, slaughter of enemies are unquestionably effective. Automobile accidents and air pollution, given a little encouragement, could do much more to reduce life expectancy. Starvation, already fairly effective, will step up its work without any encouragement, provided only man does not exert heroic efforts to stop it. Any political authority with sufficient power and ruthlessness can "solve" the problem. But obviously some solutions are as bad as the problems they purport to solve. If the aim is to enhance the meaning and dignity of human life, no method destructive to that aim is tolerable.

For that reason the appeal to reason and voluntary decision is an important part of any ethical change. Hence there is great attractiveness in the work of the Harvard Center for Population Studies with its concern for the cultural and psychological factors that enter into human propagation. There is a similar attractiveness in Philip Hauser's attention to "the importance of the cultural milieu, the problem of incentive, of motivation, of devising a package that becomes understandable and acceptable to the people involved."

However, powerful voices insist that volunteerism is not adequate to meet the emergency. Paul Ehrlich and Garrett Hardin, pointing out that society exercises coercion in waging war and in imposing taxes, insist that some coercive measures are both necessary and justifiable. When free choice becomes socially destructive, inhibitions upon freedom become ethical.

In assessing this argument there is some help in starting from the awareness that neither total freedom nor total coercion is an option. Society always involves both voluntary and compulsory qualities.

Society itself, living in finite space amid finite resources, is not totally free. When unrestricted reproduction seriously threatens a society, the society is likely to decide to direct the cost of the offense against the offenders. There are many devices — including propaganda, taxation, availability of housing, and restriction of ration cards — by which some societies now exert pressure upon people to limit family size.

The trouble is that rigorous enforcement of any restriction of reproduction involves methods — compulsory sterilization or abortion — that intrude upon personal freedom in ways that are intensely offensive to many people. The prohibition of child-birth — beyond, for example, two children to any mother — is likely to prove as difficult of enforcement as the prohibition of abortion has proved. Such prohibitions work only if there is an immense social consensus to support them. Since the consensus will not be produced by compulsion, the importance of educational and voluntary methods is obvious.

In recent years a number of thoughtful people have asked whether modern western man can meet the crisis of population and ecology without a profound religious reorientation. Paul Goodman sees the need of and evidence of "a kind of religious transformation" analogous to the Protestant Reformation of the 16th century. Kenneth Boulding, urging western man to "learn to live within nature as a member of a great ecological system, and not as a conqueror," advocates a dialogue with the religions of the East. Lynn White in an address to the American Association for the Advancement of Science, an address that has become famous, says that technology, science, and the dominant Western version of Christianity are so infected with "arrogance toward nature" that they cannot resolve our crisis. "We must", he says, "rethink and refill our nature and destiny."

There are resources available for so doing. Science, technology, and theology need not be arrogant. Anthropologist Loren Eiseley has written:

> Man has a belief in seen and unseen nature. He is both pragmatist and mystic . . . . I shall want to look at this world from both the empirical point of view and from one which also takes into account that sense of awe and marvel which is part of man's primitive heritage, and without which man would not be man.
>
> For many of us the Biblical bush still burns, and there is a deep mystery in the heart of a simple seed.

Theologian H. Richard Niebuhr, after showing how "radical monotheism" secularizes nature, removing from nature the gods and spirits and making it amenable to scientific investigation, then goes on to show how the same faith imparts a derived sacredness to nature:

> Now every day is the day that the Lord has made; every nation is a holy people called by him into existence in its place and time and to his glory; every person is sacred, made in his image and likeness; every living thing, on earth, in the heavens, and in the waters is his creation and points in its existence toward him; the whole earth is filled with his glory; the infinity of space is his temple where all creation is summoned to silence before him.

No religious or ethical conviction can do the whole work of solving man's portentous problems. Especially in areas so complex as population and ecology, man must use his best wits and technological reason. But technology serves human purposes, good or bad. It may be that man's intelligence, not his stupidity, will doom him — unless that intelligence serves some loyalty to mankind, some vision of a better society, some gratitude for this planet Earth given to man as his home.

POPULATION GROWTH AND
AMERICAN IDEOLOGY

A. E. Keir Nash

Dr. Nash considers the political implications of population control. Of all the obstacles in the American political system to achieving population control, the greatest is our ideological commitment to the classical liberalism of John Locke; historically, we have always resisted government intereference with "the private sector."

Given this traditional opposition, what is the political feasibility of various proposals for dealing with the problem of overpopulation? Dr. Nash classifies these proposals and discusses them in relation to the likelihood of their acceptance by the American public.

Dr. Nash is a member of the Political Science Department of the University of California, Santa Barbara. Currently he is on leave of absence serving as the Director of Political Research on the National Commission on Population Growth and the American Future. He is the author of numerous articles and senior author of a forthcoming book, Off-Shore Oil Pollution and the Public Interest.

A governmental policy of abstaining from intervention in population growth, whether a reasoned decision or the result of inaction, constitutes a political result as freighted with consequences as a decision to intervene. There is, thus, no gainsaying the conclusion that the population explosion constitutes a political and not merely a technical or informational problem. One inescapable question is, then, what sort of a political response by the United States is likely. It is the aim of this essay to attempt to delineate the major characteristics of the American political system which augur something less than a speedy response.

Barriers to Treating the Problem in the American Political System

An age is sometimes best defined in terms of its salient problems. And, the viability of a political culture in that age rests heavily upon two characteristics: (1) its capacity for timely perception of such problems as problems; and (2) its ability to solve them within its existing governmental contours. Without perception and without solution, the society runs grave risks of disaster — whether that disaster assume the form of societal extinction or of political revolution. At the very least, the society's politics must be able to temporize with the problem — and be able to hand it on, recognized even if only partially dealt with, to the succeeding political generation.

That the phenomenon of nuclear power has been an overriding problem of the mid-twentieth century scarcely admits of doubt. That an equally important problem of the final third of this century will be the population explosion scarcely admits of greater doubt. The mid-twentieth century accomplished the minimum of deferring the nculear issue: the outbreak of World War II now lies closer to the end of World War I than to the present, and we have not yet blown ourselves up. But there are at least two reasons why social scientists may be less optimistic in prognosticating even such limited success with respect to the population explosion. First, the nuclear problem had one great comparative "advantage" — its obviousness. After Hiroshima, it was perceptually inescapable. By comparison, population is a quiet issue that creeps up on us, particularly if we are middle-class or upper-class. If the nuclear age began with a bang, the age of the population crisis manifests itself with the intermittent distant whimper of a black baby starving in the forests of Biafra or (can we really believe it?) among the magnolias of Mississippi.

The second reason is that American political, economic, and ideological structures were far better geared to grappling with the nuclear issue in at least four ways. One, before Hiroshima, significant members of the decision-making elite, i.e., the scientists working on the Manhattan Project and the politicians around the President who knew of it, were already well aware of the problematic *political* nature of the bomb. Two, nothing in the structure of American politics (except for the strain of isolationism to whose virtual dissolution it notably contributed) weakened that grappling. Rather it grew directly out of an ever-present problem — national defense. The onset of the Cold War made its crucial political character patent to politicians and to the public. In contrast, the perception of population growth as a problem is not "built into" the normal decision-making patterns of American politics. Consequently, there is not much general pre-occupation with it among the elite or the public. Instead, although the American political scene is by no means wholly devoid of political laeders aware for some time of the population threat — the names of former Senators Gruening of Alaska, Clark of Pennsylvania, and Tydings of Maryland, and former Secretary of Defense McNamara spring to mind — American politics is hardly characterized by a pervasive sense of its overwhelming seriousness. Despite their efforts the former Senators became "former" by acts of the electorate not two years after Tydings rightly singled them out as "pioneers." It is similarly suggestive of structural resistances in American politics to timely problem-perception that not until Robert S. McNamara washed his hands of administering the Pentagon and moved to the World Bank did he find an adequate "site" from which to attack wholeheartedly the problem.

The third structural barrier to adequate grappling is economic. Population control has at least a short-run disadvantage to American business: unlike defense, if successful, it provides less, not more, consumers. As an economic interest-group pushing for massive government financial aid, G. D. Searle Co. and its competitors in the contraceptive market are hardly a match for aerospace and defense industries.

While it is difficult to believe that this third barrier will prove too formidable in the future, a fourth structural disincentive appears potentially serious enough to warrant much more detailed examination. Grappling with the problem of overpopulation threatens to be gravely complicated by ideological factors. To put the matter bluntly, on its face at least there is something "un-American" about the notion of nonvoluntary methods of control. Furthermore, at least for significant sectors of the American population, even the idea of voluntary birth control cuts against the ideological grain. Let us examine these ideological factors.

"Lockean" Norms of Individualism as a Perceptual Barrier

As Louis Hartz has so brilliantly argued, probably the single most distinctive characteristic of American political life as compared to the politics of other industrialized countries has been its wholehearted yet largely unconscious commitment throughout its post-revolutionary history to the classical liberalism of John Locke. This is not to deny the "realness" of American political conflict since 1789. It is simply to suggest, after Hartz, that its major contending factions have been essentially, in the European sense, liberal. The United States, with the debatable exceptions of a few early New England Federalists and a few antebellum Southern apologists for slavery, simply has not seen genuine conservative politicians. American advocates of the Divine Right of Kings and of the inherited rights of aristocracies have been chiefly conspicuous by their absence. So too, at least until very recently (and here the issue is yet in doubt), genuine socialism has been virtually impotent on the American political stage.

What passes for American conservatism — whether that of the 19th-century Business Whigs or of contemporary Goldwaterism — is not the American equivalent of the European conservative tradition. Rather it has virtually duplicated the values of *grand bourgeois* European liberalism. Hardly any United States conservatives have advocated the major tenets of European conservatism: belief in the natural irrationality and inequality of man and consequent insistence upon his inability to govern himself without extensive governmental constraints upon his pursuit of liberty and property. Typically, American conservatism has advocated precisely the opposite: the inalienable right of the individual, be he entrepreneur or laborer, to work out his own destiny in the absence of, or at least in the minimal presence of, political restraint. In short, the American conservative has virtually duplicated the rationalist view of human nature and the economic laissez-faire of the great liberal European philosophic descendents of John Locke — Adam Smith, Jeremy Bentham, and the early John Stuart Mill — and of the liberal political parties of 19th and 20th century Europe.

In the economic sphere, the most conspicuous characteristic of the American Liberal Left has not been advocacy of the prime political tenet of socialism — abolition of private property. Rather, from the days of the Trust-Busting Progressives through the New Deal to the present, its two dominant reflexes have been different not merely in degree but in kind: one, "regulating against" monopolistic concentrations of business power in order to return to a "golden Jeffersonian" day in the past of small rural and industrial enterprises; and two, building compensations into capitalism — whether tempering the natural swings of Smithian boom-and-bust cycles by very modest application of Keynesian control techniques, or aiding the more widely distributed enjoyment of still-very-private property rights by progressive income taxes, by unemployment compensation, and by encouraging that *bête noire* of true Marxist socialism, trade unionism. The net is a very curious paradox of comparative ideology: the economic "solutions" of the Democratic Left which the American Right has denounced as "creeping socialism" have been precisely those which European Marxist-Leninists have most bitterly attacked on the grounds that by ameliorating rather than exacerbating "the internal contradictions of Capitalism" they would frustrate the coming of the Socialist Revolution.

But to say this is to point to more than a quaintness in the history of ideologies. Rather it is to suggest that the very consensus on basic American political and economic values may have — in respect to population control — precisely the opposite effect upon "problem-solving" from that which it has customarily had in past American political conflict.

In the past, with the notable exception of the American Civil War and its social residue — the inequality of racial minorities, the Lockean consensus has expedited the resolution of conflict. Agreement upon fundamental ideals and basic procedures has — in the view of many political scientists and historians — made possible effective "articulation and aggregation" of interests within a two-party system whose office-holders have viewed the political stage as a brokerage-house of interests rather than as the battleground of conflicting world-views. Thus, so the argument runs, the American political system's essential unity on perceived goals and the means to them has permitted far more effective and peaceful political "problem-solving" than has been vouchsafed to continental European systems since the French Revolution of 1789 set loose upon the European political stage the grand ideological conflicts of genuine conservatism, classical liberalism, and socialism.

Yet, by contrast, in respect to population control the reverse may hold true: the American political system may display less, rather than more, capacity for problem-solving than its European counterparts. Why? Because population control appears to bode extensive government control over the private sphere of individual autonomy. And, if the classical European political style has been to debate endlessly the merits of government control, the American political style has been to react "axiomatically" and "emotively" against such a specter. The spectrum of European political ideologies is able to encompass such a political proposition without undue alarm. By contrast, the narrow range of

American political ideology is not. Rather it magnifies and, by ideological reflex as it were, raises a barrier to problem-solving.

Four Types of Population Control Proposals

To perceive the likelihood of such a barrier is not to pass upon the question of its height. The first necessary step in attempting to answer that question is to venture into the risky realm of speculating about the logical "necessity" of conflict between individualist norm and population control policies. Consequently, it may be expedient to divide population proposals into groups according to their clash both with the ideals of that norm and with contemporary American relationships between government and individual. Such a division arguably yields four groups.

The first category of proposals is composed of those which would make possible greater self-determination by individual couples. These include programs which seek — by contact with individual physicians, public health institutions, marriage counselors, and educators — to disseminate as widely as possible reasons for, and methods of, family planning and fertility control. Also I would include here proposals for liberalizing abortion laws — since whatever else they may be, they share with information-proposals the common objective of increasing the possibilities of autonomous individual choice. The one furthers optional access to information, the other permits a greater degree of choice based upon that information.

In the second category I would place all proposals for the adoption of population dynamics courses as a regular part of public educational curricula. It could be argued that this is merely a subdivision of the first range of proposals for better dissemination of information but there is an important difference. The first type merely "offers" the information to a willing hearer who presumably can "turn the information off" at will. The second requires "sitting through."

A third range of proposals involves the government in inducements to voluntary restrictions upon the number of children. The welter of such proposals may be subdivided into two sorts: *one,* positive incentive payments for limiting births, for voluntary sterilization, and for spacing children through periods of non-pregnancy or non-birth; and *two,* negative incentives built into the tax-structure — for instance, taking away exemptions, for exceeding 'N-children,' or levying fees on births above the Nth.

A fourth set of proposals would establish involuntary controls: for instance, "marketable licenses to have children," temporary sterilization of all females or males or permanent sterilizations after N-births, required abortion of illegitimate or post-Nth pregnancies, and finally "general fertility control agents" added to, say, the public water supply, with counteracting agents distributed to individuals who have demonstrated economic and emotional readiness for parenthood.

Scaling the Conflict Between Proposals and Ideology

These four types of proposals are scaled here in order of their increasing potential conflict with American concepts of individualism. From the standpoints of both ease of acceptance and amount of change required in the contours of American political values, the "best" solution to the population problem is that which does the job by relying as heavily as is feasible upon the lower numbered types. Yet here time is clearly of the essence of freedom. Delay as crisis builds may necessitate greater reliance upon more restrictive governmental controls. That which might suffice today may not suffice tomorrow. *Ergo,* the importance of meeting the population explosion before such controls become inevitable. In turn, therefore, it is imperative that timely consideration be given to the ideological bases of attitudinal hostility to the proposal types.

In respect to the first type of proposal, I am not persuaded of the long-term political force of a commonly raised issue — Roman Catholic resistance to birth control. If the American Catholic lay reaction to Pope Paul's encyclical reaffirming traditional Roman Catholic abhorrence of interference with "natural processes" be any guide, it is hard to believe that, despite the attitudinal tensions presently imposed upon the Catholic population, in the long run the encyclical will have a significant effect upon lay behavior. Rather, I am more concerned with other varieties of resistance which until recently have gone largely unperceived – attitudinal resistance to voluntary control among non-Catholic poor. Essentially, there are two related difficulties manifested here. The first is one of lower-strata views of the optimal number of children per family. As Judith Blake has argued recently in a provocative article in *Science,* an inescapable fact remains when all allowances are made for religious views: all the statistics point away from the assertion of family-planners that poverty-sector mothers have too many children simply because they are ignorant of contraceptive techniques. Rather, since 1952 a gap has appeared between upper and lower income groups. Where the ideal number of children in the eyes of upper-status non-Catholic women has fluctuated closely around a median of 3.1, lower-status non-Catholic women's ideal number has been much closer to 4. That difference is sufficient to cast a dark shadow over traditional family planning assumptions that government provision of "how-to" information and "tools" will begin to do the job. The second manifestation of resistance in this sector is an ideological justification of hostility to family-planning schemes put forward by militant leaders of racial minorities: namely, the charge that such schemes directed at the poor are — in view of the coincidence of poverty and minority racial status — nothing but sugarcoated genocide pills. The point here is, of course, not the abstract merits or demerits of such interpretations of family-planners' motives. Rather, it is the "realness" of such attitudes among these sectors. On balance, I find it difficult to believe that such hostility will evanesce or even diminish in the face of persistant marginal standards of living. Surely, on the contrary, the increasingly ruffled racist waters of American politics during the late 1960's argue for at least a short-run increase in such attitudes.

With that in mind, I am led to the belief that the American population problem will require the satisfaction of at least three political and economic conditions before it begins to be met: (1) raising the living standards of the "forgotten fourth" to the point where the norm of a small family has even a vague possibility of taking hold, (2) structuring abortion laws such that mature couples have freedom of choice in respect to carrying pregnancies to term, and (3) widespread adoption of the second range of proposals — integrating population dynamics courses into public education curricula.

While it lies beyond the province of this essay to prognosticate about the first condition, I shall venture judgments in respect to the second and third. Barring a violent pendular swing toward Right or Left in American politics during the 1970's, it seems reasonable to anticipate a scattering of minor reactions among state legislatures to "sex education" overcome by a stronger long-run trend toward both more permissive abortion laws and the incorporation of population dynamics courses into public educational curricula. Essentially, I have four reasons for so anticipating. First, resistance to changes in abortion laws is primarily based on a combination of legislative inertia and a neo-Fundamentalist anxiety that easy abortions increase sexual promiscuity. Such anxiety, compounded perhaps by residual Victorianism in respect to the birds and the bees, lies similarly at the base of recent movements to prevent or repeal sex education courses in the public schools. I doubt that such motivation for resistance can long dominate in the face of the larger political truth of the relationship between large families, poverty, and urban unrest and in the face of the obvious inability of such statutory structures to alter post-Kinsey sexual behavior, to prevent the acquisition of such knowledge in extra-curricular fashion, or to prevent illegitimate pregnancies. Second, neo-Fundamentalist anti-abortion laws clash with another tenet of American belief-structures — individual self-determination. There is, then, an inner contradiction in the value-structures of many opponents of liberalization of abortion and sex education. Such contradiction does not make for maximal long-run strength. Beyond that, and third, it is not obvious that residual hostilities to sex education courses would necessarily carry over to curricular innovations entitled "Population Problems" — whether separate from or integrated with existing sex education courses. Fourth, as today's university students become tomorrow's opinion setters and as their generation swells the ranks of voters it is likely that more permissive attitudes will prevail. Thus, samples of university student opinion in two states which have recently liberalized abortion laws suggest strongly that the present liberal position requiring therapeutic judgment by the physician rather than decision by the couple involved will not suffice in a decade's time. Despite California's abortion law reforms, 92.6% of a sample of University of California students wished further liberalization. Indeed, asked to judge the desirability of changing ten different types of present laws — including marijuana prohibitions — they came down most heavily in favor of abortion reform. Similarly, a sample of second year medical students at the University of North Carolina disclosed a heavy commitment to voluntarism. None of the 43 sample-members opposed family planning, but only 9 thought that they would suffice to solve the American population explosion. Over 90% of the medical students found adequate grounds for abortion when carrying to term would threaten the emotional or physican health of the mother. It is important to note that these students would not require any showing of potential danger to life itself. One hundred percent of the students would proceed beyond statutory allowances for abortion in the event of "first trimester" *rubella* with its very clear linkage to birth defects. All would permit abortion on a showing that *any parental condition* posed a substantially greater than average chance of a defective child. Lastly, and perhaps most indicative of the commitment to individual self-determination, 90% would legalize abortion without interposing a "physical-veto" — if both wife and husband jointly desired one. This survey did not ask directly about compulsory courses in public schools on population dynamics. However, it seems fair to infer from the fact that less than 1/4 of the medical students believed voluntary measures would suffice, that medical opinion of the coming generation should be considerably in advance of present educational practices, as revealed in a survey undertaken by G. D. Searle and Company in 1967. Replies from 45 of the 50 State Superintendents of Public Instruction from whom information was requested disclosed that, although only three states barred incorporation on a statewide basis of routine sex education courses in the public schools, only one state required it. Further, only ten State Superintendents knew of even limited discussion of family planning methods in their states' high schools resulting from local level curriculum decisions. In sum, there are strong grounds for anticipating that, if medical students in a state hardly renowned as a hotbed of liberalism favor such voluntarism, general medical opinion of the coming generation of physicians will do so too.

The third range of proposals for positive and negative incentives to limiting child birth raises issues of a more serious yet potentially soluble political nature. In this respect I can only declare a perhaps too optimistic view that general attitudes will shift — in due time. Rather, the question is: will "due time" be "in time"? The medical student survey showed an interesting split in opinion on this issue — considerably greater support for tax incentives over direct payments. Thus, 12 of the 43 favored incentive payments for voluntary sterilization, while over a third favored reversing tax exemptions for exceeding a certain statutorily-determined number of children, and over half favored limiting the maximum number of such exemptions.

It is possible that the opinion samplers were here tapping an attitudinal reflex-difference peculiar to members of a profession among whom the less obvious reward of a tax write off conflicts less with notions of self-help than direct dispersal of funds by the government. On a purely economic basis, however, such a distinction is hard to defend. Just as there is nothing procedurally novel in the relationship between government and individual in such tax exemptions, there is nothing really new about direct incentive payments. In both, the government simply reverses a former substantive policy of reward for "helping the national interest" by having children, and promotes another "national interest" by rewarding restraint. Whichever way the exemptions run, or whether there are more or fewer child welfare payments, the government is carrying out policy through inducement. Additionally, there is no genuine economic difference between direct and indirect reward in terms of threat to the American democratic ethos. On balance, the only real distinction is in the specific terms of "who is affected?" Tax exemptions for not having children are more likely to take hold on middle or upper income brackets. Unless there is a general minimum standard of affluence and concomitant pervasive adoption of the small family norm, direct payments may be necessary if this third range of proposals is to be sufficiently effective to avoid ultimate recourse to the fourth type of proposal, compulsory general legislation, whose sharp conflict with American Liberal Individualism is patent.

Conclusion

If the foregoing analysis of the potential clash between population proposals and American norms of freedom is substantially correct, only the fourth category of proposal offers a logically tenable showing of "inevitable conflict." The first three types are, by contrast, consonant with American norms of individualism and consistent with fiscal inducement policies typical of compensated capitalism and, at least since the New Deal, broadly practiced in related realms. Objections to these three types of proposal are logically sustainable only on the basis of Victorianism, religious fundamentalism, and finally on the basis of a recent radical "Black Power" ideology whose practical sustenance lies in the persistent coincidence of racial minority status and poverty.

Such is what might be called the ideological logic of the population problem. But what Oliver Wendell Holmes once suggested characterized the law — that its life lay not in logic but in experience — may be paralleled here. The life of American politics, and particularly the speed of its evolution to the point of dealing actively with population growth as a pressing political problem, cannot be readily predicted.

In this sense, it may be generally helpful to look at what the political elite think now, in 1970 — if we are to predict at all. Specifically, the responses of members of the upper legislative house of the largest state in the Union, California, are worth briefly examining.

In January, 1970, I had the good fortune to interview the California Senate on this subject. The number of State Senators interviewed was relatively small — 26. Nevertheless, given the circumstances that this represented 2/3 of a political elite which has been much concerned with deterioration of the environment and that these represented a fair spectrum of the two major parties and of rural, urban, and suburban districts, the attitudes expressed may be fairly taken as symptomatic of advanced political elite views on this subject.

The first point of interest is that there was no sharp party division relative to the Senators' sense of the seriousness of the population explosion. 9 of the 12 Democrats, and 8 of the 14 Republicans, viewed it as one of the more serious issues requiring legislative action during the early 1970's. Only 4 of the 26 — two from each party — were opposed to dissemination of information by physicians, public health officials, and the like. However, when it came to the other part of the first range of proposals — abortion at request — the Senators displayed much less unanimity. Six Democrats, but only three Republicans, thought that such a shift would be required in the future.

Compulsory school courses on population growth drew roughly the same Democratic support as "abortion on demand." Seven thought it should come immediately, and 1 believed that it would eventually be necessary. Republicans stood 5 and 5, respectively on this issue.

The third and fourth types of proposal drew much less support. Only 2 Democrats and 1 Republican favored positive payments now, although 4 Democrats and 3 Republicans believed that they would be enacted in the future. As one might expect — though of course the figures are too small to be statistically significant — support reversed when it came to limiting or reversing tax-exemptions for exceeding a set number of children. Four Democrats and 6 Republicans supported such measures now or later. Compulsory sterilization for exceeding "N-births," oddly enough, appealed to 7 Democrats but only 2 Republicans as an eventual legislative measure. None would hear of it now. Finally, no Senator from either party would accept the "child license" or "general control agents" in the near future. And only 3 Democrats and 1 Republican were willing even to contemplate it as an eventual possibility. On balance, then, if California Senators are at all representative of elite political attitudes toward the population problem, there is little reason to expect speedy "problem-solving" in the American body politic.

POPULATION, ENVIRONMENT AND WOMEN

Elizabeth Farians

The human factors affecting the population-environment situation that we have considered so far are either fixed or relatively stable, but there are factors which are changing so rapidly that it is almost impossible to evaluate them. One of these is the role of women.

Traditionally this was to be housewife-and-mother, and it was reinforced by powerful ethical sanctions. These sanctions arose from the need for a high birth rate to counter a high mortality rate in an "underpopulated" world and the need to use both women and children to do work that is now performed by machines. With the disappearance of these needs, a traditional moral code that once promoted human survival has in some respects become an obstacle to it. Elizabeth Farians, feminist and theologian, argues for developing a code that would be relevant to the situation it is intended to control, and she considers this code especially as it would deal with the rights of women.

Miss Farians is a member of the Theology Faculty of Loyola University, Chicago, and founder and chairman of the Ecumenical Task Force on Women and Religion in the National Organization for Women. At present she is writing a book on feminist theology entitled, God Is Not Our Father.

One of the major considerations of anyone concerned with the ethical aspects of optimum population and environment must be the new dimensions of the problem. In our fast changing world it is no longer sufficient to look to the past for some immutable moral principle to guide present conduct. We can no longer take for granted that we need only to be faithful to a moral law which is ancient in order to meet future problems. We cannot continue to rely on a moral code supposedly given as an all-embracing, once-for-all moral doctrine. The modern situation calls for radical re-evaluation. Its complexity defies the simple solutions of the past and its magnitude calls for deep change. No mere new application of old ways can cope with a population doubling every thirty years, a finite world being destroyed by man competing for power, the increasing awareness of the value of the individual, and the demand by women for the recognition of their personhood.

The Moral Code

Before considering the new dimensions of the problem it might be helpful to recount how a moral code develops; what is its origin and purpose. A moral code is formed slowly. As man experiences life he gradually organizes his reflections on it. Finally, after many years, perhaps centuries, of such experienced reflections, a codified system for living is handed down from one generation to the next.

The central principle of a moral code is that it promotes the good of the civilization it regulates. It comes out of the experience of life of the people; it is intended to protect that life. In this sense it can be said to be given and natural, or the natural law made specific according to the needs of a particular society. It is immutable or unchanging inasmuch as it fosters respect for life, however this is expressed specifically.

Any code that is moral seeks the good and avoids the evil. What is apparently good and what is truly good may be confused in particular times or places, and even particular goods or how to promote the good may be disputed, but all would agree that respect for life is the basic value advanced by any moral code. This the old moral code and the new moral code have in common. Of course with respect to any moral code a distinction must be made between what the code holds as the ideal to be sought and what people do in practice.

The Past Age

In the agrarian culture of the past, life was hard. The world was underdeveloped, and society was underpopulated. Existence itself was at stake. To stay alive was the challenge. All of the energies of society had to be mustered around survival of the human race. Many children were needed to do the work of the land, and at a time when war was the way to settle disputes many children were needed to man the military. In order to provide workers and soldiers it was necessary for women to bear as many children as possible. This was all the more true since these were times when more children died than survived into adulthood.

Respect for life during the first period of humanity meant peopling the earth. Everything was directed toward that end. Thus the moral code placed great value on large numbers of children. It was the quantity of life that was important. The quality of life could not be stressed.

Since the major emphasis was on survival the life experience of the people did not include a consciousness of the value of the individual or of the personhood of woman. Society was conscious of itself only as a group which must be sustained. The individual merged into the group and the function of woman was reproduction. Hence the old moral code was silent about the quality of life of the individual or about the personhood of woman.

The land itself was underdeveloped and wild. In some ways the land was supportive of man, but man had to subdue it to reap its value. In many ways the earth was like a fierce enemy. It was mighty and it seemed infinite. The reflected experience of man contained no awareness of scarcity. Natural disasters, even those of famine and flood, were not the result of scarcity; they were the result of insufficient taming of the land. In such a society life depended on power: power over nature, over women, over other men. The most powerful survived. Competition was its dominant characteristic.

The Modern Situation
The post-industrial age is different. Much of the world is developed, some of it even overdeveloped. While there still remains the third world, partly in both periods, the world itself is now seen to be finite. We are running out of space, air, water, and other resources. Technical progress has increased the life span and insured the survival of most children. Hence women have many years to live after their fertile period, and not as many children must be borne to keep the population stable.

The demand for children has also lessened. Before, children were a means to the survival of the race either as workers or as warriors. Now automation has reduced the need for labor, and hopefully some day soon men will find ways other than war to solve problems, and sharing rather than competition will eliminate the need for power. Then children will not be a means of filling armies; they will be valued as ends in themselves, as unique individuals.

The change in attitude toward children has been one of the main factors in the change in the status of women. When the quantity of children is no longer stressed, then their production need no longer be the major function of women and women can be seen as persons in their own right.

The style of life has also changed. A number of factors have converged to make it possible to be concerned with the quality of life. Life is not just a question of survival. Life is not as hard as it once was. Man has tamed the earth, and the industrial revolution has given man confort and leisure.

All of this has led to a new kind of life. There is time now for education, and this in turn tends to expand social consciousness and to bring out individual awareness. These produce a shift in emphasis from quantity of life to quality of life.

New Dimensions for the Moral Code

Ethical problems arise when the moral code lags behind the current situation. In some cases the traditional moral code is outdated in its evaluations, and in other cases it is silent concerning issues that were not the concern of past ages.

It is obvious that there has been a shift in values. Nowadays respect for life stresses quality of life rather than quantity. Mere existence is no longer seen as an end in itself.

Mankind has also reached a stage of overpopulation and overdevelopment. We have gone from overabundance to scarcity of natural resources, and from underpopulation to more people than the earth can support. Hence we need conservation rather than continued expansion, and birth control rather than unlimited reproduction.

Coupled with the need for conservation is the need for a new form of economics based on sharing and cooperation rather than competition. This would seem to be a necessity in a finite world where limited resources means that one country's or individual's gains are another country's or individual's loss. A sharing, cooperative spirit in the world would surely change the character of man. Some say it is natural for man to be greedy, aggressive, and power seeking, but we do not know how another economic system would modify human nature. We do not know whether man is naturally cooperative or naturally competitive or even whether man could be a happy combination of both, because as society was organized in the past only the aggressive survived. Even in our modern world, man is forced to be competitive in order to succeed, if not to survive. The moral code has been silent about this, except to encourage moderation or balance in any attribute of the individual. The moral code has never been able to successfully deal with morals on a national level. The prophets of old tried but in general succeeded only in becoming martyrs. Nowadays respect for the moral code has retreated almost entirely to the private sector of life.

It must also be pointed out that part of the present population crisis is caused not by too many people but by a competitive power-hungry economy. Much of the present starvation and wretchedness in the world is caused by mal-distribution of food and goods. Here the moral code has not been silent; but it has not been insistent enough. It has not been insistent enough on the immediate issue, the love for one's fellow man which should control and counteract greed and indifference.

At the moment there are some who are seriously considering the population problem as one of poor distribution. The Roman Catholic Church has taken this line, but it has done so to support its claim that artificial birth control is morally wrong. Other groups, especially certain minorities and certain other underprivileged groups, maintain that genocide may be the aim of the white rich, who will not voluntarily give up power and privilege.

Many are also becoming concerned about trying to solve population problems too quickly by somewhat simplistic proposals for birth control. Groups like the Friends' Service Committee and the New University Conference point out the dangers in allowing governments to decide who shall live, because it also means deciding who shall die.

Nevertheless, even though mal-distribution of the world's goods is the immediate cause of untold unnecessary suffering of mankind today, there is a population crisis — and a pollution crisis directly related to it — which can only be adequately eased through birth control. Here the shift in understanding the bases of any moral code which urges respect for life, from quantity of life to quality of life is crucial, whether the method of birth control is abstinence, sterilization, contraception, or abortion. It is to be hoped that we can make this change in our moral code in time. When we realize that the purpose of a moral code is the good of society and when that society is in serious danger of overpopulation and total pollution, then it becomes clear that birth control of some kind becomes a moral imperative. There is no moral dilemma here once we recognize that respect for life as unlimited reproduction reflected the good of society in a very different situation. Now that adequate population is assured, understanding of respect for life can and should have a deeper meaning. The moral code must stress the quality of life rather than just quantity.

A note of caution must be introduced here. Quality of life does not confer a license to murder. To respect the quality of life is to respect life itself as the base of that quality. But to respect the quality of life does mean not to bring into being life that cannot be adequately supported or life that will be deformed.

Several further comments should be made about birth control:

1. To accept sterilization as a means of birth control does not mean that involuntary sterilization can automatically be considered moral. I can conceive of times when involuntary sterilization might be absolutely necessary, but at the present time I do not think we are able to determine when that condition exists for certain.

2. The distinction I have made between quantity and quality of life is not adequate to solve the abortion dilemma for those who hold that abortion is murder. It merely adds weight to the arguments in favor of abortion by showing that respect for life is consistent with abortion, because respect for life means concern for the quality of life as well as concern for mere existence. The respect for the quality of life meant here is not only for that of the child but also that of the parents, both father and mother. If they cannot support another child psychologically, physically, or economically, then the quality of their life may also be in jeopardy.

Besides, the whole burden of this paper is to show that the moral code as we now have it was developed by a previous age when the needs and awareness of society were different. If the need of society is to control birth, and if in the modern situation respect for life means concern for the quality of life, then the anti-abortionists may find their position to be self-contradictory.

It should also be pointed out that abortion came to be considered morally wrong at a time when women as individuals were not considered important. Their right not to bear unwanted children was never considered. Again the modern situation is different. Social awareness has been refined.

3. A further word should be said in favor of sexual abstinence as a means of birth control. Few today have any regard for sexual abstinence or virginity. Many indeed deem it harmful to a heterosexual relationship, and some even consider it harmful to the adult individual, However, there is very little evidence for this, and countless people lead happy and successful lives despite sexual abstinence. Moreover, some experts with

their eyes on the future, such as Marshall McLuhan and Margaret Mead, claim that sex is "cooling off," so that abstinence may become more popular than anyone previously thought possible. I mention this only so that we avoid a too ready discarding of something we do not adequately understand.

As mentioned earlier, another consideration of the modern situation which gives use to a new dimension to the moral code is the new awareness of the personhood of women. Again, a number of causes have converged to improve the status of women, but the one with which we are mainly concerned here is birth control. Regarding birth control, a reciprocal interaction is involved. A new regard for children resulted in a new regard for women, but at the same time, an increased respect for women in justice demands a lower birth rate, even if there were no population crisis.

In a previous age, women moved from being a chattel or plaything of man to a position of respect as the producer of children, as mother. Now that role is being somewhat modified. When society needs less children the role of women must change. Women can no longer be defined totally by their function as reproducers. Some women understand this, as does some of society.

But some women resist this change, and so do some segments of society. Once again, in order to understand this resistance and overcome it, we must call to mind the origin of the moral code which stressed the role of childbearing and thus enhanced the concept of motherhood.

Also, some women may tenaciously cling to the role of mother because they realize that it is at present their major source of status. These women must be helped to see that a more fundamental dignity comes from being a person in one's own right.

If birth control is to become a means of obtaining optimum population and environment and for the sake of justice itself, the moral code must broaden its evaluation of women. There must be a shift from identifying women solely as mother to identifying her also and primarily as a person in her own right. Society must be supportive of this fuller role for women, and the moral code must begin to actively call for fair, just, and equal treatment for them. Whereas before the moral code was silent on the rights of women, it must now make this a new dimension.

POPULATION, ENVIRONMENT, AND MINORITY GROUPS

Douglas E. Stewart

Any proposal to limit population is bound to arouse mixed feelings among the members of minority groups. When the argument is made that it is in their own interest, they sense that it also threatens to freeze them permanently in a minority position, and history justifies their unwillingness to accept that. No minority in any society can afford to rely solely on the good will of the majority.

Thus the population-environment situation confronts minority groups with choices harsher than any of the members of the majority have to make. If they "overbreed" for the sake of numerical strength, they condemn themselves to continuing in the misery of ghetto existence; if they co-operate in population limitation they are threatened with the usual fate to minorities.

But this dilemma also affects those members of the majority who seek population control and the restoration of the environment, urban as well as rural. Without the co-operation of minority groups they cannot achieve their ends; and as we have said, assurances of good will are not enough.

Without resolving the dilemma — perhaps only history can do that — Douglas E. Stewart argues that the best ways to gain the support of minority groups for population-environment movement are to raise their standard of living and put an end to the indecency of race prejudice.

Mr. Stewart is Director of the Department of Community Affairs for Planned Parenthood-World Population in New York.

The problem of overpopulation is everybody's problem. This includes minority groups and everyone who presently lives on this finite planet of ours. This simple and logical statement should be obvious and readily understood by all who read it. Yet, for many complex reasons this is not the case in 1970. However, if our world is to survive and if we are to maintain a high quality of life for all, it must be made obvious and readily understandable.

It is because of the complex reasons that this paper will attempt to deal with the peculiar problems of minority groups in relation to the question of overpopulation and environmental degradation in the United States. The main thesis of this paper is that though on a world-wide basis minority groups and poverty-stricken whites have a higher interest in helping to resolve the problem of overpopulation because they suffer the most from its deteriorating effects, this is not the case in the United States, where the problem of overpopulation has a different face and its resolution must be approached in a different way. In the United States minority groups and poor whites are victims not of overpopulation but of racism, prejudice, and discrimination. It is for this reason that more minority group persons and poverty-stricken whites are not actively involved in attempts to solve the population problem. This latter statement should be obvious and understood by all. Yet, due to the nature of human beings in our society and in our nation, it is not obvious and understood by all. However, if the common problem of overpopulation in the world, which includes the contribution of the U.S., is to be solved collectively, these problems of racism, prejudice, and discrimination must be dealt with honestly. They constitute the economic, political, and social communications barriers that keep our nation apart.

In his historic message on Population and Family Planning in July 1969, President Nixon stated in his comments on the developing nations:

"... Their standards of living are not rising quickly, and the gap between life in the rich nations and life in the poor nations is not closing.

"There are some respects, in fact, in which economic development threatens to fall behind population growth, so that the quality of life actually worsens ... it is still difficult to feed these added people at adequate levels of nutrition. Protein malnutrition is widespread. It is estimated that every day some 10,000 people — most of them children — are dying from diseases of which malnutrition has been at least a partial cause. Moreover, the physical and mental potential of millions of youngsters is not realized because of lack of proper food ....

"The burden of population growth is also felt in the field of social progress. In many countries, despite increases in the number of schools and teachers, there are more and more children for whom there is no schooling ... more and more families are without adequate shelter. Unemployment and underemployment are increasing and the situation could be aggravated as more young people grow up and seek to enter the work force.

"... Many parents in developing countries are still victimized by forces such as poverty and ignorance, which make it difficult for them to exercise control over the size of their families. In sum, population growth is a world problem which no country can ignore, whether it is moved by the narrowest perception of national self-interest or the widest vision of a common humanity."

President Nixon, just as grimly, could have been discussing the *have-nots* in the United States, as the following exerpts from the article entitled, *A Nation within a Nation,* which appeared in the May 17, 1968 issue of *Time* magazine attest:

"Yet in the midst of this unparalleled abundance, another nation dwells in grinding deprivation. It comprises the 29,700,000 Americans who are denied access to the wealth that surrounds them — a group three times the population of Belgium. They are the men, women and children — black, white, red, yellow, and brown — who live below the poverty line.

"The nation of the poor is often invisible to the rest of America.

". . . Few phenomena in human history have been so closely scrutinized by statisticians as American poverty. From Michael Harrington's 1962 study, *The Other America* to last month's report by the Citizen's Crusade Against Poverty, *Hunger, U.S.A.,* which found that 10 million Americans are chronically malnourished, the condition of the U.S. poor has been catalogued in a sierra of statistics.

". . . According to the Office of Economic Opportunity . . . the poor make up 15% of the U.S. population. Contrary to the impression given by riots and all the other conspicuous problems of the slums, Negroes are not the major component of that group, at least not in numbers: two out of every three poor Americans are white. Of the 11 million rural poor, nearly 9,000,000 are white. Since 70% of the Nation's citizens live in cities and towns, it is not surprising that more than 60% of the poor are urban dwellers. In age, nearly half of the poor are 21 or younger; a quarter 55 or older. Indeed, a third of all Americans of 65 or older — 5,400,000 of them are poor.

"The jobless total in the poorest neighborhoods of the nation's hundred largest cities stood at 7% during most of the year, and shows little sign of improvement. That poverty breeds poverty can scarcely be denied: according to one recent study, 71% of all poor families have four or more children (v. 1.35 offspring for the nation at large), and though two-thirds of all poor mothers are married and living with their husbands, half the husbands do not hold regular jobs. The other half hold full-time jobs that do not pay enough to lift them above the poverty line.

"Statistics at best can only delineate the bare perimeters of poverty. The sensations of being poor are scarcely comprehensible to the 170 million Americans who are not poor: The hollow-bellied, hand-to-mouth feeling of having no money for tomorrow; the smell of woodsmoke that hangs over southern shanty towns — romantic to the suburbanite, but symptomatic of scant heat and pinchgut rations to the poor; the bags of flour delivered by a well-meaning welfare agency, in a household that has no oven; the pervasive odor of urine and rat droppings in perenially damp walk-ups; the bite of wind or snow through a wall of rotten bricks and no hope that the landlord will repair the crack. Poverty is the certainty of being gouged — particularly by one's own kind. For if the poor share anything it is oppressors: credit dentists and credit opticians; credit furniture stores and credit food markets where for half again as much as the affluent pay, stale bread and rank hamburger are fobbed off on the poor. Poverty spells the death of hope, the decay of spirit and nerve, of ambition and will.

"'Poverty is a psychological process which destroys the young before they can live and the aged before they can die,' says Yale Psychologist Ira Goldenberg. 'It is a pattern of hopelessness and helplessness, a view of the world and oneself as static, limited and irredeemably expendable. Poverty, in short, is a condition of being in which one's past and future meet in the present — and go no further.'"

Certainly the message contained in these excerpts from the *Time* magazine article must be considered as presenting some of the real social and psychological aspects of the Population/Environmental crisis. Is there any wonder that there were so few poor, especially poor minorities, involved in the recent Earth Day activities? It is difficult for those who are trapped in the environmental conditions which were so vividly described in this article to understand the recent urgent concerns in the nation about environmental deterioration. Whose environment? they ask. It should be obvious why they cannot comprehend the anxieties of the affluent, because they are on different communication wave lengths. This communication gap will only be bridged when minorities and poor whites are given the same economic and social opportunities as affluent Americans. Lerone Bennet, Jr., Senior Editor of *Ebony* magazine and author of *Before the Mayflower* and *The Negro Mood* in his most recent book, *Confrontation: Black and White* amplifies this in the following passage from that book:

"If we are to avert a disaster here, there must be a massive re-education of white Americans. There must be, at the same time, a massive attack on the evidences of the mis-education of white Americans. A necessary prerequisite is the immediate cessation of segregation and discrimination and a massive program of national atonement for hundreds of years of soul-destroying oppression, a program that would involve *as a minimum requirement* the expenditure of billions of dollars and the engagement of the energies of all our citizens.

"Anything less is a lie.

"Anything less is deceit, fraud, silence.

"This program should be spelled out in a series of federal, state, and local plans setting out in great detail phased approaches to integration in housing, employment and other areas. To be effective, these plans must be based on community-wide recognition, locally and nationally, that this problem can be solved and that it will be solved."

Dr. Paul R. Ehrlich, Professor of Biology, Stanford University, and author of the popular book, *The Population Bomb,* discussed the same problem relative to minorities and poor whites in a letter dated, November 26, 1969 which he wrote in response to an inquiry to Mr. Walter Thompson, a Black reporter for KQED in San Francisco. Dr. Ehrlich wrote:

"As I am very deeply involved in the population control movement, and since press coverage of my statements sometimes leaves something to be desired, I would like you to know my exact position on the genocide issue.

1. The most serious popluation growth occurs among the affluent whites of the U.S.A., and their analogues in western Europe, the Soviet Union, and Japan. These people are the prime looters and polluters of our planet — the ones who are destroying our life support systems. From the point of view of pollution every American child born is 50 times the disaster for the world as each Indian child. From the point of view of consumption each American is 300 times as bad as each Indonesian.

2. The slight edge in birth rates of poor black Americans over poor whites is relatively insignificant, because in their depressed economic condition neither poor blacks or whites make any significant impact on the world situation. Affluent blacks tend to have *fewer* children than affluent whites.

3. In my estimation perhaps 1/3 of the people who talk population control mean population control for someone else — blacks, the poor, those on relief, etc. To that extent the "genocide" accusation is valid.

4. If people want black reproductive performance to resemble that of whites they can do this simply. *All they have to do is give the blacks the same economic and social opportunities as whites have.*

5. I am in favor of making free contraception and subsidized abortion available to all Americans, white or black, married or unmarried. No one should be subject to compulsory pregnancy. Government support of such programs is necessary — but these should not be presented or thought of as population control programs. I suspect blacks will get more power if they have smaller families, because they will be able to advance economically more rapidly. But I colud be wrong, and the choice is up to the blacks.

6. I have one child and will have no more; population control begins at home.

In his July 1969 message on Population and Family Planning, President Nixon asked the following questions and made the following comments about the problem in the U.S.:

"Where, for example, will the next hundred million Americans live? . . . Are our cities prepared for such an influx?

". . . How, for example, will we house the next hundred million Americans? Already economical and attractive housing is in very short supply.

"What of our natural resources and the quality of our environment? Pure air and water are fundamental to life itself. Parks, recreational facilities, and an attractive countryside are essential to our emotional well-being. Plant and animal and mineral resources are also vital. A growing population will increase the demand for such resources . . . The ecological system upon which we now depend may seriously deteriorate if our efforts to conserve and enhance the environment do not match the growth of the population.

"How will we educate and employ such a large number of people? Will our transportation systems move them about as quickly and economically as necessary? How will we provide adequate health care when our population reaches 300 million? Will our political structures have to be reordered, too, when our society grows to such proportions? Many of our institutions are already under tremendous strain as they try to respond to the demands of 1969. Will they be swamped by a growing flood of people in the next thirty years? How easily can they be replaced or altered?"

The President was obviously discussing "quality of life" in the U.S. in these questions and comments. He is President of all of the people in the U.S. Yet it must be clearly recognized that he was not discussing "quality of life" for 30,000,000 members of minority groups and poor whites, and they are keenly aware of it. In fact, the "have-nots" in our nation know that he was discussing "quality of life" only for 170,000,000 "haves" in America. The questions the President raised have historically been raised by minorities and poor whites. They have never received an adequate answer however. But, if the common problem of overpopulation, which threatens total destruction for all, is to be solved the gap will have to be closed between the "haves" and the "have-nots."

Blacks have historically lived in squalid slum conditions, lived in overcrowded and inferior housing, attended overcrowded and inferior schools, had an unemployment rate twice as high and sometimes three times as high as that of whites, and have had poor or non-existent health services. This was true when the nation's population was just a little over 100,000,000. In point of fact, the N.A.A.C.P. was organized in 1909 and the National Urban League in 1910 to work toward improving these conditions. They are still working to improve them. The problems have been compounded, however, because there are more people for whom they must improve them and because *racism* continues to exist. Blacks are pragmatic realists and therefore, are keenly aware that as long as *racism* continues to exist and the population continues to grow, their problems in housing, education, health, and employment will continue to be compounded.

Activist Blacks (not necessarily militant) are also political and economic realists. They know that American society functions not as a rational society but as a political society. In a rational society, there would be no racism. In a political society, it takes numbers of people to elect a man to public office, and the holders of public office are the holders of power. He who holds power can change things to what they ought to be. Most Blacks are keenly aware that there aren't too many whites chafing at the bit to elect any Blacks to public office. They, therefore, feel that the black population should double while the white population slows to less than a zero rate of growth. This way, they feel, they will have an opportunity to acquire the political power thatiis essential to improving the living conditions of Blacks in America. They feel the same must be done for Black Capitalism. That is to say that in order for Black Capitalism to succeed, there must be large numbers of consumers for the goods and services that will be produced by Black Capitalists. It is felt that there aren't enough whites willing to purchase goods and services from Black entrepeneurs to insure success. Thus their consumers will have to be Blacks and members of other minority groups.

This is a political and economic strategy for survival which is irrational because it does not consider the practical problems of raising large numbers of children in an existing racist society. Yet it is strongly felt by many Blacks and is one of the communications barriers that must be overcome if we are to solve our collective problem together. The obvious answer is not to try and change the minds of Blacks about this strategy until the nation rids itself of the cancer of racism.

Federick Douglass, the great Black abolitionist, wrote about the strategy for Black survival over 100 years ago. These are his words:

"Let me give you a word on the philosophy of reforms. The whole history of the progress of human liberty shows that all concessions yet made to her august claims have been born of earnest struggle. If there is no struggle, there is no progress. Those who profess to favor freedom and yet deprecate agitation are men who want the crops without plowing up the ground. They want rain without thunder and lightening. They want the ocean without the awful roar of its many waters. Power concedes nothing without demand. It never did and it never will. Find out just what people will submit to, and you have found out the exact amount of injustice and wrong which will be imposed upon them. Men may not get all they pay for in this world, but they will certainly pay for all they get. And if we must ever get free from all the oppressions and wrongs heaped upon us, we must pay for their removal. And this we are prepared to do."

No one who knows the history of our nation and society can realistically quarrel with this statement by Douglass. The question is: is there sufficient concern about the problem of overpopulation to deal with the real issues as discussed here?

Blacks tend to function like whites on this issue. That is they are willing to cut off their noses to spite their faces. This is ludicrous and foolhardy and can only be categorized as brinkmanship. On the other hand, whites who continue to permit racism to exist are also cutting off their noses to spite their faces. This too is ludicrous and foolhardy and can only be categorized as brinkmanship. In fact, in view of the available statistics about the problem of overpopulation, environmental degradation, and the eco-catastrophe, it could be considered suicidal, not so much for Americans over the age of 25 but for those under it: the ones who are inheriting this world. *The obvious answer is to attack both racism and overpopulation simultaneously with equal vigor.*

It must also be noted that Blacks have historically recognized the relationship of large families to poverty and the effectiveness of contraception in the prevention of unwanted pregnancy. The difficulty has always been what it is today: the lack of an effective and safe method of contraception and the unavailability or inaccessibility of those methods which do exist.

Dr. W.E.B. DuBois, editor of the N.A.A.C.P. Crisis magazine and leader in Negro thought, wrote the following in 1932, in an article prepared for *The Birth Control Review:*

> "The American Negro has been going through a great period of stress, not only in this present depression, but long before it. His income is reduced by ignorance and prejudice, and his former tradition for early marriage and large families has put grave strain on a budget on which he was seeking, not merely to maintain, but to improve his standard of living.
>
> ". . . There comes, therefore, the difficult and insistent problem of spreading among Negroes an intelligent and clearly recognized concept of proper birth control, so that the young people can marry, have companionship and natural health, and yet not have children until they are able to take care of them."

Elmer A. Carter, Black editor of *Opportunity,* wrote in the same issue of *The Birth Control Review:*

". . . On the higher economic levels, Negroes have long since limited the number of their offspring, following in the footsteps of the higher classes of white America. Although statistics are not readily available, it would appear that the Negro, aware of the tremendous handicaps which his children must face under the most favorable conditions, is even more compelled to limit their number than his white compatriots similarly placed."

Similar thoughts are expressed in the same issue of *The Birth Control Review* by Professor Charles S. Johnson of Fiske University; Dr. G.W. Alexander, general secretary of the National Medical Association of Negro Physicians and Surgeons; Dr. M.G. Bousfield, Chairman of the Public Health Committee of the National Negro Insurance Association; and others who contributed articles to it.

Minority groups are clearly identified as being in the "have-not" category in the U.S. The "haves" are saying our ship is sinking and we must work together to save it. The "have-nots" respond that their ship has been sinking for a long time and the "haves" did nothing to help them. The "have-nots" do offer a way out of this dilemma if they are listened to and sincerely heeded. They say all will sail on an equal plane together or all will sink together. The decision is in the hands of the "haves".

OPTIMUM POPULATION AND ECONOMIC EXTERNALITIES

Philip E. Sorenson

Dr. Sorenson considers population growth — and, by implication, the uses of the environment — from the point of view of an economist, assessing the costs involved. These costs are internal when they are borne by the producers of goods or of children and external when borne by society as a whole. Obviously an industrial polluter is imposing heavy external costs on the rest of us; less obviously, the couple that overproduces children does so at the expense of society. This is true even of the couple that can afford to raise a big family; their children exploit "the commons" as much as, or more than the children of the poor.

The present population of the United States is now large enough for any economic advantage can be gained from numbers. If population were stabilized, per capita income would rise faster than if population growth continued. Thus neither the economy as a whole nor the average individual worker would gain from an increase in population.

Dr. Sorenson goes on to argue that we must try to internalize as many as possible of the costs of production and child-raising, and like Keir Nash, he considers the ways in which this might be done. Finally, like Stewart Udall in Part III, he questions the validity of defining our economic welfare in terms of "gross national product".

Dr. Sorenson is Associate Professor of Economics at Florida State University. He has published a number of studies on optimum resource use and environmental economics, and has served as a consultant in these areas to the United Nations and to Federal and state governments.

The density of population necessary to enable mankind to obtain all the advantages both of cooperation and of social intercourse has been obtained . . . . If the earth must lose that great portion of its pleasantness which it owes to things that the unlimited increase of wealth and population would extirpate from it, for the mere purpose of enabling it to support a larger but not a better or a happier population, I sincerely hope, for the sake of posterity, that we will content to be stationary long before necessity compels it to us. — John Stuart Mill, *Principles of Political Economy,* Book IV, Chap. VI.

One must be impressed in re-reading Mill's *Principles* with the contemporary relevance of his assessment of the population problem. Our admiration for the beauty of his logic is tempered, however, by the realization of its date. It is possible that our present concern over population growth is much ahead of its time, as was Mill's? Those of us who disagree must recognize that probably a majority of the public is settled in its belief that population growth does not constitute a clear and present danger. After all, most world societies have survived and even flourished despite expert predictions of impending disaster.

Historically even economists have put only minor emphasis upon the population variable. It is true that Ricardo and his followers embraced the Malthusian population hypothesis in order to explain the asserted long-run tendency of wages and profits to fall to a (variously defined) subsistence level, but even in their writings factors affecting the birth rate and the impact of rising population on other aspects of the economy were only superficially analyzed. In like manner, some contemporary students of economic development have adopted the Malthusian hypothesis to explain the long-run supply curve of labor. But in general modern macroeconomic theory treats population growth as an exogenous variable and puts major emphasis on the determinants of the rate of investment, in order to explain the growth of productive capacity and of income over time.

The population question is dealt with explicitly by resource economists and in that part of the literature of welfare economics concerned with defining "optimum population." I believe the studies of J.L. Fisher and H.J. Barnett will reflect the contemporary economic assessment of the population-resources problem, and it must be said that neither author shares the alarm of many non-economists concerning the quantitative aspects of resource depletion. In respect to optimum population, economists have tended to focus on changes in per capita income as a measure of the worth of additions to the labor force, or in more sophisticated analyses have looked at the present *net* value of each prospective child, meaning the value of his future marginal production plus the psychic utility he brings his parents and minus his consumption stream through life. This last approach treats the child as a potential factor of production and implicitly ignores any positive welfare gain to society from his own consumption, which is treated entirely as a cost. The difficult question of whether it is selfish to prevent additional births in order to maximize the standard of living of those now living is neither asked nor answered in these studies.

Any index of welfare involves value judgments, the population-welfare index probably more than most. "The greatest good for the greatest number" is mathematically indeterminate and makes economic sense only if there exists an agreed upon social welfare function which weights the increased per capita "good" in relation to the utility of increased numbers. It is important that we recognize that not all Americans would agree to the same index of relative weights.

Programs for the limitation of population size must meet the test of political acceptability. In my opinion, the majority of the American people will not presently accept arbitrary limits on family size, whatever their views concerning optimum population and in spite of the body of evidence indicating that the probable alternative is a future increase in the death rate. There is another approach to population control which relies mainly on market constraints on individual choice and is therefore more likely to be accepted. This approach assumes that there is a demand and a supply curve for children, as there is for every economic good. To change the equilibrium birth rate, we must shift the demand curve to the left by effecting a change in tastes or by introducing rationing devices (such as childbirth permits, to be used individually or sold, after which various penalties are imposed), or we must shift the supply curve to the left by increasing the private costs of child rearing and by constructing birth control clinics, distributing free contraceptives, permitting abortion without qualification, and encouraging sterilization — the last-named methods all tending to increase the individual's capacity to objectively determine his family size. It would appear likely that a combination of approaches would have a greater chance for success than any one alone. I shall emphasize two public policy measures here, recognizing that they complement rather than replace other current and proposed programs.

As an example of the first approach, consider the case of smoke from a refinery which damages nearby crops. In the absence of some tax or liability mechanism, the internal (private) costs of the refinery will not equal its total social cost. Assuming a competitive industry structure, the fact that some of the refinery's costs (the crop damage) are external means that the value of its output will be less than the total (private plus external) costs of production; or in simpler terms, the output from the refinery will exceed the socially optimal level.

Contrary to first impressions, external costs such as the smoke damage involve a reciprocal relationship. If the refinery presently "damages" nearby crops, the farmer's success in forcing installation of control mechanisms for the smoke will as surely "damage" the refinery. The question of who should pay whom for what damage must generally be decided in the courts. But it is not certain that the optimal economic decision will be reached there — the decision according to which the most productive economic activity survives.

Without belaboring the theory here, the essentials of the matter are these: for optimal outputs of all economic goods (including children) it is necessary that costs external to the firm (or the family) be internalized. This may be accomplished by means of an appropriate tax, by legal action, or by government regulation. If a tax is applied, the proceeds must be paid to the damaged party or parties, if an economic optimum is to be obtained. Legal action can potentially eliminate inequities, but it may substitute a less productive for a more productive activity (as would be the case if recreation interests were able to close a major harbor to commercial traffic by injunction). Where external costs are extremely high, difficult to estimate or to police, government regulation (such as zoning) may be required. Indeed, an economic optimum sometimes requires a combination of a tax and proper regulation.

Although the emission of effluents is the most obvious case of external costs, it is not necessary that a "guilty" and an "innocent" party appear in our model. As nations compete for the limited supply of fish in the ocean, each raises the cost of fishing for every other nation. Farmers drilling wells into the same water table likewise impose reciprocal external costs on one another, as do drivers on a suburban freeway at rush hours. In each of these cases, because they are not required to do so individuals fail to take account of the full cost of their activities in exhausting the capacities of a common property resource.

This model of external costs can fruitfully be applied to the population problem. We may assume at the outset, I believe, that the present population of the United States is large enough to permit the achievement of all technical and market economies of scale and to afford us a freedom in foreign policy which is, if anything, excessive. If per capita income is used as a measure, we have probably surpassed the optimum population size, and this is true despite the fact that per capita income continues to rise. The essential indicator is not the simple *level* of per capita income over time but its direction with respect to changes in population alone. In fact, other things being equal, per capita income will grow at least one percentage point *more* per year given a zero rather than a two percent rate of population growth. Thus neither the economy as a whole, nor individual workers on average, will gain from additional population. This is not to deny that some sectors of the economy stand to reap substantial benefits from a continuation of the population boom, most particularly real estate and resource-based industries. But a redistribution of the economic benefits of zero population growth would more than compensate for the losses of these sectors, since the total benefits are positive.

The basic economic explanation for excessive population growth is that individual decisions concerning size of family do not take account of the total cost to society of additional children. What each family wants is not what all families want. The problem is that significant external costs are not included in the family's estimate of the supply cost of an additional birth. Externalities such as the increased cost of education, public health, police services, and highways readily come to mind. But more important external costs arise from the environmental blight that follows population growth: pollution of the air and water, disappearance of undeveloped land, over-crowding of recreation sites, and the reduction of space and of privacy.

An excellent economic rationale exists for the provision through public agencies of certain educational and health services based upon the positive neighborhood or spillover effects of those services. That is, the social benefit to a free and democratic society from public education for citizenship and from public health services for the control of communicable disease exceeds the private (individual or family) benefit. Provision of basic education and health services for all children might be imposed as a requirement on parents (just as auto insurance is required in many states in recognition of the external costs of non-insured accidents), assuming that every family had the financial capacity to meet the cost. In fact, however, many parents could not afford to provide general education for their children or to obtain the basic medical services which are required for optimal public health. Society therefore provides these services as public goods, recognizing that the social benefits of the arrangement exceed its social costs.

On this ground I reject the suggestion that parents should be assessed additional taxes as the number of their children entering public schools rises. There is, however, a point at which the external benefits of additional schooling become very small in relation to the internal benefits; indeed, the latter are great enough that the individual will rationally choose additional schooling at his own expense, with student loans and scholarships providing some added incentives. This does not mean that public higher education should be eliminated, but only that a larger proportion of the costs would be borne by parents or individual college students. One economic justification for the tax and subsidy measures proposed below is that parents with larger numbers of children have a higher expectation of profiting from public higher education services and therefore are imposing significant external costs upon society.

Since the most important external costs of population growth involve nonmarket based utilities such as esthetic values, clean air, and recreation sites, some method of estimating these values must be found. The economic approach here is to attempt to discover what the consumer would be willing to pay to retain privacy or to avoid noise or the destruction of scenery: an imperfect procedure, admittedly, but necessary for rational social choice. It has been asserted that economists are too narrow, materialistic, or man-centered to provide a proper analytical framework for the evaluation of utilities emanating from the environment. I cannot debate that issue here except to contrast the economist's position with that of the extreme conservationists who regard every endangered species as priceless and who look upon some past age as a sort of environmental ideal. It is possible that, at some point, the protection of a species will require public expenditures of such a magnitude that it will be neglected in favor of other social investment programs of higher priority. The economist's argument is that all public spending projects, including conservation projects, be judged in terms of alternatives rather than absolutes.

The external costs of population growth may be likened to the costs imposed by a polluting firm on a downstream user of water. The economic remedy in the latter case is an effluent charge, perhaps combined with some regulation. The counterpart of the effluent charge in the case of population growth is a tax which approximates the external costs to society of additional births.

In summary, the American economy does not need more people. Each of us will suffer a loss of real (market-based) income and sacrifice substantial non-market utilities if population growth continues.

A number of fiscal and institutional changes are required to internalize the external costs of children and to otherwise shift the population supply curve to the left. These include (a) elimination of the personal income tax exemption for dependent children; (b) creation of new tax schedules favoring single taxpayers, childless couples, couples who choose to adopt children, and, in general, families having smaller numbers of children; (c) subsidizing male or female sterilization (in the spirit of the present subsidies for not growing cotton); (d) liberalization of abortion laws nationally; (e) distribution of contraceptives freely through public health clinics to all individuals who request them; and (f) reduction of immigration quotas.

On the side of demand, programs should be initiated to reduce the psychic income benefits of, or "need" for additional children. We should recognize that where other utility alternatives are available and known, the birth rate will fall; thus by raising the average level of income and education we encourage smaller average family size. Increasing professional and leisure time alternatives for women in our society will similarly reduce their desire or willingness to accept additional pregnancies.

More generally, I propose the launching of a widespread national campaign (along the lines of the current cigarette-cancer campaign) to change public attitudes concerning appropriate family size. The program needn't rely on heavy-handed dramatics, but it requires more than discreet references to parking problems. Americans want the family size they obtain, in most cases. If they are made sufficiently aware of the fact that the quality of every man's life is diminished a little by each birth announced by his neighbor, concern for community approval will bring some reduction in the number of children wanted, on average. J.S. Mill summarized the issue perhaps too bluntly when he said, "Little improvement can be expected [in population control] until the producing of large families is regarded with the same feelings as drunkenness or any other physical excess."

All ethical principles are based upon the individual's recognition of his interaction with other men, the reciprocal nature of human relationships, and the efficacy of cooperation in achieving any social order. Population limitation must become an ethical principle, just as respect for another's property or person. But this kind of moral principle will not develop spontaneously; it requires repetition, demonstration, education through the agencies of government, schools and churches. To develop the required conviction among responsible authorities will be a tremendous challenge.

Putting my conclusions in simple form, I propose that the costs of rearing children be raised to include all (or most) of the external costs they impose upon society and that, at the same time, the utilities associated with increases in family size be reduced. Whether the tax penalties proposed earlier should be retroactive is a political question. From the point-of-view of incentives the answer is probably "no" on the ground that in economics bygones are forever bygones. The differential sacrifice of the younger generation is a requirement imposed by our current perception of the problem; analogously, only limited numbers of a population actually fight in any war.

I do not ignore the hard problem of the high birth rate among the poor. Their income and education levels must rise substantially if they are to respond to economic incentives affecting the birth rate. But I would oppose exempting them from the tax measures suggested above. A negative income tax program which raises all family incomes to a minimum level might include additional bonus payments to encourage smaller family size. It is obvious that present welfare programs create negative incentives for regulation of child-birth. They should be altered to do away with these negative incentives.

As a final suggestion, I propose a revision of our national economic accounts in the direction of measuring the state of our total environment. It is time we put into practice what Kenneth Boulding has called "the economics of spaceship earth." In the econosphere, the total resource stock is the important point of reference, not simply the gross value of the throughput. We have too long accepted the "cowboy economy" mentality — that with technology as our handmaiden, infinite stocks of raw materials may be converted into a maximum quantity of consumer goods whose waste products may be dumped into a number of infinitely accommodating reservoirs. We seriously underestimate the long-run cost of the high Gross National Product we presently enjoy. It is not only concern for posterity which should prompt an early revision of our national income accounts to include the depreciation of such essential values as air and water quality, the state of the land, and space. Fiscal and employment policy should be based on an index of national income adjusted to account for changes in these fundamental commodities. It is possible, for example, that a reduction in the present output of goods (through reduced working days and early retirement) might increase the present value of all future income streams, where the latter include environmental utilities.

I believe that the greatest benefits from the achievement of zero population growth in our society would be enjoyed by those now chained to the cycle of poverty. The real wages of these groups are kept at minimum levels both by the absence of organized labor markets for their services and by the excessive supply of labor in these markets created by a high birth rate. Too few of the children born into poverty find it possible to escape its vicious circle. Population control is not the only measure to be recommended here, but it has the greatest chance for long-run success. Again quoting Mill, "Only when, in addition to just institutions, the increase of mankind shall be under the deliberate guidance of judicious foresight, can the conquests made from the powers of nature by the intellect and energy of scientific discoverers become the common property of the species, and the means of improving and elevating the universal lot."

THE DILEMMA OF TECHNOLOGY

James P. Lodge, Jr.

The enormous development of technology that accompanied the Industrial Revolution has liberated men from a total preoccupation with gaining the means of subsistence, and very few of us would be willing to forego its benefits. At the same time, our use of technology has become inordinately wasteful, and it threatens to do permanent damage to the biosphere, the overall ecosystem we inhabit. Nevertheless we need it: in the words of Dr. Lodge, "While it is largely responsible for the present mess in the environment, technology is our hope for getting out of this mess."

For Dr. Lodge, re-education in the uses of technology is the key to the situation. We need to know more about the specifics of waste and pollution and the consequences of living in an economy not geared to constantly increasing production for a constantly increasing population, and acquiring this knowledge will take time.

In the meanwhile we need not be inactive about combating obvious abuses of the environment. Dr. Lodge indicates some ways in which we can reduce pollution and waste as we work toward our further goals. Finally, he suggests that the attainment of these goals is particularly the responsibility of the younger generation.

James P. Lodge, Jr., is Program Scientist at the National Center for Atmospheric Research, in Boulder, Colorado, and Affiliate Professor of Chemistry at Louisiana State University. He is Chairman of the Colorado Air Pollution Commission and the author of over seventy original publications largely dealing with atmospheric science.

It has become increasingly popular, especially among the impatient young, to place most of the blame for the present environmental crisis on science and technology. It seems worthwhile to review the situation dispassionately, weigh the real issues, and see whether in fact the blame has been properly assigned.

At the outset, it seems possible largely to exonerate science. Research activities in and of themselves contribute very little pollution, and the products of science are words and equations, not beer cans or smog. It is only when the findings of science are translated into technology that they become causes of pollution.

It is less easy to excuse all scientists. Scientists as humans like to see their findings put to use, and must certainly share some responsibility when they promote the implementation of their findings without regard to the environmental consequences.

Technology, obviously, is another matter. Let us examine one simple measure of its environmental impact. It was, so far as I know, first pointed out by R. Buckminster Fuller that our living standard can be expressed by the concept of "energy slaves". This concept can be represented by a number derived as follows:

The total liberated energy is calculated for all sources over the United States, whether for home heating, heavy manufacturing, or transportation; this quantity is divided by the total population to give the per capita energy — far too large a number to be comprehensible; this large number is then divided by the work energy of a single human being, to give a quantity small enough to be grasped. It expresses, if you will, the number of slaves that would be needed for each present inhabitant of the United States if all the work performed mechanically were done by unaided human efforts. A recent recomputation of the figure by R.I. Larsen suggests that each man, woman, and child in the United States has at his beck and call, on the average, the equivalent of 500 slaves. (In fact, some have far fewer, while some have many more.) As was remarked before, this is a true measure of our standard of living, well above that of the most affluent Oriental potentates and Roman emperors.

The "energy slave" number is also the truest measure of our total impact on the environment. The United States is inhabited by a bit over two hundred million people and one hundred billion energy slaves! The wastes of these slaves comprise the true pollution problem, for energy slaves, like humans, must inhale air, excrete wastes, consume fuels (food), and dissipate their bodily heat. Overall, the per capita waste from energy slaves is probably comparable to that of humans, and, being foreign to the normal biological processes, many of the wastes from the energy slaves are far more difficult for the environment to cope with.

Is this number of energy slaves really necessary? The answer must be that they are not. We build houses with total disregard for their architectural fitness to the climate, confident that a large enough furnace and/or air conditioner can compensate for our mindlessness. We build automobiles of superfluous bulk, with engines of 450 housepower, although less than 10 percent of that horsepower is used 95 percent of the time. We design aircraft to cut in half the travel time between distant points without questioning whether anyone really wishes to arrive that much sooner. We expend electrical energy to transmit television programs devoid of information or value. We cut down trees and expend power to print newspapers too thick for anyone to read, stuffed with information that no one wants, advertising goods that no one needs.

However, while technology is far from blameless, it does not bear its guilt alone. The product that no one wants soon vanishes from the market. The television program without a listener quickly vanishes from the airwaves. The house that no one will buy is soon leveled for a parking lot. We may write letters to our Congressmen, but the surest way to kill the supersonic transport is to organize a unanimous refusal to fly in it.

But beyond these frills, fripperies, and foibles of our culture, there is a solid need for technology. Men will not of their own free will live like the poor of India, of Egypt, or of the ghettos of the United States. Without technology, without pesticides, without rapid transportation and communication, without farm machinery, we cannot hope to house and clothe and feed the present population of the world, or even of the United States. This is the dilemma of technology. While it is largely responsible for the present mess in the environment, technology is our hope for getting out of this mess.

We need education on a global scale. The developing countries need help to avoid the ecological mistakes that we have made. We ourselves must labor to undo the damage that we have done. We must limit our own population, it is true, but it is even more necessary to impose rigorous birth control on our energy slaves. To say that this requires an enormous program of rethinking priorities is to state the obvious, but it is nonetheless true. And in order to do this, we need quantities of information that we now lack.

The greatest need for action today, it seems to me, is in the areas of applied research. I recently heard a speaker at an ecological meeting call for an end to disposable paper napkins and handkerchiefs. He may have been right, but I suspect that he had no idea of the comparison between the ecological impact of disposable paper goods and that of the additional detergents necessary to wash the durable product. I myself have suggested that a great deal of travel could be eliminated by a really good system of video-equipped telephones, but I recognize the possibility that the energy necessary to manufacture all that equipment might be greater than that required for travel. But these questions have answers. It is simply that no one has taken the trouble to determine them. I submit that there is not an economist in the country who has seriously examined the consequences of a static economy.

None of this should be construed as cause to do nothing today. There are obvious ecological insults that could be brought under control. Gross pollution of any medium of the environment can certainly be decreased or halted, wherever it occurs. All reasonable means to slow the growth of population should be made available. Polluting products should be removed from the market, and polluters whose products are not of sufficient value to justify continued production should be, if possible, forced out of business by boycott. If there is the will to do so, early steps can also be taken to identify and modify the numerous features of our laws which favor pollution. For example, I own an old automobile which is economical to run almost entirely because its value for tax purposes has depreciated to zero. Compared to a new vehicle, it certainly generates more pollution, and it puts as much strain on the roads, the police, and everything else supported by taxation. Yet the owners of newer, cleaner automobiles are subsidizing my owning an old wreck. The same kind of tax mathematics keeps in business a number of leaky old factories which generate far more pollution than new ones, and whose diseconomies are compensated entirely by low tax valuations. Taxes on fuels seem to decrease as their potential pollution increases. The post office charges well above cost to carry necessary communications in order to subsidize the delivery, below cost, of "junk mail." These subsidized rates are so low that it does not even pay the advertisers to check their lists to avoid duplicate (and multiplicate) distribution of the same material. In my own household, at least, nearly 50 percent of the trash that becomes the problem of our municipal waste disposal facility is composed of this gratuitous paper.

Lists have already been compiled of things that the individual can do to minimize his environmental impact. Although most of these suggestions are fairly obvious, there are a few which seem not to have occurred to anyone. For example, the federal law forbidding re-use of liquor bottles has probably served its purpose and could be repealed, thus eliminating one item in the solid waste problem. Doubling the postal cost of "junk mail" would be a greater contribution, but probably harder to achieve.

In nearly all the "aerosol" products on the market, from insecticides to whipped cream, freons are used to generate pressure. Freons also escape when old refrigerators are junked. So far, these chemicals seem harmless to man, beast, or flower — but they also appear to be nearly immortal in the atmosphere. Since nobody has investigated the long-term effects of world-wide accumulation of freons in the air, perhaps their use should be avoided or minimized until their long-range impact can be assessed.

While it seems clear that in the long run the automobile is on its way out, there are many steps that can be taken to make its declining years more pleasant for all. Exhaust pollution can be decreased significantly by insisting on synchronized traffic lights. The inevitable stops cause less pollution when they are made gently, not screechingly. A "panic stop" causes more exhaust pollution, as well as adding rubber dust and asbestos from brake linings to the air.

Finally, we can insist on quality in the possessions we acquire. The environmental impact of skilled craftsmanship is no greater than that of inferior workmanship, and high quality products do not require replacement as often as shoddy ones. Whether we consider automobiles, homes, furniture, or toothbrushes, the poorly fashioned product sooner becomes a part of the waste cycle and, in addition, may well generate more pollution than a longer lasting commodity.

Overall, then, technology, which got us into this mess, is going to have to get us out again, strongly aided by real changes in our way of living. It seems to me that this is the specific responsibility of our young people. They have demonstrated, as no generation in the recent past has done, their ability to innovate. It is true that some of the innovations are not viable, that some are anti-social, and that a fair number are distinctly upsetting to their elders. But innovate they can and do. If they will take up the challenge, embrace it wholeheartedly, and think it through to its consequences, they can well be the force to save the world in fact and not in fancy. The greatest danger is that they may not display the necessary staying power. They cannot escape these problems, like a bad program on television, by turning a channel switch. Pollution will inevitably get worse before it gets better. Population will inevitably get larger before it is brought under control. But if the "now generation" can learn patience and persevere, they can spark the changes that must occur if an optimum environment is to be achieved.

POSSIBILITIES FOR ACTION

PART THREE

Anyone who seriously considers the trends that have created the population-environment situation and the human factors that complicate it must recognize that its solution will be revolutionary in its scope and character. The changes to be made are so big that at times we are tempted to regard the whole enterprise as hopeless.

Our pessimism would be justified if the ecological revolution were something we had to create out of thin air, so to speak, and impose on the general public as an unpleasant but necessary remedy for the world's evils. Fortunately, that is not the case. Revolutions of the sort we have in mind are not invented by small groups of conspirators. They are responses by society as a whole to institutions that have lost their relevance to human needs and aspirations, and they arise not out of misery but because the needs and aspirations of energetic people are being frustrated. Considering the extent to which the general desire for quality of life is now frustrated and the fact that intelligent people everywhere feel that existing institutions are insufficiently responsive to their needs, it is not too much to say that the ecological revolution has already begun. But if it has, it is still in its early stages, and the job of those of us who are concerned with the population-environment situation is to understand this revolutionary process and to help to give it the right direction. It is as if a river were seeking a new channel; the waters are backing up and at times they are turbulent, full of cross-currents. The revolution, in some form, is inevitable, simply because the human race is not going to allow itself to be destroyed without fighting back; but a proper, which is to say humane outcome is by no means certain. We have to work for it.

There are two dangers. The first is that energies frustrated by existing institutions may erupt in pointless violence, and we have seen some of that in the past ten years. The other is that for lack of unity these energies will be dissipated in quarrels within the movement and in reform efforts that lack enough general support to be effective.

So the question is, how can we promote our revolutionary cause and at the same time keep it from destroying the human values, or "quality of life" it is intended to preserve?

We have spoken of the need for dialogue, but dialogue unaccompanied by action soon becomes sterile and academic. The dialogue we call for is one engaged in by activists.

In Part III our contributors discuss from a background of practical experience the kinds of action that would further the process of achieving a humane resolution of the population-environment situation.

First they consider the possibilities — and limitations — of direct political action, and it appears that for success here we need a much greater public acceptance of our political and economic aims than now exists. This acceptance, in turn, depends on education in the broadest sense of the word, which would include not only formal schooling but the kind of education that comes from experience in coping with social problems and from group action to secure particular reforms. If the direct results of such action sometimes appear small by comparison with what remains to be done, the indirect result can be immense: a climate of opinion in which larger reforms become feasible. Finally in this section we return to the question of what kind of political action would be possible and effective once sufficient support for it had been generated.

STABILIZING U.S. POPULATION SIZE:
A POLITICAL STRATEGY

Joseph D. Tydings

With the passage and approval of S. 2108 in December, 1970, the first family planning bill in American history became law. This bill, which was introduced in the Senate by Joseph Tydings of Maryland, provides funds not only for family planning services but for population research, manpower training, information, and education as well.

From a background of long experience in practical politics former Senator Tydings outlines a political strategy for eventually stabilizing the population of the United States. He argues that at the present time compulsory population control is not feasible and that talk of such extreme measures only alienates the general public and is thus a disservice to the population-environment movement. In order to be effective the advocates of population limitation must resolve their differences and unite in a program of public education. Mr. Tydings enumerates the steps necessary for achieving general acceptance of population stabilization in this country.

Joseph D. Tydings, a practicing attorney, served in the United States Senate from 1965 to 1971 and has received many awards for his leadership in population and environmental causes. He is the author of Born To Starve, *a recent book about the population crisis.*

The United States must begin immediately to develop the public policies needed to stabilize the size of its population.

This important proposition can be supported by careful reasoning and an abundance of demographic data; and before most audiences, the full case for population stabilization should be presented. However, given the purposes of this National Congress on Optimum Population and Environment and the backgrounds and predispositions of most of the delegates in attendance, I feel at liberty here to treat the need for population stabilization as an accepted fact.

I would like to move beyond the expression of concern over the problem of population growth and focus instead on the critical question of *how* this nation should actually go about stabilizing its population. For despite nearly a decade of actively discussing the population problem, we still lack an accepted political strategy for translating our concerns into effective public action.

On the broadest plane, determining *how* to stabilize U.S. population size is more an issue of philosophy and politics than of biology, for much of the debate regarding the best means to slow population growth has centered on the question of whether population programs should be voluntary or compulsory.

The basic principle governing the disposition of civil liberties in a democratic society posits that the state only gains the right to deprive the individual of freedoms when the exercise of those freedoms constitutes a clear danger to the survival or well-being of the community; and that state abrogation of such freedoms can occur only *after* all reasonable alternatives short of compulsion have been tried and found wanting.

The United States has had no previous experience with attempts to slow the birth rate. We have no way of ascertaining yet whether voluntary incentives and public education will be sufficient to stem the population growth that is beginning to threaten us. Until we exhaust the possibilities of developing effective voluntary programs, recourse to compulsion is inconsistent with our traditional commitment to maximize individual freedom.

Furthermore, even if a compulsory program of population control were deemed necessary, such a program would not be politically feasible at this time. Strong resistance still exists in Congress to programs promoting voluntary family planning and even more to compulsory population control. Indeed, at this time, talk of compulsion constitutes the greatest threat to the success of the population stabilization movement — a point I shall elaborate on shortly.

Thus, both for philosophic and political reasons, proceeding along voluntary lines to achieve population stability is the only practical course in the coming decade.

If we can fashion at least a temporary consensus around the necessity for a voluntary approach to population stabilization in the foreseeable future, then I believe we can begin to act now.

A successful political strategy for stabilizing U.S. population size must be a multi-stage process.

As you well know, most issues — regardless of their import and urgency — require a political gestation period before the public and Congress are prepared to deal with them. Therefore, it makes sense to start a legislative program in any area with those proposals and ideas that have been in the public eye sufficiently long to secure a degree of acceptance.

In the context of a campaign to stabilize U.S. population growth, this means starting with the establishment of a national family planning policy, a policy to eliminate all unwanted births in this country.

Thanks to the pioneering efforts of people like Margaret Sanger and organizations such as Planned Parenthood, voluntary family planning is practiced or tolerated by a vast majority of Americans. As a result of this broad public acceptance, open debate about public family planning programs is finally no longer considered politically taboo by most members of Congress.

In addition to being the most politically acceptable population measure, an effective family planning program also promises a reduction in our birth rate — though the exact size of that reduction cannot be determined *a priori.*

Thus, providing family planning services to all who desire them and developing safer, more foolproof contraceptives offers a relatively inexpensive and politically acceptable first step towards stabilizing our population.

The second important stage in an effective political strategy to stabilize U.S. population size must be the reform of our abortion laws. If contraception fails, families must have the opportunity within a reasonable period of time to terminate unwanted pregnancies. It should not fall within the purview of the state to either compel a woman to have an abortion or constrain her from having an abortion. Such decisions are best left to individual conscience.

Finally, since contraception and abortion are methods only for preventing unwanted births, it is imperative to go beyond family planning to insure that the number of wanted births is consistent with a stable population size. In other words, the crucial third stage in our political strategy must be the creation of a national population policy; a policy to develop non-compulsory means to reduce the size of the average American family sufficiently to produce a stable population.

Creating such a policy constitutes a much more difficult task than establishing a national family planning policy.

To begin with, science has not yet discovered the psychological determinants of family size. We know very little about why one family wants two children while another wants six.

As a result, we simply do not know what kinds of voluntary incentives, economic rewards, and educational programs might reduce the birth rate to a level consistent with securing a stable population. Proposals such as those to limit income tax deductions in order to encourage smaller families — while useful symbols and vehicles for debate — are still only blind experiments lacking an empirical basis.

Furthermore, even if we knew what kinds of programs would substantially reduce the birth rate, the public has not been adequately prepared for the application of such knowledge through a national population policy. The idea of population stabilization as a public policy still frightens most Americans. In many respects, population stabilization is an issue whose political gestation period is just beginning.

Therefore, in my judgment, implementing this final stage in a political strategy to stabilize U.S. population size will require the following steps:

First, Congress and other national institutions and organizations must go on record in support of stabilizing U.S. population size. At this juncture, the population movement needs the kind of legitimacy and respectability in the public eye that can best be provided by the open endorsements of churches, business groups, medical associations, elected officials, newspapers, and civic organizations.

We have got to take our case to opinion-makers in the country and quickly win for population stabilization the non-controversial acceptance that family planning increasingly enjoys. For as long as population stabilization is viewed as a divisive, controversial issue by the majority of public officials in the country — which is currently the case — the likelihood of establishing an effective national population policy remains slim.

Second, the federal government must underwrite a national campaign to educate the American public on the dimensions and consequences of U.S. and global population growth.

Unfortunately, most of the information the American public has received to date on the population problem has been the product of a counterproductive academic debate that has dominated population circles for several years. This debate, which has become increasingly polarized and polemical, has centered on the precise nature of the consequences of unchecked population growth and the degree to which effective family planning programs would stabilize the U.S. population.

Each side — the one preaching urgency and the other less haste — has been guilty of grave oversimplification in taking its case to the public. One side warns Americans that unless U.S. population growth is halted immediately with whatever means necessary, the survival of the nation is in deepest jeopardy. The other side retorts with reassurances that population growth presents no real problem for the foreseeable future; that improved family planning programs are all that is required.

Now, few of the parties to this debate would actually subscribe to these simplified, extreme versions of their positions. Yet, it is these simplified versions fashioned largely for propaganda purposes that currently are shaping public debate over the population issue across the country and in the Congress.

Unless we break out of this polemical trap and change the character of this debate, we are going to default the opportunity to deal intelligently with the issue of population growth, for the public is either going to be convinced that there is no population problem, or people will be so frightened and repelled by some of the alarmist proposals for population control being offered largely for dramatic effect — such as compulsory vasectomies after two children or sterilants in the drinking water — that population stabilization will become a politically impossible issue. Either way, the population movement is the loser.

Nor can a successful population education campaign be built with Madison Avenue techniques. We are not pushing a product or promising a fad. Nothing less than public comprehension of the problems created by unchecked population growth and a grasp of the geometry of that growth can produce the climate required for a sustained effort to stabilize our population.

The experience of those who sought to promote public support for nuclear disarmament is particularly relevant to our task of designing a population education program. The campaign to "ban the bomb" in this country relied on scare techniques, catchy slogans, and even some slick T.V. advertising. But the campaign failed to create more than transitory concern.

Most people, after all, test their images of reality through simple observation. When ten, fifteen, and then twenty years passed without a nuclear war or accident, Americans were no longer convinced of the urgent need to disarm.

Disarmament advocates had failed to provide the public with even an elementary understanding of the probability theory on which the scientific community's fear of the continued deployment of nuclear weapons was based. People could not visualize Kenneth Boulding's picture of the hand of fate dipping each day into a bag containing one black ball amid many white balls, the black ball being nuclear disaster. Though the hand of fate has brought up a white ball each day since Hiroshima and Nagasaki, the black ball is still in the bag. And for those who can grasp this basic concept of probability, it is impossible to feel secure about the future until the black ball is removed from the bag.

In other words, disarmament educational efforts assumed that a problem created by the application of the scientific method — the existence of nuclear weapons — could be successfully solved by propaganda rather than sound scientific argument.

The population stabilization movement must not make the same mistake. Somehow we must inculcate in the American people a scientific approach to the problem; otherwise we will encounter endless opposition from well-meaning Americans who deny the existence of an aggregate population problem as the result of casual observations made while flying over uninhabited areas of the nation. Somehow we must teach enough familiarity with the demographer's calculus to enable people to grasp the mathematical inevitability of population stabilization in a nation with finite resources and space.

Third, we desperately need research and new data from which to develop non-compulsory methods for reducing the birth rate. Without reliable information on the determinants of family size and parental motivation, efforts to stabilize U.S. population size by voluntary means will surely fail.

To the best of my knowledge, very little research of this nature is currently being conducted by the National Institutes for Health or in our universities.

In conclusion: the population stabilization movement is passing out of the pamphleteer stage. We now must turn to political action and public education on a massive scale.

I believe the First National Congress on Population and Environment represents an opportunity to take the first meaningful step in this direction. Hopefully, the academic hairsplitting over whether the U.S. will add 70 million or 100 million more people during the next thirty years will be abandoned for a hard look at the strategies required for stabilization.

Unless we begin to act, the public will tire of our words. And if we fail, we will be forced to confront an over-crowded, misery-ridden world with only the hollow apology of Eliot's J. Alfred Prufrock: "That is not what I meant at all; that is not it at all."

BEYOND GNP: A PLEA FOR
A QUALITY OF LIFE ECONOMY

Stewart L. Udall

One of the major obstacles to achieving ecological sanity is the suspicion of many people, and especially economists, that the population-environment movement is utopian and unrealistic. Stewart Udall advocates a dialogue that would make allies of the economists who now regard us as impractical. Our arguments in this dialogue would dispose of over-simplified notions of our aims and principles. "We are not," says Mr. Udall, "proposing a return to a Walden Pond economy." He suggests that in some ways it is the conventional economists who are unrealistic, particularly in their adherence to the outworn belief that "gross national product" is a valid way of measuring the economic well-being of the United States.

To use GNP as a yardstick is to accept the idea that economic expansion and progress are synonymous. Unfortunately this is an idea which most Americans still take for granted long after it has lost whatever relevance it once had to an underpopulated and undeveloped continent, but it persists as another major obstacle to the attainment of the goals of the population-environment movement.

Stewart L. Udall, former Secretary of the Interior, is not only an outstanding conservationist but one who is highly conscious of the "people" aspect of the conservation cause. In his own words, "the total conservation approach demands concepts large enough to relate conservation to the overriding issues of our age. You cannot save the land unless you save the people. True conservation begins wherever the people are and with whatever trouble they are in."

Mr. Udall is the author of The Quiet Crisis *and* 1976: Agenda For Tomorrow.

The counterattack against the population-environment movement is already under way. Not long ago one of the *New York Times'* best writers on economics, Erich Heinemann, authored an article entitled, "Babies vs. the GNP: Demographer Finds Population Curb No Panacea For Nation's Various Ills." Heinemann asserted that environmentalists have "been quick to acquire an orthodoxy and a litany all of their own," and he approvingly quoted a recent statement by Herman P. Miller, Chief Demographer of the U.S. Census Bureau, that trying to deal with current social problems "by persuading women not to have babies is like trying to treat cancer with a sedative. It might relieve the pain, but it won't make the problem go away."

On a similar note, even the good, grey *New Republic* has gone out of its way in recent weeks to describe our movement as "the ecology craze," characterizing it as little more than "a cop out for a President and a populace too cheap, or too gutless, or too frustrated or too all of them to tangle harder with current social problems."

It is vital, in my view, that we meet such arguments head on. We must conduct an ongoing discussion with our critics that is both rational and productive. We are already type-cast as idealists (which we are), as alarmists (which, to a degree, we must be), and as crusaders who are critical of establishment economics (which, to a further degree, we must also be.) To achieve maximum effectiveness as individuals and as a new organization, I believe we must keep our ideals rooted in reality, our alarms based on foreseeable consequences — and our crusades must be sufficiently pragmatic and convincing that in the months ahead we can win over important politicians, economists and demographers to our side.

Let us, then, base our arguments and our program on foresight and sound analysis, and avoid myth-making of our own that will make our cause vulnerable to critical comment. When it comes to discussion of a bedrock subject like economics we must acquire prestigious allies who can keep our ideas and arguments on the sure footing of sound theory.

So, in this light, consider my remarks as a friendly epistle to the economists. My aim, then, is to open up a dialogue between the nation's economists and its environmentalists. I have no new truths or theories about the U.S. economy to offer. I am not even an amateur economist. However, I do want to provoke a hopefully constructive reaction from the practitioners of the once-dismal profession. In the search for a humane environment we desperately need the guidance of some of the nation's best economists.

The dialogue up to this point has been both limited and unenlightening. On the one hand, environmentalists have expressed outrage at the anti-human effects of much economic expansion; and most of the economists who have bothered to reply have, in cavalier fashion, oversimplified our arguments or pictured us as emotional hand-wringers wholly ignorant of the "Iron Laws" of economics.

So let me begin by clearing out some of the verbal underbrush. In the first place, I want to suggest a few "don'ts" for economists who may be ready to enter into serious discussion about redirecting our economic system toward what I will call a quality-of-life economy:

1. Don't turn us off by oversimplifying our arguments into easily demolishable strawmen. We are not, for example, proposing a return to a "Walden Pond economy" — even though, like most economists and other affluent Americans, we are engaged in a search for quiet, unspoiled enclaves to vacation in, or live out our lives in. We deeply believe that our economic system has made all of us producers and consumers first and has caused us to neglect the whole range of humane values that give true meaning to life. We believe something is seriously wrong with a system that creates a fat life of empty affluence — but can't even learn how to recycle its wastes or build livable cities. We believe that many of Thoreau's truths are more piercing and pertinent today than ever before, for it is plain far more men and women live "lives of quiet desperation" in 1970 than in 1847. But understand us, please: the proprietor of Walden Pond is a life-philosopher we read and respect; he is not the "in" economist of the environmental movement.

2. Don't dismiss us as an angry wave of neo-Luddites. When the youth among us bury combustion engines, they are expressing the fear that unbridled faith in technology may destroy us. We are not machine-smashers. But we are convinced the time has come to civilize and restrain technology and make it serve men. We have a paramount bias for Earth — for life. We are skeptical, therefore, of the gifts offered by such technological extravaganzas as the SST and manned exploration of the lifeless otherworld of outer space.

3. Don't assume that we propose zero population growth as an economic panacea. As we believe another generation of more-of-the-same economic growth is a prescription for catastrophe, we are convinced that the one sure way to reduce long-term demands on the life-support system of the planet — and to make all of our social problems more manageable — is to level off population increase in this country. We are aware that per capita consumption must also be leveled off, and this is why we argue for a new lifestyle of restraint. Therefore, we are convinced that the managers of our economy must question all the old assumptions of quantitative growth and help us develop a different, more balanced, life-centered economy.

4. Don't assume that we have a quarrel with the truly immutable principles of economics. We do ask however that you turn creative thought to those theories and concepts that are subject to change.

Our quarrel with conventional economists and conventional economics arises out of our conviction that the time has come for changes in economic thought as profound and productive of change as those of John Maynard Keynes. The current economic system is based on ideology of maximum production and maximum consumption. It may have been appropriate in 1932 or 1945, but it could lead us down a path to disaster in the remaining years of this century. Can we continue to optimize indiscriminate growth, and ignore those new patterns of growth that might create an optimum environment for man?

Is it right, we ask, in a nation that spends nearly 10 per cent less in the public sector than some countries in western Europe to assert that the *only* way our country can solve its social and environmental problems is by an unlimited upward spiral of the Gross National Product? As we fear that ours is becoming a corpulent acquisitive society, we must quarrel with the assumption that America can continue to consume one-third of the resources and raw materials of the world — and produce over one-third of its pollution.

Consequently, we plead for a less deterministic, more life-centered economy, whose managers are ready to re-evaluate all of the shallow trend projections that dominate our planning today. Are we prisoners of our past? — are we environmentally and economically already prisoners of Santayana's dictum: "What matters most for each man has seemingly already been decided for him"?

Environmentalists are, I believe, dismayed most by the trend projections that dominate U.S. planning today. There is an insidious, self-fulfilling thrust to these forecasts of growth. They foster a Juggernaut mind-set. They utterly ignore the human effects of such expansion. They convince us that we have no opportunity to remake tomorrow.

We are told the year 2000 already assured by the momentum of the present includes:

—One hundred million more people;

—One hundred fifty million more motor vehicles;

—Five or six times as many aircraft;

—An energy system that demands three or four times as much fuel;

—An industrial machine that demands three or four times as much resources and raw materials;

—Another thirty years of suburban sprawl and bulldozed "progress";

—A production system that spews forth three or four times as many wastes and poisons and pollutants.

Is this our "land of lost content"? Is this the American Eldorado? Or will the pursuit of such materialistic goals take us down a road to world unrest and the wrecking of the environment of this country — and the planet as well? These are some of the questions this congress was convened to ask.

It is hard for us to envision the year 2000 of these trend planners without the dread that it will surely mean dehumanized cities, a buildup of unbearable stress, the crowding and over-mechanization of nearly every aspect of life, and the disappearance of most of the amenities we associate with the way of living we now prize.

It is not alone the environmentalists who are appalled by such a brave and bulging new world. Eminent economists and historians have already voiced misgivings about it.

Listen to John Kenneth Galbraith:

> The penultimate western man, stalled in the ultimate traffic jam and slowly succumbing to carbon monoxide, will not be cheered to hear from the last survivor that the Gross National Product went up by a record amount.

—Or to the historian, Daniel Boorstin:

> Perhaps more and more Americans, surfeited by objects, many of which actually remove the pungency of experience, now begin to see the ideal — the ideal of everybody having the newest things — being liquidated before their very eyes. Perhaps the annual model has begun to lose its charm.

—Or, finally, to the profound pessimism of E. J. Mishan, the young British economist, who has dismal views of the future of man and who has written in his new book, "Technology and Growth: The Price We Pay":

Business economists have ever been glib in equating economic growth with an expansion of the range of choices facing the individual; they have failed to observe that as the carpet of "increased choice" is being unrolled before us by the foot, it is simultaneously being rolled up behind us by the yard. We are compelled willy-nilly to move into the future that commerce and technology fashions for us without appeal and without redress. In all that contributes in trivial ways to his ultimate satisfaction, the things at which modern business excels, new models of cars and transistors, prepared food-stuffs and plastic objets d'art, electric toothbrushes and an increasing range of push-button gadgets, man has ample choice. In all that destroys his enjoyment of life, he has none. The environment around him can grow ugly, his ears assailed with impunity, and smoke and foul gases exhaled over his person. He may be in such circumstances that he will never enjoy a night's rest at home without planes shrieking overhead. Whether he is indifferent to such circumstances, whether he bears them stoically, or whether he writes in impotent fury, there is under the present dispensation practically nothing he can do about them.

Another distinguished economist, Kenneth Boulding, has attacked what he regards as the outdated concepts embodied in conventional GNP economics. Boulding, with one eye on the finiteness of the planet's resources, believes we must begin now to move toward an economy of equipoise, in which what the economists call "throughput" is minimized and kept in balance. More than any other economist, Boulding has sought to look beyond full-employment economics to a more subtle science based on qualitative yardsticks. It is curious that a nation which rejects economic determinism should blindly accept the idea that the shape of our future is already decided by the twin forces of plain greed and the profit motive, wearing the common cloak of "consumer sovereignty," and not show warmth toward the "spaceman economy" concepts of Boulding.

On another front, I urge the economists to survey the long term future and give us insights into the world community and its geo-economics. If we continue our gluttonous course, consuming indefinitely over-one-third of the world's resources, do we not foreclose the option of the under-developed countries to aspire to our standard of living? Indeed, is a stable world possible if we persist in conduct that is already charac-terized by some nations as economic imperialism? I would suggest that we are already witnessing — in Canada perhaps, and in parts of Latin America and the Middle East — the first faint beginnings of a protest that will undermine the very assumptions of our year 2000 growth projections.

To conclude, I would ask our friends in the world of economics to weigh our arguments that over the long haul of life on this planet it is the ecologists — and not the bookkeepers of business — who are the ultimate accountants. We need you as advocates and allies in order to explore the feasibility of an optimum population and an optimum environment for this country — and an optimum economy geared to the quality of life as well.

ENVIRONMENTAL EDUCATION

Martha T. Henderson

Is there an ecological instinct in human beings? Whatever the precise scientific answer, we are justified in using the term metaphorically; the evidence is the interest of all children in nature, an interest on which formal schooling relies heavily in the primary grades. But the environmental awareness that is cultivated in the early years of education is usually allowed to dwindle as the compartmentalized learning of "subjects" takes over in secondary school. As a result, the average adult American may remember a few scraps of biology and of geology and the other earth sciences, but his sense of environment has been stunted and he lacks the ability to relate the abstractions of science to the concrete facts of his surroundings.

Martha Henderson considers how formal education could remedy this defect. She argues for cultivating what we have called the ecological "instinct" not by adding ecology as a subject to the already overloaded curriculum but by relating environmental concerns to the subjects that are now being studied. Environmental awareness would be developed by an interdisciplinary approach, and it would lead naturally to awareness of population problems. Miss Henderson suggests way in which environmental studies could be continued throughout the years of high school and explains how existing curricula could be modified to include them.

Martha Henderson is Education Associate of the Public Broadcasting Environment Center, of Washington, D.C., and Secretary of the North American Committee, Commission on Education, of the International Union for the Conservation of Nature and Natural Resources, whose headquarters are in Morges, Switzerland.

All of us are involved in the environmental crisis. Man is an important biological part of it, and people in their increasing numbers create many of its problems and suffer from them. Merely cleaning up the mess around us is unsufficient. As James L. Aldrich of the Education Development Center puts it, "To many of us concerned with education, these crises are the symptoms of more fundamental social distortions which dictate a major re-ordering of educational priorities . . . . The need is for a concentrated effort to develop the materials, teacher training, and style of classroom operation which provide the basis for exploring the vast web of relationships of man with nature, of man with man, of the partnerships which must exist if we are to re-establish a life worth living.''

Clearly we are discussing changing the value system, the cultural set, of people. The job is not easy, but it is the task of education to try, though performing it will require major changes in education as we know it today.

American society has recently tended to offer a declining range of options for the ways in which we should live. The emphasis in setting national and personal goals has been on material progress. We must provide a far greater range of options for the future. It may involve a different standard of living, new forms of social groupings, smaller families, and a shifting of values to non-material gratifications, all of which challenge our fundamental assumptions as to what life actually is or should be.

A look at history may give us some leads for our own action. As a child, I lived in a college community in New England. Looking back at my grandparents' generation, which was still active then, it seems to me that they represented a life more in harmony with their surroundings than ours, and certainly they had interdisciplinary concerns. We cannot and do not wish to replicate their society. It was traditional in outlook rather than future-oriented. They represented one class instead of all of society. Still, their experience has value for us.

First, the social circumstances of that earlier time virtually forced people to share ideas across different concerns. They observed the various life styles of professions and the training and work needed to enter them and operate within them. If one man was a lawyer, his brother was possibly a doctor, another might teach history, and cousins be in business. Since they had grown up together and continued to meet at family affairs or as neighbors, they knew one another's interests. Children were privy to discussions of adult concerns at Sunday dinner or might observe members of the family at work. Visits to the father's office were common. The relationship of the extended family to its surroundings was relatively clear.

Second, they had an over-arching frame of reference, a philosophy, derived from their Judeo-Christian heritage. Although many might be agnostics or atheists, they operated far more consciously than most of us do within the broad set of concepts of that heritage. Specialization has narrowed us. If you ask people nowadays to cope with more than a few specialties, they are unable to do so, because they lack concepts which would enable them to integrate many concerns. A broader, humanistic philosophy allowed those of an older generation to take in more variety and find a place for it.

Third, they had a feeling that they were able to influence their world. They could act upon it and had some power over its direction. They controlled the universities, business and the professions, although most in those professions no longer had much direct political power. It was worth striving for a harmonious life, because you could make pretty good strides toward achieving it for yourself and your heirs.

In this earlier era, as James Coleman has pointed out, the child was in contact with the realities of his world. The schools could then be left to handle codified knowledge. At present children need to be taught in school about their environment. This requires a radical change of the role of the school in society. A multi-disciplinary, problem-solving approach is demanded by the complexity of our environmental problems.

Not all schools are in a position to make immediate major changes. In some it may prove impossible to break down disciplinary lines, particularly at the secondary level. Only use of population and environment data in all the various disciplines may be possible.

But many teachers are moving toward an interdisciplinary approach. Maybe two teachers share a common program or team-teach. Possibly several share a project. In some cases it may be possible to get a whole school to take population and environment problems as a focus, as is being done at colleges such as the University of Wisconsin at Green Bay and Hampshire College.

Whatever the arrangement, it would be helpful to have a tutorial group for a small number of students held either in a classroom or at lunchtime.

This group would provide a small "society" where many interests could be clarified and developed. The group could set to work to plan for a future environment which seemed to represent good ecological and demographic principles, for it is in the future that students will operate. To focus on the future is to avoid over-emphasis upon immediate short-term problems such as pollution in favor of more positive ideas of long-term change.

How could discussion in these seminar groups start? There are some interesting suggestions in the work of a clinical psychologist, Barbara Ellis Long. She tries to "drop a pebble" into the group to stir discussions and then lets the ripples spread from it as they will. Students pursue different directions of concern at their own pace. They are able to make the material their own and relate to it personally. They bring up their hopes and fears, and discover how they are shared, and find their own relationship to expressed goals. Students discover alternative courses of action to which they have contributed ideas and through which they may gain the power and responsibility to make changes.

The group can explore not only individual needs, but how to operate together. They learn to be considerate of the others, rather than always competitive, and to devise common goals and coordinate routes to reaching them. The teacher acts as "midwife," setting up situations in the form of games or role-playing to clarify issues, questioning to bring out structure of skills, and providing leads to necessary information.

What are some of the projects to focus upon? After starting in with themselves and discussing their views about the future world, the tutorial group might try to create an interesting small environment in the room where sessions are held. In some cases students would be able to move things around in the room in order to discover different spatial and temporal relationships and feel how they effect human response. They could cut off the light or shade it in different ways. Plants in the classroom can be observed over a period of time. Through such experiments they could achieve an initial sense of power to change their world. This immediate environment should receive the greatest emphasis in elementary schools.

Older students will want to know how to move out from their room to deal with broader areas for their work on population and environment. Teachers will need background materials for them; certain curricula which might be useful for a multi-disciplinary, problem-solving approach could be gathered. There are numerous curricula already available in most of the disciplines.

These programs offer only leads. Especially at the secondary level, few are integrated around a specific location or across disciplinary lines. Students and teachers might learn a great deal from adapting available curricula to problems of their local environment and its future.

Whatever focus is chosen as a start — it might be early man or the population-housing situation in the neighborhood or a specific pollution problem — what is needed is to reach past the small immediate situation to the broad basic principles which underlie it. Recognition of air pollution can lead to discussion of population density, industrial waste, and health. The automobile problem leads to consideration of alternative sources of energy and new social groupings.

Social and ethical considerations should be paramount. Students in a neighborhood study can consider the role of religion in the lives of people and whether it or economic considerations seem more important. They can examine a specific problem such as abortion and begin to consider legal means to solve it. This in turn could lead to deeper considerations of the role of law in our society. Law versus violence is a possible focus. The legislative means to change should also be examined. Computer-based courses on politics and urbanism are available and useful.

Discussions of these matters would help students to understand how to participate in the decision-making process. If a topic proves to be too sensitive to be discussed in terms of the immediate community, some other city or a foreign culture can be studied.

We need to develop in students a sense of style and a sense of history. If they recognize change from the past, they will consider it more easily for the future. They should be able through the arts to dream of this future and express their dreams in poems, in music or plays or films.

Within the school, games and role-playing may help to make problems real, but how can older students learn to change the reality of the world around them unless they are out in it, dealing with it? Too many students think of the world as run by "they," a distant, untouchable group which controls them. We must give them a sense that this is *their* society, that they do have a place in it and can make changes to improve it.

Participation in the real world around the school is essential for most students; and planning for field work is vital. In many cases a few students will want to look over curricula and set up their own program. Many will seek immediate involvement in an organized project and will revise available curricula materials as they find them necessary to their program.

There are any number of ways to tackle an environmental problem. Students might take up the study of their neighborhood and do the ecology in science class, anthropology in social studies, and so on. With the co-operation of a group of teachers an interdisciplinary effort might become part of the school program. Teachers could discuss and integrate the different segments in the tutorial and try to project the present into the future. No matter how it is arranged, some students will obviously be more interested in one subject than another. In the small groups they can see how their interest fits within the whole. Goals can be reshaped as more is learned.

Explorations outside the confines of the school have many variations. The Parkway Program has businesses, government offices, museums, architectural firms, over one hundred places, cooperating with schools. In this manner students are apprenticed to actual operations affecting their world. They begin to feel they are participants in reform. They start to understand the training required to engage themselves more deeply and the challenge and fun of that involvement. Not all will want this apprenticeship made of study, but it should be an option.

Students can also work on a site such as a swamp or island and record ecological factors. The Thomas School in Connecticut reports its findings about a local area to the Fish & Wildlife Service. In England, student-recorded changes in land use during the development of new towns became data for town planners.

There are other routes. High school students can arrange to teach in elementary schools, which helps both. Or students may join with community action committees in public hearings on the Air Quality Act and similar legislation.

These arrangements with the outside world need to be planned and take time to set up. Students can do some contacting, but the teachers will be obliged to help establish the actual programs and be among the ultimate evaluators of work done outside, if credit is to be given. The students will themselves be increasingly able to make evaluations, but to meet the laws, teachers must stay in the picture throughout the operation and make sure appropriate goals are set and work accomplished.

The local League of Women Voters or Planned Parenthood group can be of great assistance with contacts. In some inner city sections, community groups can be most useful; this is a fine way to involve parents with the school. Once the ball is rolling, one group will lead to another.

The home-base tutorial must remain the place of integration, of trying to project plans into the future, of relating the student to his work. Otherwise there is a mere scattering out into the community, without focus on a central problem.

By these outside contacts, the world of teachers and students alike will be enlarged. But teachers may feel rather at sea trying to coordinate all these new fields. New curricula alone will not suffice, and people with jobs are often busy. Where is help?

The local universities or technical schools are a source of assistance. If qualified undergraduates or graduate students could sit in with the tutorial regularly, teachers could get extra advice in fields such as law or planning that are rarely included in their training. If one wanted to do field work, students in ecology or sociology would be an invaluable help.

This participation by college and university students in schools is becoming steadily easier. Undergraduates can now occasionally teach in schools for credit. Law schools, environment and population centers, design and planning programs, and medical schools have field projects in which secondary school students may occasionally participate as survey takers or in other appropriate roles. Graduate students, too, can now sometimes teach in school as part of their studies at the university.

The sort of university student assistance indicated provides all kinds of potential intellectual and practical help to schools. The only point to remember is that a reasonably structured program is vital. A student needs to have his role and responsibilities clearly defined in advance, with a teacher.

This discussion has taken a single school's possibilities as a focus. But we have hundreds of thousands of schools. How can we get environmental-population studies more widespread?

In one city or town, an environment center in the neighborhood might be a useful focus for community projects undertaken by many schools. The National Park Service and others have some centers; others might be established.

But there is a need for better materials and learning arrangements for the programs in any given locale and for better dissemination of programs across the country. A national effort similar to that involved in the science curricula programs of the last decade should be launched in the environment-population field, to build up units which coordinate existing materials around environmental problems and develop new ones to fill gaps. A few schools can manage to do so for themselves. Most cannot.

Such a national effort could only develop prototypes for selected regions or locales. Subsequent workshops should not only adapt units to specific regional or local situations, but should set up a network of interested local professionals to work on the development and use of these materials in the schools. Teams of teachers, students, and administrators, university deans and students, community action groups, and professionals should be organized around school programs. Not all involved in adapting and developing materials could work continuously with all the neighboring schools, but they could help to arrange introductions to their colleagues.

Of course, teacher-training is a vital ingredient. Pre-service training might be conducted along lines similar to those discussed above for students. Teachers must be key participants in curriculum development, and in-service methods have to be initiated as part of new learning situations. The children are ready for open programs. Teachers need more help.

Steady contact must be maintained by many local centers with a central organization. A newsletter would help. A series of workshops would be effective.

It should be noted that the organization of such complex learning programs would greatly benefit from the advice and involvement of people who understand areas such as technology-assessment or policy-planning.

The media are another important factor that should be used to spread the word about good programs, locally and nationally. TV should develop specific teacher-training programs in the environment-population field, possibly taking ideas from successful BBC programs in the arts fields. Locally, if teachers with exciting projects wrote them up for their neighborhood paper, sent a notice to a national group, or wrote their Congressman supporting appropriate educational legislation, then more of the citizenry who ultimately control our schools would be knowledgeable about good programs.

Nor should the network described be only national. We live in one world, in a closed, interdependent system. We must cooperate internationally. The International Union for the Conservation of Nature and Natural Resources (IUCN) based in Morges, Switzerland, has an education commission which maintains extensive contacts all over the world. American organizations should arrange closer contact with the Union and its North American Committee on Education. The United Nations is sponsoring a major conference on Human Environment in 1972. Many other international meetings will lead up to this session. American educational participation should be supported.

We are proposing here that environment-population education be directed not merely to specific, immediate issues such as population or pollution control, but address itself as well to helping people develop new values, a new set of priorities for their world, which emphasize not material growth but the concept of one world, with man in harmony with nature and technology. As in earlier generations, members of society should be able to achieve communal sharing of many concerns, a grasp of philosophic, ethical frameworks, and a sense of the individual's and the community's ability continuously to influence their environment.

To reach these goals, students will need many new options in their education, including the opening up of schools, universities, and the community to a beneficial interplay. Students will also need as part of their studies a secure tutorial base that offers human warmth and a sense of mutual sharing of hopes and responsibilities.

For ultimately it is the confident person, prepared to set wise, realistic goals and devise sound operative alternatives for reaching them, who will be able to participate in building a future world fit for man and all other living things.

THE USE OF ARTISTS AS ARTISTS IN
THE STRUGGLE FOR POPULATION CONTROL

Alan Gussow

"Artists are the antennae of the race," and as such they are more readily aware of and responsive to their surroundings than the rest of us. But their sensitivity — and with it the ability to produce real works of art — can be lost if it is misused to create propaganda. Paradoxically, the social usefulness of the artist rests on his refusal to modify his individual, personal vision to suit the apparent needs of society. So we may wonder what role, if any, he has to play in the population-environment movement.

Alan Gussow, an artist who is also a conservationist, believes that role is to give depth and concrete imagery to our understanding of the concept "quality of life" — and quality of life, in the final analysis, is what the population-environment movement is all about.

Mr. Gussow describes two programs in which the interests of artists coincide with the interests of conservationists, to the benefit of all of us, and suggests that similar programs might also serve the cause of the population control.

Alan Gussow is a well-known painter and a consultant to the National Park Service of the Department of the Interior. He has worked to secure grants in aid to artists who, like himself, are engaged in projects related to the restoration of the environment. He is now preparing a book to be published in the fall of 1971, entitled A Sense of Place, *in which he writes about American artists and their response to the natural landscape.*

We have all seen the Volkswagen commercial about the heavy snow which asks the question, "have you ever wondered how the snow plow operator gets to work?" and then smugly reveals that he drives his VW over unplowed roads in order to plow the roads for everyone else. The artist is a little like the snow plow operator and (though he might dispute the metaphor) his art functions like the VW in the commercial.

Art is the vehicle that transports us to the road that needs clearing. Viewed this way, an artist's role in the population crisis would be to bring the public to an awareness of the need for population control. It isn't enough for the artist merely to change his own life, rather he must gear up to persuade others to change theirs.

If we want artists to use their skills as artists to serve a social end, it is necessary first of all to identify what it is that artists uniquely do. What the artist does is to recreate an experience, to communicate in some sort of visible form what it was that he felt or witnessed or observed. Feelings exist in all of us, but the artist is trained to take his feelings and substantiate them. The critical phrase here is "his" feelings. We are all familiar with the outcome when art is forced to play a social role. We have seen enough of Soviet "socialist realism" to know that art created under fiat to ennoble the labors of the common man is no art at all, and in the end debases itself by illustrating not the common man's ideals, but the ruling bureaucracy's idea of what the common man's ideals ought to be. There are notable exceptions, of course. Daumier in France caricatured the hypocrisy of the law courts; Goya in his etchings marked forever on our minds the horror of war. In our own time, Picasso's *Guernica* stands as art and symbol of the horror-filled night in which the light of life is extinguished. In each of these works, the artist took his skills — his eye and hand — into battle, and indicted the society around him. In these situations of stress, horror, and repression, he emphasized the distance between that which should be and that which was.

But none of these enduring comments on the problems of the world— on man's inhumanity to man — was commissioned. Each motif was freely chosen, determined by the artist's own repulsion at the way things were. For artists value freedom; yet, as these works movingly illustrate, freedom to an artist is valuable only in so far as it can be willingly surrendered, given up for something. The real artist wants freedom for one purpose only; to be able to choose what it is he wants to do. Artists do not set out to solve the world's problems. To say that what I do best as an artist may often have nothing to do with the problems of the world may seem like a terrible admission, but it is the truth. Art has to do with life, not with problem-solving. And if an artist, before the fact, says that he intends to reckon with the world's problems — problems like population growth — he runs the danger of neither solving the problem nor creating art. Tell of love beforehand, as

Blake says, and it loses flow without filling the mold; the cast will be a reject.

From a social standpoint there is another, perhaps even greater risk. The inherent danger for any artist attempting to indict is that he will aestheticize terror, that he will make beautiful what is horrible, make acceptable that which should be repugnant.

Knowing something then of what it is that artists risk and at the same time caring deeply about the problems of this planet, and of population growth specifically, is there anything we can do to engage the energies of artists — directly — in heightening awareness of the problem and in getting people to act differently? Is there any artist, however great, who can, by force of his mind and symbols, enter the bedroom and make people "stop at two"? On the lowest level — and I'm not speaking genitally — we can suggest that artists enter the arena of mass culture and create, cynically, and with Madison Avenue aforethought, new fashionable modes of art. Since we have lived through Op and Pop Art— perhaps what we should commission is a new art movement — Vas Art, celebrating the new found freedoms of tubal ligation and cut *vas deferens*. In our commercial, fashion-minded times, of mini-and maxi, should we request, politely — but with a hint of financial reward — that artists focus on the altered organs?

Maybe what is called for is a new *machismo*. Artists, like Blacks, symbolize for many a hedonistic potency. Perhaps rather than a change in art, we should suggest a change in artists — a voluntary loss of procreative potency (after two children), coupled with a rising current of artistic creativity. Yet, perhaps this role should be left to the novelist — the voluntarily sterilized hero as a cultural ideal.

What I am saying is that artists can be used, of course, but used in this way, they cease to remain artists. They become tools — and just possibly, impotent tools. Is this anyway to use an artist? You bet it's *not!*

So then we come to the key question: what, if anything, can artists —*as artists*—contribute to awareness of the population problem? We all know that the world is changing. People experience its changes in many personal forms — longer lines of cars into and out of our cities, more dialings before our call goes through, more crowds at our national parks (turned urban slum for the summer season), more frustration and antagonism on the streets, both in simple exchanges and in violent confrontations. About the fact of change — generally in a bad direction —

there is broad agreement. But what is hardly ever considered is the changes wrought in each of us as the result of changes we are making in the world. This it seems to me is fertile ground for the artist. Artists inevitably make qualitative judgments. Artists are moved less by quantity than by quality. If there is anything art can make vivid it is qualitative changes. Artists can say what the scientists know but can't prove. Artists — real artists — do not confuse data with experience. And the experience of life is qualitatively different today. Artists attach a value to things — not the merely material — but to things with resonance. It is appropriate for artists to place a value on tranquillity, on the capacity of people to meditate. As an artist, I can — and do — say there is a value to the natural, as opposed to the artifact. In so far as our world is polluted, we are polluted. Art can establish a model of purity, which on a religious level, aspires to saintliness. The natural landscape which I value — and depict in my paintings — exist as reminders of what many men choose to forget, namely that we are part of a much larger system than merely our civilized and socialized spaces. Much of what I have just indicated as having value is, of course, directly threatened by a continuing growth in population. I cannot fight population head on; I can say, however, "See what we stand to lose if we drown in numbers."

The kinds of changes I am talking about are locally occurring. We see them easily, with no great effort, in our daily lives. I work against the stream of these changes, commenting on what we may lose. But these are not the only changes going on. There are other, perhaps more profound changes which suggest new realms for the artist to reckon with. We cannot see the hands of the clock move. We cannot see life growing. We cannot see either the stars or the atomic components move though they move at fantastic speeds. We cannot see our oceans being destroyed. We cannot see ecological systems going under before they go under. We have hints and guesses. We can infer, we can predict, we can sense. Perhaps there is a role here for another artist — an artist who serves as an early-warning system. Viewed this way the artist — through his art — can suggest in the present moment what the alternative to a predictable future may be. The artist may be able to provide us with the "experience" of a future based on the logical implications of our daily acts, sped up as it were, if we were to make no alteration in our present course. And the key word again is experience. What is the future likely to be? With respect to the Shadow of yester-year, "The Artist knows."

I would like to describe two programs, one in the works and one about to commence, in which artists are participating in self-determined projects for environmental conservation. Let's not confuse environmental conservation with population control. As a lover of unpolluted places, the natural landscape, and one who makes continuing reference to such places in my work, I set out two years ago to see if something could be done to get artists working as artists in the conservation effort. What I am about to describe does not relate directly to population problems, but I think the conception and early indications of success of these two programs offer some intriguing possibilities for an approach to getting artists involved in the population problem.

America the Beautiful Fund of the Natural Area Council, a small, Washington-based foundation with limited resources, was persuaded to expand their seed-grant program (grants from as modest an amount as $250 to perhaps a maximum of $1,500, averaging around $600) to individual applicants for open space preservation, park design and restoration, and ecological research and beautification. Beginning in February of this year, the Fund announced that it would for the first time give seed grants to artists. Since I had urged them to inaugurate this program, I was asked to serve as chairman of the Review Committee. In a letter sent to hundred of art schools and universities, asking for applications we said, in part, "the purpose of the expanded program is to encourage young American artists to become involved with environmental conservation and to contribute, as artists, to a greater public understanding of the natural in the landscape. America the Beautiful Fund has no bias whatever for any art mode or trend, and indeed welcomes applications from all artists — representational and earthwork alike." The letter also suggested some possibilities, "the artist as social critic, the development and testing of a nature education program through art, participation in natural areas surveys in conjunction with ecologists, planners and landscape architects; and development of new ways for artists to comment on either natural beauty or environmental destruction." The letter concluded, "What (the Fund) hopes to do beyond engaging the talents of gifted artists is to get artists out into the natural landscape, experiencing — and hopefully responding — in whatever way seems appropriate to sensations of season and place." Within four weeks the Fund had dozens of applications, wires and phone calls from artists asking support for a wide range of programs. Two deadlines had been established, one on March 1, the other May 1. Some wanted to travel to Alaska to sketch and paint the landscape there before it was destroyed, another wanted underwriting for a trip to gather material for a college art and ecology course. A third wanted funds to complete photographic documentation of the Louisiana architectural heritage. Four grants were made — only two weeks after the program was announced.

One went to a young earthwork sculptor in Iowa who had a plan for an environmental-sensing art form. He proposed to work in a large metropolitan center (we have sent him to Los Angeles) shooting a laser beam from one tall building to another. When the air was "clean" the beam would be green; when the air became polluted, the beam was to turn orange and a strange sound would be emitted. After checking the effect of this sort of laser beam on birds and planes — no effect, we found — we gave him his grant. How could we resist? Another artist, working in a major eastern art school, was given funds to make a film and related graphic material to save an urban lake. A third grant went to the artist (turned art director of an environmental magazine) who planned a series of ten posters on environmentally impacted areas — helping, hopefully, to attract attention to the problem and contribute to saving of these places. His publication had offered to print the posters, and one government agency, at least, said it would print and pay for the posters if the magazine did not. And finally, a young artist from New York City was given a small grant to work with city children at a summer camp in the mountains, combining man-made materials and natural processes into a kind of participatory landscape architecture.

Would these efforts by artists to involve themselves in "environmental conservation" have materialized without the Fund's support? We have no way of knowing. That we have successfully engaged the energy of artists, I have no doubt. And most important, they are functioning as artists.

The other program has perhaps even broader implications. As a painter of natural places, I proposed to the National Park Service in June of 1968 that they institute a program whereby artists would be designated "Artist-in-Residence to a National Park," much the way many universities and colleges have artists and poets in residence. My thought was that some artist would be named, for example, "Artist-in-Residence to the Grand Canyon" and for a brief period of approximately three or four months, would be a kind of spiritual caretaker for the place. In order to test the feasibility of this idea, I was named Artist-in-Residence to the Cape Cod National Seashore in September 1968 and immediately took up quarters on the Cape as the first American artist ever to serve in residence in a National Park. After the two months stay — a period which profoundly changed my life — I returned, imploring the Service not to let this splendid idea begin and end with one artist. After two years of form filling, report writing, and general nuisance making, I have persuaded the Director of the National Park Service to call for a workable plan of action. It appears now that by this fall we will see the first wave of American artists living in residence in eastern national parks as diverse as the Vanderbilt Mansion in the Hudson Valley, Acadia in Maine, and even the Statue of Liberty.

I recognize that much of the foregoing concerns itself broadly with the environment and not specifically with population control. What I hope is that some of us may be encouraged to develop similar programs, calling upon artists as artists, to add their unique energies to at least spiritually defuse the population bomb.

Francis Bacon, the English painter, once said, "Art is not the description of an object; it is the recreation of an event." It is the events of life which shape our character. In fact it is these events, happening somewhere, which not only form our nature, but also predict our future. We are each a history of occurrences, situations affected by the quality of the place and people we come in contact with. If we are forced to experience a world faulted by a population gone numerically mad, then art, which depends for inspiration on the reality of life's events will also suffer. It is clear, therefore, that we can appeal to the artist for help, not only because the artist's life is at risk, but because his art, too, is in danger.

SOCIAL ISSUES OF
BUILT ENVIRONMENT

Andrew F. Euston, Jr.

*In all our discussions of a strategy for the population-environment movement the
need for education has been emphasized, and we have seen that education, in
the broad sense of the word, can take many forms. In this essay Andrew Euston
considers the educational effects of architecture, especially the architecture of the
public housing we must build in the next thirty years — and plan for in the next
ten.*

*It is no accident that most people who are now concerned with the
quality of our environment had the good fortune to grow up in surroundings that
inculcated high standards for environmental quality. By contrast, most of our
public housing appears to have been designed by planners whose poverty of
imagination we may well find reflected in the generation that is growing up
in this housing. People who know nothing better than urban drabness and
monotony can hardly be expected to envision — and fight for — a more humane
environment.*

*Mr. Euston argues for the development of a "socio-physical technology" with
respect to housing, to support creative and constructive life-styles, and he calls for
the adoption of this technology by the governmental agencies that must underwrite
the costs of construction of most of our new housing.*

*Andrew F. Euston, Jr., is an architect now serving as Urban Design Program
Officer in the Environmental Planning Division of the Department of Housing
and Urban Development. He is the author of two books:* Check List For Cities
and Socio-Physical Technology, *and of many articles and reviews.*

The design of our urban environments serves to facilitate or to
handicap the individual's sense of personal well-being and his sense of
community. The building and rebuilding of these urban environments
are destined to raise social issues of greatest moment to American

society — issues which science is not prepared to resolve and of which those who design and build are presently unaware.

There are buildings with firm and even elegant façades made for more prosperous inhabitants where today people sleep in shifts. The families who cannot choose must be content to remain buried behind these deceptive façades, often forced to endure severely distorted life styles. As we know, these living styles can involve dope, illegitimacy, malnutrition, illiteracy, skillessness, personal failure (i.e., alcoholism, ennui, anomie, irresponsibility, etc.) and rebellion. The least that may be said of such faulty environments — antique or modern, is that they *influence* behavior in negative ways. It is becoming apparent to us, where such malignant environments are concerned, that what is experienced within can no longer be hidden — it takes forms we ultimately have to face.

The issue of environmental quality in the United States has now become a task of utmost urgency. For the man-made or -built environment this will require reforms and innovations in client participation, in building technology, in the use of manpower, in the allocation of resources, and in the governmental procedures that are meant to cope with the built environment. National resources must be allocated to the development of a balanced, socially responsive, overall environmental design technology that includes socio-physical technology. The main reason for the lag in socio-physical technology has long been and still remains a lack of focus upon the social consequences of environmental quality.

Housing and the Need for Socio-Physical Technology in Building

To secure progress in housing production is only part of the story. There is widespread agreement that the urban crisis is basically a social crisis. Meaningful progress in housing development must come to terms with more than a production technology. Viable social technology is also needed to serve the decision-making that lies ahead.

Since production and investment in the next thirty years are expected to double our entire inventory of built environment, we may anticipate cultural changes far in excess of those we have previously experienced. Few would challenge this, perhaps because change is now an accepted part of our life, yet preparation for change — above all social change — is not yet accepted in the field of housing. Instead there is reliance upon the traditional sources of judgment (i.e., the professional, the marketer, the Federal program administrator, etc.) for the criteria, the preferences, and the problem identification that apply in urban physical development. This is not to exclude the possibility that conventional wisdom, tempered by scientific verification, can ultimately supply the data needed with respect to change.

Serious questions are being asked now by government about how to change the delivery systems, the labor practices, the production systems, the codes, the government structures, etc., to deliver *more of what we have.* In terms of the social impacts of housing, however, social science has not been applied in questioning what we have; and there is ample reason to question it. Systematic analysis must be applied if we are not to repeat the mistakes that are being built into our present housing stock.

Why Have a Socio-physical Technology for Building?

There are many reasons why a need for deliberate and scientific examinations of the housing environment has come about. Given vastly intensified production goals for "decent, safe and sanitary" housing, the main problem is that existing information and the techniques for employing it do not identify all the choices and the consequences where our individual life styles are concerned. It is not sufficient, for example, to base the planning and design of large-scale, mass-produced, mixed income residential environments on "homeowner reaction surveys" that have their current application in the marketing of speculatively developed, private, middle-class housing. Nor are "windshield tours" the answer to the analysis of our existing low-income housing inventory. When we look at buildings to judge what they are like to live in, we can be very much deceived. Slums can be found in every style of architecture. If, as is being widely proposed, the nation is soon to commit itself to the building of factories to build new cities, then we must recognize that far more than a year-to-year market survey of customer trends must be involved in the way housing itself is fundamentally conceived. Evaluating the deficiencies of slums is a complex problem that confronts all of today's housing rehabilitation efforts. When we rehabilitate housing or when we build it new therefore, we have to consider what life-styles the final physical housing product will be able to support. Raymond Studer, Head of the Man and Environment Division of the College of Human Development at Pennsylvania State University, has expressed the problem of a socio-physical technology in this way:

> Increasingly complex, technologically sophisticated cultures cannot long survive complacency and gross ignorance regarding effects of the man-made environment upon human affairs. The vicarious attributes of designer experience, conventional wisdom, and intuitive guessing all have a role in the design process; but alone they are not good enough. The move toward a more refined understanding of man-environment relations as they impinge on the design process is as irreversible as it is necessary.

Another investigator of the socio-physical environment, Dr. Humphry F. Osmond, of the New Jersey Bureau of Research in Neurology and Psychiatry, states the issue in terms of the psychic environment:

> There is a great need to recognize the social consequences of the environment. There is an urgent need to humanize the physical environment. There must be a clearer understanding of social goals toward which physical programs may be directed. In order to achieve this objective there needs to be an effective use of multi-disciplinary know-how.
>
> The relationship between psychic environment and its physical counterpart, as we are beginning to understand them with the mentally ill, are simply an exaggeration of situations in the urban community. Similar forces prevail, and the design criteria are just as valid for so-called normal individuals as for the mentally ill since, at a critical time, the elements are just as significant.

Dr. William Michelson, a sociologist at the Institute for Studies in Education of the University of Toronto, has been commissioned by the Canadian government to conduct studies that will seek to answer questions such as:

> Aren't the lacks in suburban residence a partial impetus for young adults to split off from their families at the earliest opportunity?
>
> To what extent would *high rise* improve as a location for family living with a) expensive sound insulation, b) children's facilities within control distance from the parent, and/or c) more tenant responsibility for maintenance and remodelling?
>
> What is the "tipping point" in class difference between neighbors such that on one side they will interact and on the other ignore each other.
>
> Taking as an assumption current notions that neighborhood integration should properly involve residentially separate groups of people who meet on the common turf of facilities and schools, what sizes should each of the separate blocs be, and at what ratio should they mix?

To what extent does the threshold of housing aspiration *rise* with exposure to improved housing?

Do people *learn* to seek certain *ends* from their housing (apart from their overt housing preferences)? Can they learn to achieve these ends through *other means?* For example, can public open space accumulate functions traditionally performed on private lots?

What is the ability for humans to adapt to higher densities? What form does a positive response take?

We have all heard about the cultural shock suffered by the urbanizing refugees of depressed rural areas. With many such people the farm house porch is built into the entire life style. Even the urban born poor have clung to the front stoop and the fire escape landing while the street has served them as a *public* common. We need to deal with the habits we have kept by respecting these habits, if we can, or else by helping ourselves to otherwise adapt. Instead, as we now find, the hardened institutional character of much building in cities today has failed to provide either the sense of human scale — of things being meant for human use, or the actual facilities for social intercourse — places like the laundromat, the farmers' market, the poolroom, the workshop, or the neighborhood pub.

There are many long-perpetuated examples of the resulting social frictions that involve the housing environment. Entrances for public housing remain a favorite arena for trouble. Elevators do not come equipped with urinals for children, so that something else really ought to yield here. Perhaps high-rise should be out for the time being, where families are concerned. In the absence of design solutions an Act of Congress has decided *this* issue for us! Even so, how *do* we compensate equally for the traditional street life of the front stoop or the leisure world of the farmhouse porch within our new urban environments? Perhaps ground-level sitting areas and lounges are an answer to the porch, and perhaps a way *can* be found to make youngsters use a first floor public toilet. These are "here and now" issues that have never been systematically examined by either the design professions or the behavioral sciences.

The Need for Federal Focus on Social Needs
and the Housing Environment

Federal actions will substantially influence what is built, how it is built, and consequently, how it must be used. Establishing sound socio-physical technology that identifies the real social needs and the real social consequences of what gets built is a national problem to which Federal government must give focus and investment. Our range of future life styles will in many ways depend on what gets built. It is this central question of life styles that is behind the choices that a free market place has traditionally been able to offer, but increasingly this is getting beyond the control and understanding of the developer or the marketer — whose subdivisions and apartment structures are dependent upon a galaxy of other community facilities and services over which the market place has little control or profitable interest.

Clearly, however, there cannot be adequate investment without focus. Despite our having sponsored over a million dwelling units for public housing, military families, and the like since the period of the depression, the U.S. government has been effectively absent in fostering a user need or social technology for the housing environment. Yet even amongst those calling for social advisors and other major national social policy reforms, the social impacts of built environments have consistently been overlooked.

Government policy and assistance is becoming the basis for strength or weakness of the housing production market. Despite growing demands for housing, the housing market increasingly looks to government for its health. Government already intervenes in housing by (a) leading the way for investment through laws, mortgage supports and direct financial assistance, (b) impelling the "fly-wheel" of production through special technical subsidies and the assembly of large markets, (c) the assembly of land through powers of eminent domain, and, (d) acting as developer of last resort for portions of the low-income housing, the military, Indian tribes, etc.

A few aspects of this pervasive impact upon housing may serve to illustrate why Federal government should invest in the means for a viable socio-physical technology:

> First, government at all levels affects taxing and code provisions which retard or stimulate investment in groups, but the need for housing is a national problem that crosses all jurisdictional boundaries. Federal government substantially influences what products and services are most profitable. To get beyond the status of a "shelf item" a product must be reasonably well assured of a profitable "cost performance trade-off curve." Government can either stimulate the private sector to assemble sufficient

markets for an innovation or else pay for it directly as with the aircraft industry.

Second, the power of state government is being employed to generate housing. New state agencies such as the New York State Urban Development Corporation are getting underway and Federal government will be expected to provide them with technical and financial assistance.

Third, as the potential "builder of very last resort" the government increasingly imposes its own final judgment of user needs criteria upon the housing tenant. In this circumstance, therefore, government has a consumer-oriented obligation to assure that the highest level of social and physical technology be applied to the task of building. In the absence of other sources government must generate and systematically validate the criteria by which it determines the priorities, the levels of amenities, and the balance of community development which it directly creates.

Last, the positive trend toward reliance upon Federal and state powers of eminent domain for large-scale land assembly makes the need for sound socio-physical criteria of critical importance. Community rebuilding, new town and resettlement programs have the greatest need for social technology and performance standards for community planning — HUD or HEW should be generating this criterion as they should for any Federally-assisted community development.

Who's Watching the Store?

The provision of adequate housing and the achievement of a nationwide production breakthrough in housing is a first order of business today. Given this urgency it is all the more crucial to provide criteria and guidelines for the delivery of an effective product. Housing *must* be built, but how *must* it be designed? When and if America's housing stock is doubled can we expect to live in our accustomed way? Will this housing environment be as anyone expected? or as anyone intended? Who is "watching the store" here?

The Federal establishment has frequently filled this role. The impact of Federal assistance and its attendant policies have already determined the character of urban development in America since World War II. Government programs for highways, sewers and for housing finance itself have, for better *and* worse, encouraged this development to be mainly exurban and suburban, automobile and middle-income oriented and, as a bonus, racially divisive. However, "popular," some of the results of our building are costing us dearly already.

We may anticipate that in the coming thirty years the U.S. must replace 90 per cent of all existing buildings and, must build in addition new structures to accommodate an estimated population increase of

50,000,000 people. Let us make several assumptions and explore the implications of this phenomenal building program. With respect to production let us assume that: (1) the means of housing production is established within the first ten-year period; (2) the second ten-year period will find the country largely caught up with concurrent housing demand; as a consequence (3) our response to housing needs will be in full swing by the final decade of this century. In addition, let us assume that existing policies permit our investments to conserve existing architectural and community settings. It should be evident that the magnitude of such changes involving merely one generation's span of time (i.e.: thirty years) will be of such magnitude and nature as to alter every urban physical arrangement we now know.

The import of any such assumptions means that ten years from now our then current knowledge about the complexities of social needs and the housing environment must be applied in the creation of physical environments for new and evolving life styles and social possibilities. The consequence of this — whether we like this or not — must be recognized as the inevitable redesign of our culture.

Under these circumstances, can we Americans expect to have a wide assortment of healthy and humane residential neighborhoods that support creative and constructive life styles, or will there be merely blocks upon blocks of well-engineered and leak-proof human storage space? If the technical means for housing delivery is developed, will there be a social technology of any usefulness at all to those who must decide and deliver? If we delay further in promoting the development of such a social technology, there will come a time when no one *can* watch the store.

ORGANIZING ACTION

Pieter Byhouwer

As the governmental apparatus of the United States grows bigger, it also becomes more remote from the life of the ordinary citizen and less responsive to whatever pressures he can exert on it as an individual. In consequence a kind of extra-governmental politics has developed: the politics of community action, in which the individual has not only a vote but a voice. Community in this sense can mean either a geographically defined neighborhood or a nationwide organization representing some particular interest; in either case the purpose is to secure enough collective power to influence the existing governmental structure.

But group action is effective in other ways as well. By presenting live issues to the public and stimulating controversy about them, it performs an educational function, and, as the long history of the labor movement demonstrates, it gives its members the political experience and sophistication they need to deal effectively with government. Moreover, because they are oriented to action, community groups can recruit adherents as mere argument never could.

On the other hand this kind of politics is prone to certain weaknesses, chiefly a tendency to exclusiveness and a kind of idealistic narrowness that fails to take account of human weaknesses.

Pieter Byhouwer, who is experienced in the politics of community action, discusses the strategy and tactics of group organization and of action once a group has been organized. Bearing in mind the most common failings of action groups, he calls for permissiveness, tolerance, willingness to co-operate with other groups, and especially a real awareness of community needs. (In the essay that follows Mr. Byhouwer's, Dr. Bennetta Washington points up his argument that insensitivity on this score alienates many potential supporters of group action.)

Pieter Byhouwer, a teacher and social worker, has served as a consultant for the American Friends Service Committee in the promotion of their report Who Shall Live? *and as an editor of the* Encyclopedia Britannica.

Sooner or later any organization passes from the stage of initial recruitment around ideas into a stage where it will have to prove its value to the community by action aimed at concrete results. Often, the bulk of recruitment will occur in this later stage, when people actually experience how the group can be useful to them as individuals and as a community.

Let us take the anti-draft movement as an example. In its initial stages an ideology was developed, and people started burning their cards, leafleting induction centers, refusing induction, and speaking at colleges and high schools. But not until good draft counseling services started proliferating did the movement actually prove its usefulness to all the people who are faced with the draft. Ever since, draft counseling has been a sustaining force to the draft resistance movement.

Again, let us look at the abortion reform movement. The first and continuing stage of the movement is the effort to educate the public on the results of the present illegality of most abortions and on the alternatives to that state of affairs. But the movement is a going concern because it has a concrete action program, including lobbying to get abortion laws repealed, provision of abortion counseling and referral services (whether abortion is legal or not), and, once laws have been changed, making abortions really available to all classes of people. Those three actions are all closely tied in with education, but they go beyond it in actually producing social change.

Now let us look at a group that is still pretty much in the propagandistic stage: Zero Population Growth, a movement that has already recruited vast numbers of students. The thrust of the concern of its members is generating some action at once. For example, Chicago members have found that vasectomies here are expensive and hard to obtain. They have communicated this to Planned Parenthood, and now there is a plan to include vasectomy in the Planned Parenthood clinic services. It seems clear that if ZPG growth is to continue during the next academic year, the organization will have to go on reaching out by arranging more action programs and providing services to its constituency.

Chicago ZPG chapters have had many speakers in high schools and stimulated budding ZPG chapters in a number of them. How can this high school constituency serve and be served? A number of possibilities for action occur to me. For example, the high school community is different from the college community in that most students live with their parents and therefore have a closer relation to the "adult world."

Perhaps the high school chapters can form a link with that world if the students can be helped to reach out to growing families. In addition to its own speakers, ZPG could make speakers available from such organizations as the National Organization of Women and the Open Door Society, an organization of parents who adopt hard-to-place children and promote interracial adoption as an alternative to having children by procreation.

But in the high schools themselves there are crying needs to be met. Many students are on the point of becoming sexually active, and a great many unwanted pregnancies result from inexperience, with associated abortions, forced marriages, or illegitimacy. ZPG is one of the few grass-roots organizations with an active concern about those problems that relate to the high schools. It would therefore seem useful for ZPG to organize workshops for high school students where they are made aware of the resources the community has in the way of abortion counseling services and of doctors or family planning clinics that prescribe contraceptives to teenagers without requiring their parents' consent. At these workshops various contraceptive methods and their applicability could be discussed, along with the hang-ups and exploitative myths that spoil sex relations in our society. Organizations like the Women's Liberation Union and Planned Parenthood might cooperate in setting up the workshops.

Consultation with other organizations will open up additional courses of action. For example, Planned Parenthood is setting up a family planning clinic in one of the Chicago suburbs with the idea of turning it over to the local Board of Health once it is a going concern. They are afraid that the center will discontinue its no-questions-asked service to teenagers and students as soon as it is turned over to the Board of Health. ZPG, because of its consultations with Planned Parenthood, can anticipate trouble, send young people to the clinic as soon as it changes hands, and put on the heat if services to minors are in fact discontinued. Action could include letters to local officials and newspapers, picketing, and seeking backing of various civic organizations. If the action is unsuccessful, ZPG could perhaps stimulate the establishment of a special teen clinic.

Another problem that needs work in many states is the harassment of doctors by malpractice suits for tuboligations and vasectomies. Although in most cases both husband and wife sign consent papers, those papers are disregarded in court unless by legislation they protect doctors from suits. People may sue for many reasons: remarriage may change their minds; sometimes a lawyer talks them into it. The main job here is letter writing and lobbying to have a law passed protecting doctors from such suits. But other actions should be considered too; people have different talents, and some people prefer demonstrations to letter writing. Whenever an action program is developed, it is important to provide many channels of action for people inclined in various ways. There is no reason why, for example, there should not be picket lines in front of the homes of some of the people who bring such suits, exposing them to their neighbors as opportunists who do a disservice to the public by making doctors reluctant to perform sterilizations.

And here we have hit upon one of the important factors making it possible for a group to be action-oriented: our members have to have a permissive attitude toward what various people want to do. In too many organizations an action for which some people are ready will be discouraged because of the intolerance of vocal other members. It would be much more fruitful if we encouraged everybody to do his thing. Let us recognize that change in our society is usually the result of many different actions. Some people will be offended by picketing, but others will become aware of an issue only in this way. Those who will respond to letter writing are unlikely to be upset by demonstrations.

Another condition for the development of successful action programs is a fearless determination to respond to community needs. To become responsive, our group should spend time researching community needs. Volunteers should test the performance of relevant services in the community. What does sex education in the schools consist of? Is it inadequate because of timid teachers, a conservative Board, or general community uptightness? Which doctors are willing to prescribe contraceptives and to whom? To married people only? How can poor people get them? Is stilbesterol treatment available? What is the policy on tuboligation at the local hospital? Where are sources of pollution, and where is the landscape being disfigured? What laws regulate pollution, and are they enforced? What land can be set aside for parks or wilderness? How do different kinds of people feel about these issues? Our members should not only talk with many people in the community — people should be encouraged to vent their ideas to our group.

Another condition for action is readiness, no, eagerness!, to cooperate with other organizations toward concrete goals. If the Junior League seems like a very ungroovy organization to some of our members, do not let that prevent us from inviting its members to help us with suitable work. And let us find out how this organization operates, so that Junior League members can earn their required volunteer work-credit hours by working for us as an offically accredited organization. On the other hand, some of our members may be allergic to religiousness, but let us not have that keep us from recruiting the aid of churches or of the workers of organizations such as Church Women United.

Do not assume a negative attitude toward certain groups without testing them first. For example, officially the Catholic Church is dead set against abortion, but we may find that some priests in the community are open-minded and that there is a study group in one church that would like to explore all aspects of the problem, using speakers pro and con. Of course the pro-abortion speaker should perform like a pro. She should carefully prepare herself in the issues of importance to Catholics: Father Drinan's position, the large number of abortions requested by Catholic married women who were tripped up by the rhythm method, and the distinctions between private morality and the proper realm of law.

Usually, the recruitment of individuals and organizations will serve to get work done on a specific problem, such as processing sewage before draining it into the river. In approaching people to work on such a problem, it is always important that they be asked to contribute their advice. It is difficult to sell people on a predetermined program of your own making, but people will move if they are given an opportunity to participate in planning, if their opinion is sought and valued.

Few things will serve more admirably to keep a movement ineffective than an appeal based largely upon idealistic statements and self-righteous stances. People who are unready to swallow the party line of a true believer may very well be willing to cooperate on the reaching of goals that they see as important. The larger questions will no doubt arise in the course of our working together, and at that time we may have established a climate which was absent at first in which real communication is possible. And we may find out a few things ourselves.

In working with other groups it is important not to be one-sided. Let us not assume that the businessmen and the upper middle class of our town are the only people needed to get something done. People whom we thought to be of no consequence may react in ways that effectively block change. One weakness of Zero Population Growth may well be its exclusive focus on the middle class, leaving too many people to the teachings of the Catholic Church or to fears of genocide and of further deprivation by taxation discriminating against large families. To counteract concern about the environment, industry can raise the specter of threats to the jobs of its workers. Are environmental action groups sufficiently in contact with laboring people to counteract such propaganda effectively? In our programs, are we sensitive to the needs of workers and poor people?

Let us see how lack of social awareness can prejudice programs. In Chicago a proposal has been forwarded to close the expressways to private cars on days of heavy air pollution. The underlying assumption is perhaps that the expressways serve suburbanites who drive to work even though they could use public transportation. The reaction by one of my neighbors to this proposal was very hostile. He is a factory worker at a Cicero plant, forced to live far away on the Southside because he is black. Public transportation to his job is so poor that he stays home when his car has broken down. He concludes the plan is drawn up by people who do not understand his predicament and who possibly do not care, and I think he is probably right.

Fortunately, ZPG chapters are becoming more aware of the problems tax schemes designed to penalize large families may present to the underprivileged — and, to speak from my own predicament, to adoptive parents. The fact is that there is insufficient commitment in our society to see to the welfare of poor people, and population action groups should insist on solving that problem as a prerequisite for tax penalties for large families. (Personally, I cannot see any merit in tax penalties at all.) The way to become aware of such social pitfalls is to start actively communicating with poor people instead of being afraid of them and concentrating only on the middle classes. If no poor people participate in our decisions, our policies will tend to victimize and alienate them, no matter how loudly we proclaim that poor people are not the problem.

Let us see how this kind of thinking might apply to the simple concern with an auto junk yard that disfigures your town. The initial idea in your organization might be to try to zone the junk yard out of existence. But it is pointed out that the junk yard performs a useful service to many people, especially those without much income, by making second-hand auto parts available cheaply. The concern now becomes one of disposal of hulks and fencing the yard instead of discontinuing the operation.

The preceding example presented a small local action, and you may feel that it would take a disproportionate amount of energy. But it is in such local actions that many fruitful community contacts are made. They may provide the life blood of your organization. There is always the temptation to concentrate too much on the "big" and "important" issues. Some feel that only legislative action really matters — but we Americans rely too much upon laws. To involve people, we also have to do things in our immediate community. Others — and I count myself among them — feel that the evils of our society are so fundamental, so interdependent, and so all-pervading that their eradication (by now a prerequisite for survival) cannot be achieved without total revolution — but how can we build a revolutionary constituency if we cannot co-operate with our neighbors on a little project like labeling low-phosphate detergents in the supermarket? We should always work on several different levels at the same time; but be aware that the small projects may be as frustrating as the large ones.

An important question to keep in mind while we plan for action is: can we hope to involve enough people to succeed? This question cannot be answered beforehand, but it requires experience. Our preliminary research may answer it in part. The recruitment, culminating in public meetings, will show our strength. Maybe it seems hopeless, but if the issue has really impressed us by its importance we will struggle on in the face of great odds, gathering more strength, applying it, perhaps experiencing set-backs and sudden, unexpected progress. And even as the action is carried out, other problems arise — some caused by our own solutions to previous problems — and other actions are defined that will task our strength in turn.

And so we will organize for change and hope to accomplish something useful here and there. Lectures, speak-outs, and teach-ins will be held, volunteers recruited, coalitions formed, strings pulled, demonstrations and picket lines organized, letters written, and media contacts pursued. We will be a force or be reckoned with locally, state- and nation-wide, and — it is to be hoped — world-wide. And, if our species is to survive, in the end we will get results.

We will get results because in all our contacts and actions we will strive to be aware of the best interest of all people — we will not lose sight of the fact that the welfare of all human beings is the focus of our movement to limit population and restore the environment. We will get results because we will be sensitive to dehumanization, deprivation, and exploitation in all their many guises, because we will not separate means from ends but — without assuming that all people are of good will — subject all our actions to the criterion of respect for human beings. We will get results because we will welcome the participation of all kinds of people in our councils and seek to learn from them as well as teaching them, and try to involve ourselves in cooperative action with them. We will get results because we really commit ourselves to "power to the people," in its most humane and inclusive sense.

THE IMPACT OF THE
POPULATION-ENVIRONMENT CRISIS
ON MINORITY GROUPS

Bennetta B. Washington

Long before Americans began to engage in large-scale environmental destruction they were far advanced on a course of population destruction in the forms of genocide against Indians and enslavement and segregation of Blacks. Struck mainly by the monstrous injustice of it, we are apt to overlook the equally enormous irrationality of depriving the nation of the constructive and creative energies of millions of its people. We are still so far from a real understanding of the psychological effects of racial injustice and the potentialities of a minority group once it has outgrown these effects that even now our racial minorities exist among us as a great unknown. Who knows what a Black child, or an Indian or a Chicano might produce and contribute to American society if he were really free? We can be certain, however, that any population-environment policy which rests on the assumption that the status of minority groups will not continue to change is totally unrealistic.

How can we deal with this variable factor as we work for common survival in a world that is fit for all of us?

Without trying to give a complete answer to the question, Dr. Washington discusses one great obstacle to gaining the cooperation of minority groups: lack of awareness of their complex natures as survivors of centuries of injustice and poverty, and especially of their well-founded suspicions of the intentions of the majority.

Bennetta B. Washington is the Director of the Women's Centers of the Job Corps and the wife of Mayor Walter Washington of Washington, D.C. As an educator and administrator who has long experience in dealing with the problems and potentialities of minority groups she believes that "all children want to learn, and when you expect them to achieve, they do," and her professional experience, she says, has strengthened that belief.

Joseph Wood Krutch, writing in 1954, said:

> Moralists often blame races and nations because they have never learned how to live and let live. In our time we seem to have been increasingly aware how persistently and brutally groups of men undertake to eliminate one another. But it is not only the members of his own kind that man seems to want to push off the earth. When he moves in, nearly everything else suffers from his intrusion — sometimes because he wants the space they occupy and the food they eat, but often simply because when he sees a creature not of his kind or a man not of his race his first impulse is "kill it."

That Krutch's view of the world and the warnings he voiced are widely appreciated today is indicated by the admiring editorials that appeared following his death this year. He loved the desert and the glories of the wilderness, but he also knew and appreciated the gifts of cities — imperfect though he found them.

His was a sensitive and informed view of the world — one in which he wanted all men to share and which his writings helped many to appreciate more deeply.

His recognitions of the interdependencies among all living things, which many of us are only beginning to share and his conviction that human beings are influenced not only physically but emotionally by their environment are important for us to consider.

It is also vital for us to understand the wide variety of environments in which different Americans are nurtured. And we must not forget the emotional climate which may vary from life-giving warmth to the extremes of heat and cold that militate against human survival. As an educator, I know from experience the effect that the emotional climate in the home, in the classroom, and in the community has on a child's ability and desire to learn.

I know, too, how young people react to the prospect of prolonged unemployment or underemployment. I will never forget the young man being urged to complete his education who said, "I don't want to be the best educated car washer in the world."

The environment of the inner city is hard but here again I would like to give you some pertinent words written by Mr. Krutch. "We grow strong," he said, "against the pressure of a difficulty, and ingenious by solving problems. Individuality and character are developed by challenge."

I think we can agree that minority groups in the United States today have faced and are facing the kinds of difficulties that must give those who survive certain strengths. However, too often the struggle implants a kind of cynicism that must be overcome if we are to achieve our goals for a stronger and healthier democracy; and deep-seated doubts cannot be overcome with a cosmetic approach couched in the choicest Madison Avenue phrases. The ability to detect the phony is NOT dulled but sharpened by deprivation. Efforts must not only be sincere, but they must be perceived by those we seek to work with as beyond suspicion. A study is being made now in Washington, D.C. to determine the probable number of small children who may suffer physically and mentally from eating chips of lead paint. The surveyors have encountered difficulties because some inner city residents suspect what they term a "hidden agenda." The National Institute of Mental Health recently undertook a project to determine whether there is a link between chromosome conditions and criminality. They have been using blood samples from underprivileged boys. Now some parents are refusing to bring children to clinics for the lead poisoning test because they believe it may be a way of obtaining samples of chromosomes. They take the view that they are the victims, not the *causes* of racism and the elimination of the condition will not be found in further studies of them. Lead paint has, of course, been used in many houses, but only in houses that are not adequately maintained do chips fall where overburdened parents cannot watch hungry and malnourished children closely.

Of late, the automobile is being blamed for traffic problems, for air pollution, and for increasing our problems of waste disposal. The inner city has its own unique view of that, too. Cities are inundated with abandoned cars which are costly to remove. But also they cannot be removed from the streets unless measures are taken simultaneously to destroy the rats who find them ideal living quarters. Remove the cars and the rats scurry to the nearest houses.

The child of the slums who escapes rat bites, lead poisoning, and a host of other poverty-born ills eventually finds himself in a run-down school with too many broken windows and too many teachers who have given up the struggle. Sometimes he is bussed to spend a few hours of his day in less crowded and deteriorated classrooms.

"School bussing," as a *New York Times* headline recently pointed out "is a United States tradition." The accompanying article stated that "by 1930 bussing had begun a period of dramatic growth. From

7 per cent of the country's enrollment in that year, it has increased to 40 per cent today, making school bussing the largest transportation service in the United States. Altogether, state and Federal officials estimate about two-thirds of the country's 45 million pupils are bussed.

"This massive growth of bussing provoked little resistance," the *Times* continued, "until court and administrative orders . . . began to require bussing for racial integration." Now "resistance has ranged from violence . . . to antibussing petition campaigns in cities from coast to coast."

The United States Commission on Civil Rights recently pointed out that "For decades black and white children in the South were bussed as much as fifty miles or more each day to assure perfect racial segregation. No complaints then were heard from whites of any harmful effects."

And you may be sure that children are not unaware of the facts of life in their communities. They watch hours of television and hear innumerable radio bulletins, and whatever their reading scores on standardized tests maybe, they *do* know what the local newspapers are saying about issues that affect them.

I too well remember the day that a story appeared in a morning paper labeling the high school of which I was principal "a blackboard jungle." No one could forget the troubled and angry faces confronting teachers that day. It did little good to explain that the reporter was really interested in awakening the community to the dire needs of inner city schools. Good intentions had paved the road, if not to hell, certainly to my office. It took time and skill to repair the ego-damage done by a well-intentioned but insensitive journalist.

To the black and the Spanish American, among other minority groups in our country, insensitivity may seem a greater pollutant of the atmosphere than carbon monoxode.

Let us listen to a grandmother telling Robert Coles what it is like for her small granddaughter, in his book "Children in Crisis." "They can scream at our Sally," she said, "but she knows why, and she's not surprised. She knows that even when they stop screaming, she'll have whispers, and after them the stares. It'll be with her for life . . . . We tell our children that, so by the time they have children, they'll know how to prepare them . . . . It takes a lot of preparing before you can let a child loose in a white world. If you're black in Louisiana it's like cloudy weather; you just don't see the sun much."

A year ago the *New York Times* published an account of a meeting in Albany to discuss the New York City Schools. I would like to read you the conclusion of the story.

> Chancellor's hall, where the community control group ended the day, is dominated by a 35-by-22 foot mural called "The United States of America." It is filled, in the best romantic style, with cherubs, shadowy figures of American history, and virgins in flowing robes representing freedom, and liberty, and justice.
>
> In the lower right hand corner is the only black man in the picture. He is attempting to rise from his knees. His arms reach out toward the American ideals. A white man stands behind the Negro, his hands placed on the Negro's shoulders. As she left the hall, a middle-aged Negro woman glanced back at the picture and said, to no one in particular:
>
> "I wonder, is he trying to help him up or hold him down?"

Do we have to wonder about the pervasive skepticism of the minority community — the reluctance to cooperate in a program to identify and attempt to help children suffering from lead poisoning? Even programs designed to attack basic problems are viewed with suspicion.

And yet there are those who do establish constructive relationships, who are accepted, with trust, and Robert Coles is one who has succeeded in breaking down the barriers. Again, in *Children in Crisis,* he reports the words spoken to him by a woman newly arrived in Boston from rural Georgia who was encountering Northern "social services" for the first time. She said:

> "They came telling us not to have children, and not to have children, and sweep up, and all that. There isn't anything they don't want to do to you, or tell you to do.
>
> "Then they say we should look different, and eat different — use more of the protein. I tell them about the prices, but they reply about 'planning' — planning, planning, that's all they tell you. The worst of it is that they try to get you to plan your kids, by the year; except they mean by the ten-year plan, one every ten years. The truth is, they don't want you to have any, if they could help it.
>
> "To me, having a baby inside me is the only time I'm really alive. I know I can make something, do something, no matter what color my skin is, and what names people call me. When the baby gets born I see him, and he's full of life, or she is; and I think to myself that it doesn't make any difference what happens later, at least now we've got a chance, or the baby does. You can see the little one grow and get larger and start doing things, and you feel there must be some hope, some chance that things will get better; because there it is, right before you, a real, live, growing baby. The children and their father feel it, too, just like I do. They feel the baby is a good

sign, or at least he's some sign. If we didn't have that, what would be the difference from death? Even without children my life would still be bad — they're not going to give us what they have, the birth control people. They just want us to be a poor version of them, only without children and our faith in God and our tasty fried food, or anything."

I also remember a television documentary about the life of the poor in the Southwest. The interviewer asked a Spanish-American woman why, in the face of such poverty, she continued to have children. "Because," she said, "children are the only things we CAN have." And I am told that among the Navaho, families grow larger as poverty grows worse.

In the *New York Times Magazine* of a recent Sunday, a student leader explained the reaction of the black students at Fisk to the deaths at Kent University: "We were sorry the students were killed, but we saw no reason to get uptight about it. State troopers killed four black students at South Carolina State and another at Texas Southern, and nobody remembered to even call 'the law,' much less march on Washington." He paused for a moment in mock reflection. "But then, you see, we are used to being killed by 'the law,' and used to having it forgotten the next day."

In so many thousands of ways men and women learn in their childhood how society views them and what they may realistically expect from society.

In his book *Let Them Eat Promises,* Nick Kotz tells us that "In this country, thousands of young children feel pain. Some do not call it 'hunger,' because they have never known the feeling of a full stomach. Countless Americans are physically and mentally maimed for life, their entire destiny and contribution to society sharply limited by what their mothers ate during pregnancy. Hungry children cannot concentrate and do not learn at school; they develop lifetime attitudes about a hostile world."

When we actually face the overwhelming hazards to physical and mental health encountered from birth by the poor and the despised in their daily environment, it is difficult not to become completely discouraged about the possibility of bringing about positive changes.

However, we can turn again to Krutch's conviction that "individuality and character are developed by challenge." We can also take heart from the conclusions of Robert Coles' and Maria Piers' study of the effects on children of life in concentration camps. In a book called,

Wages of Neglect they say, "The damage done by grossly insufficient care, is, to a large extent, reversible. If great vulnerability is part of human nature, so is the capacity for survival and a powerful urge to grow and develop."

Perhaps God, in the form of this powerful urge to grow and develop, is on our side. And perhaps one of the distinguishing marks of our age is that God and science seem to be coming closer together.

Science is losing its arrogance, and a respect for the strong forces in men and nature is reasserting itself. We are of necessity forced back to a state of wonder by the works of Joseph Wood Krutch. We must also pause when 30,000 human beings meet death because an earthquake shatters man-made dams, releasing seas of mud and water, and when our firm conviction that "cleanliness is next to godliness" results in the killing of large natural bodies of water by the phosphates in detergents.

Recently a friend who has long been concerned with the problems of maintaining the purity of our water supplies said that some years ago top men in the field tried to determine which areas of research demanded top priority, "and," he said, "we missed phosphates. How could we?"

Perhaps we should all consider the words of one of our great scientists — Franz Boas, whom anthropologists especially should contemplate today.

In *Anthropology and Modern Life* he wrote:

> I should always be more inclined to accept, in regard to fundamental human problems, the judgment of the masses rather than the judgment of the intellectuals, which is much more certain to be warped by unconscious control of traditional ideas. I do not mean to say that the judgment of the masses would be acceptable in regard to every problem of human life, because there are many which, by their technical nature, are beyond their understanding, nor do I believe that the details of the right solution of a problem can always be found by the masses; but I feel strongly that the problem itself, as felt by them, and the ideal that they want to see realized, is a safer guide for our conduct than the ideal of the intellectual group that stand under the ban of an historical tradition that dulls their feeling for the needs of the day.

I am afraid we can expect little progress in some of the most critical problems facing our society and, in fact, the world today, unless we immediately and effectively involve every population group in the necessary research and planning.

The democratic process may be slow, but it is still the surest way that man has devised. I think it was Winston Churchill who said that democracy is terrible but it's the best system we have so far.

Our difficulties are simply too deep and too broad to yield to the ministrations of an elite who dress alike, talk alike, eat alike, and think alike. If there ever was a time for us to reaffirm our belief that the strength of democracy lies in diversity, this is it. We cannot afford in this great hour of need to waste any talents, any creativity, any insights, any approaches to life.

If we are to arrive at some approximation of even the limited truths on which we can base programs, and if we hope to have programs succeed, we must elicit the cooperation of all economic, ethnic, racial, geographic, and religious segments of our population. Even as we contemplate the need to maintain some balance of nature on our small and damaged planet we cannot lose our reverence for life in a maze of statistics and body counts.

A recent magazine piece about unemployment and under-employment bore the title, "No Man Can Live With the Knowledge That He is Not Needed." Every human being has a need to give, to create, to produce some tangible evidence of his or her worth.

How can society satisfy this basic need for affirmation of the self in the best interest of the individual and of all men? What opportunities can be provided for the constructive use of the creative energies of men and women that must have outlets?

When the desperately poor mother of a large, hungry family tells us, straight into the TV camera, "Children are the only thing poor people CAN have," what is our answer?

I, for one, don't know, but I suspect that maybe she does. Perhaps we should ask her.

POTENTIALITIES OF COMMUNITY ACTION

Shirley L. Radl

Nowhere have the possibilities of grass roots political action been demonstrated more dramatically than in the nation-wide expansion of Zero Population Growth, Inc. ZPG, founded only two years ago, aims at population stabilization in the United States by 1980. Skeptics may regard the target date as indicative of an undue optimism, but Mrs. Radl's account of the development of this activist organization from its very modest beginnings suggests that a good many Americans already accept the ideas underlying the population-environment movement and need not so much to be persuaded of their validity as to be given effective organization through which they can act on them.

It might be noted that much of the support for ZPG comes from people young enough to be prospective parents, people who might have been expected to be the chief protesters against any curtailment of the freedom to reproduce.

Mrs. Radl, a housewife and the mother of two children, is Executive Director of Zero Population Growth, Inc., which has its headquarters in Los Altos, California.

In view of the magnitude of the population-environment situation, community action programs may appear to be rather insignificant. But many of us involved in these programs are convinced that community action will provide the spark for broad-scale programs designed to alleviate population pressure across the entire nation.

Many well-informed experts lament the problems of overpopulation and environmental decay; they attend conferences, write papers, and give speeches. There is a range of ideas that emerges from such meetings, including the concept that the situation is hopeless or, more commonly, that view stated by a prominent biologist that, "in the long run voluntarism is insanity. The result will be continual uncontrolled population growth."

We who are working at the grass-roots level find this view understandable but somewhat pessimistic. Voluntarism has never been given a serious opportunity for success, and yet there are those who are ready to condemn it before it is tried on a broad scale. We consider the view that the situation is utterly hopeless to be that of dedicated scholars who have become continually depressed over the population-pollution crisis but continue to write and to give talks, more often than not to groups composed of like-minded intellectuals. Perhaps the key lies here. Are our dedicated experts spending too much time talking to each other and not enough time reaching the general public? It is my opinion that grass-roots activity can bring the dialogue out of the conference hall and into the street — where it belongs, if resolution of the crisis is ever to be realized.

Community action can provide the link between the academic sector and the general public, and as such action grows, can establish the necessary links between the experts, politicians, the media, the business community, and the man in the street.

Community action programs are usually the work of dedicated individuals who refuse to believe that "nothing short of coercion can accomplish zero population growth" but instead, and perhaps because they have not yet become disillusioned from years of depressing research reflecting only sheer hopelessness, are prepared to go out into the community in an effort to educate their fellows — neither the instructors nor the students in this case being experts but rather people who genuinely fear that the species will cease to exist if we continue to reproduce and pollute at our present rate.

The efforts of a few dedicated souls attempting to bring about change in their communities can easily be dismissed as so much sincere folly. One may ask how a community action program in Los Altos, Honolulu, Stevens Point, Ann Arbor, or New Haven can be effective on a broad enough scale in sufficient time to bring about the necessary changes in traditional attitudes and legislation. But just as the example set by the United States can serve as a model for other countries, the success of community action programs can serve as models for other communities — then states, then the nation. Moreover, we in Zero Population Growth are starting to see impressive results that indicate this sort of action will sweep the nation.

To provide you with evidence that community action can work and can in fact go beyond the community itself, I will use my experience over the past months.

I became involved in Zero Population Growth, Inc. late last spring. ZPG is a grass-roots, nonpartisan, political organization that was founded in Old Mystic, Connecticut. It was just by chance that I joined it. Subsequently, I learned that there were several other individuals in my community, Los Altos, who were equally concerned about the population problem and had also discovered ZPG. At that time there were approximately 100 members, and we decided that we really should do something. The obvious course was to provide a community educational program and hopefully garner enough support to start a local chapter of ZPG.

We started with a "coffee," i.e., an evening meeting to which we invited 350 people, engaged a speaker, and were delighted when 23 people attended. Three of them joined ZPG, bringing us to a grand total of eight members in our area. We continued to hold such meetings and then became involved in holding "open to the public" meetings, featuring well-known speakers. For all of our efforts we directly acquired a scant number of members and supporters, but we learned that the number was not an absolute; rather, each new member we recruited became an ambassador for our cause and ultimately returned in numbers severalfold, and that severalfold continued to multiply.

By mid-July we had recruited several hundred members, and it seemde appropriate to call a meeting and officially form a local chapter of ZPG. The result of that meeting was that members came from all over Northern California, and we were successful in laying the groundwork for several chapters which went off on their own to repeat the programs we used here, with the full realization that it would be slow going but that rewards would be realized. The experience in Los Altos is a case of community action that exploded into a far-reaching program and expanded outside of the community, helping ZPG to grow from under 100 members in the spring of 1969 to over 30,000 by April, 1971.

Perhaps if the ZPG explosion had been confined to Los Altos, it could be thought of as just a successful community program. However, what took place in my own community has been and is being repeated continually across the nation. The indications are that dedicated individuals are not content with simply getting things started in their own communities, but have a compulsion to expand outward, once success has been realized locally. This is the reason for our success: we just explode wherever we have a successful community chapter. We have found that wherever a chapter develops it is followed a few months later with several more chapters in the general vicinity and continues to expand outward.

In all of the areas where success has been realized, one factor has been present: recognition of the value of community action. Nearly every chapter of ZPG was started because of the initiative of a handful of lay-people who made an effort to bring the problem of overpopulation and pollution to the attention of the general public. Most of them were encouraged by the success of other ZPG chapters elsewhere in the nation. People made the effort to start something within their own communities, and in no instance have we a reported failure — in every case where the challenge was met a ZPG chapter developed, and the population problem has enjoyed considerable space in the news media as a direct result of these community endeavors.

Community action cannot be put down. Pessimism based on arm-chair intellectualizing should be challenged. The concept that volunterism just won't work is open to question. How does anyone know? It has never been put to a real test — inasmuch as all forms of birth control have never been made available to all members of society. The nation and the community are being informed, for the first time, as to the seriousness of continued population growth, and for the first time in our history we are challenging some of our age-old traditions such as the belief that large families are good just because they exist. We are beginning to ask why. This beginning constitutes a large step toward providing a climate of acceptance for liberalized birth control legislation and for attitudes towards family planning relative to our present population dilemma. Once the realities of the population crisis are made clear, people planning their families are not going to be enthusiastic about bringing a large number of children into the world only to condemn them to a life of misery — if any life at all.

Another notion that will be exploded with the advent of community action programs is that the situation is utterly hopeless. It is not hopeless. There is still something left to salvage, and until such time as every member of society is given the education and the choice to behave responsibly, it is defeatist to suggest that we are all through. I've said it before — the public has not been given the full opportunity to make the choice concerning the perpetuation of our species. Until recently the media only skirted the issue. The media have been so concerned with profit, as have the advertisers, that they have actually persuaded the general public to accept the false notion that large families are fine, fun, and quite respectable; the more goods purchased for the large families, the better off we are as a nation. Why? Similarly, our legislation is outmoded, and what scant amount of advertising on television concerning the population explosion occurs is put on the tube only after 11:00 p.m. A bit late for those already in bed, I'd say.

The fact that ZPG could expand as rapidly as it has done, without substantial financial means and without substantial commitment from professionals able to contribute time, is indicative of a very good beginning for a climate of acceptance for voluntary population control. ZPG enjoyed some rather overwhelming success even before the media made population information available to the general public. It enjoyed this success operating on a very tiny budget — donations being scarce, owing to our nontax-exempt status. We are continually amazed that people of financial means, who recognize that the population crisis may well be the end of our species, are reluctant to make sizeable contributions to an organization such as ours because contributions are not tax-deductible. When we are breathing our last gasp because of pollution, a fat lot of good money will do any of us. The one interesting equalizer in all of this is that no matter what our economic status, nothing — not money, power or industrial strength — can save any of us from choking to death. We all go, regardless of race, creed, or economic status.

To point out just what community action can realistically accomplish, the success of Los Altos, Wisconsin, Connecticut, Michigan, Hawaii, and Chicago serve as excellent examples. In Los Altos we began with five members, one of whom was a "full-time volunteer," complete with typewriter and mimeograph machine. In August 1969 that manpower expanded to six volunteers, three typewriters, and the same mimeograph machine. By September the operation was moved to an office with funding provided by local members who pledged certain amounts of mnoey each month for overhead. In September the national office of ZPG was moved to the Los Altos address, and by February 1970, ZPG occupied three large offices on the same street. By early March a Washington office was opened, a lobbyist hired, and two support helpers added, while at the national office the number of full-time employees working for subsistence salaries numbered twenty-five.

The experience in Los Altos and similar experiences in Wisconsin, Chicago, Michigan, and Honolulu are only a few examples of expanding community action. There is no doubt that all ZPG chapters will reach the same level of expansion as have these chapters and federations.

Community action must begin somewhere, but it does not have to end where it starts or be an end in itself. On the contrary, all indications are that it serves only as the beginning of a continual program to educate the educable, to reach the convinced laymen, and to recruit the dedicated in an effort to realize a collective legislative voice.

It is clear that one million concerned citizens remaining separate from each other can apply little pressure to institute legislation relevant to our goals. However, if one million concerned citizens come together, there is little doubt that their collective voices will be heard. That is the value of ZPG; hence the value of community action. There is a place to begin, and we have done so — community action has brought us to our present national scope and will continue to increase. Our chapters are autonomous, but they come together in a collective unit on both state-wide and national levels. We have committed ourselves to legislation that will implement our objectives such as repeal of all abortion laws and all anti-contraception laws. We will endorse and actively support political candidates responsive to the need for clear-cut legislation and government programs in the areas of contraceptive research, appropriations for national birth-control programs, and tax programs designed to offer incentives to middle-class Americans to limit their family size.

Earlier I indicated a disdain for compulsion or coercion as a means of alleviating the population crisis. It has become clear that until such time as every opportunity to practice complete birth control along with education relative to the population crisis has been made available, the suggestion of compulsion is nonsensical and hopeless resignation unacceptable. We have not given enough of our fellow citizens either the information or the opportunity to voluntarily limit their numbers, and because we have not done so, we cannot judge the situation as "hopeless." Information will be provided initially through community action. Education begins in the community as does political action. We in ZPG have found that when people are apprised of the facts our membership (and the concern in the community) goes up just as geometrically as does the population curve.

This is grass-roots, and this is where it begins. Only one reasonable citizen in a given community need be informed, concerned, and dedicated in order to galvanize that community into action.

It is interesting that most of the innovators in ZPG are novices. Probably this is the case simply because so many of them possess the zest and energy necessary to convert concern into action as a result of their lack of experience in such matters. They are fresh and have not been disillusioned by years of attempting to initiate programs to alleviate population stress, only to be frustrated at every juncture. The present climate of opinion in the nation is favorable for our goals, and we have fresh young people who want a future and are willing to provide the energy to realize these goals.

We started out as a collection of "over-thirty idealists," and, as could have been predicted, we have evolved into a nation-wide campus movement. And why not? It's really the future of the young people that's at stake.

CULTURAL CONSUMERISM

Hazel Henderson

Shirley Radl presented us with a strategy for action on the population front. Hazel Henderson in turn, outlines a strategy aimed at reaching our environmental objectives. She urges that, instead of relying on the cumbersome machinery of government, we organize ourselves as consumers and direct our efforts toward the economic establishment, whose power to influence our cultural patterns through advertising and other uses of the mass media rests on our willingness to buy its products. Consumer action to improve the quality of products for personal use is not new; it could be extended to prevent environmental degradation and waste of natural resources.

Mrs. Henderson makes it plain that she is not attacking the industrial system as such, but rather many of its current practices, which she finds outmoded and irrelevant to the production of real goods and services. Far from being a danger to the system, 'cultural consumerism' could help it to survive in an era when waste and the misuse of the environment can no longer be tolerated by society.

It will be seen that Mrs. Henderson's strategy seeks not only to educate the corporations, but also to educate the consuming public in its civic responsibility.

Hazel Henderson, a social activist, writer, and lecturer on public issues, is a director of the Council on Economic Priorities of New York and Washington, which publishes research on the social impact of corporate policies and practices. She is also a member of the Advisory Board of the Council on Population and Environment of Chicago.

Let me begin by drawing your attention to some recent happenings in our society: a short time ago some 2,000 people, some dressed as "grim reapers" marched on the annual auto show in New York City; women's organizations have sprung up not only to liberate women from the artificially limiting stereotypes portrayed in the mass media, but also to protest the fashion dictatorship of the clothes industry and their hated midi skirt. Lapel buttons with the words "Tame GM" and "Gulf Kills" proliferate. What is all this about? I believe it is a new extension of traditional consumerism, which generally aims itself only at products. This new form of cultural consumerism now attacks directly the wholesale corruption of our cultural values brought about by powerful corporations through the mass media. These new consumers have given up on the overloaded and malfunctioning political system; and are now directing their efforts at curbing the vast, private, and often unaccountable power to shape our culture wielded by large corporations.

First, I want to describe some of these new patterns of citizen-consumer activity; second, to speculate on why they have emerged; and lastly, to try to suggest how they can modify our culture in the future.

Let us begin by surveying the current scene to see if we can recognize some patterns in this type of citizen-consumer behavior which has spilled out of the traditional political channels and is now overflowing into our courts, into direct challenges to private industry, and finally, when all else fails, into that court of last resort: the streets. When applied technology begins to produce very rapid change as it is doing currently, the traditional avenues for petition and redress of grievance become overloaded. Many citizens have found that now-adays it's often easier to picket a corporation than to picket City Hall! Likewise, citizens have found that the traditional tools of political expression, the ballot and the pen, have become increasingly outmoded and ineffective for changing official policies. The political two-party system has also become bureaucratized and sluggish as it becomes out-flanked by the mass media and the "street theater happenings" which are often staged to cater to editors' demands for action and drama.

1970 so far has seen the beginnings of a further movement of citizen-consumers away from the normal political process, and the zeroing in of protest directly against those other two sectors of the interlocking triumvirate of social power in the U.S. today: large corporations and their advertising and opinion-influencing organizations. These new citizen-consumer activities range all the way from boycotts of polluting products, such as that being conducted by California's Clean Air Council against General Motors cars, to the new wave of activism at corporate annual meetings. Such organizations as Action on Smoking and Health spearheaded the anti-cigarette crusade by successfully testing the Federal Communications Commission's Fairness Doctrine.

This released millions of dollars of advertising time and space which is now being used by health groups to air the anti-smoking messages. A similar spontaneous action by consumers sick of violence was the boycott organized against military toys, which has removed hundreds of these items from toy departments. Citizens For Clean Air, which I helped found in New York, mounted one of the first social-protest campaigns for clean air, and one of its latest ads is specifically directed at countering the advertising of the auto industry. Friends of the Earth recently filed suit against NBC to demand observance of the Fairness Doctrine by giving equal time to opposing conservationist messages for every commercial extolling the virtues of gas-gobbling automobiles and for oil company ads claiming "clean air" qualities for their gasolines.

The Washington-based Project on Corporate Responsibility and its subsidiary group Campaign GM (producer of the "Tame GM" buttons) is another prototype organization. It seeks to use existing Securities and Exchange Commission Laws to present issues of corporate responsibility before shareholders at annual meetings. Already it has lined up many large blocks of General Motors stock held in portfolios of churches, universities, pension funds and other institutions, and although it failed to elect 3 "public interest" directors at GM's annual meeting, it succeeded in forcefully placing the issues before the shareholders and the public. Other independent groups with names such as Project Gulf, Project Honeywell, and Project United Aircraft seek similar goals. A group of aldermen and lawyers in Chicago have brought a class action in behalf of their fellow citizens against the four major auto makers for damage to their health caused by auto pollution. A new organization in Washington, the Citizens Communications Center, helps citizens to understand their rights under the Communications Act of 1934 and tells them how to challenge the license-renewals of broadcasters who don't live up to their public interest responsibilities. Another new group, The Council on Economic Priorities, makes economic reports on corporations, which enable an investor to determine how much a corporation is actually spending on pollution control compared with its claims, and whether this sum is a percentage of its gross income or of its advertising budget. Often such figures are very revealing. Many companies spend many times more on advertising or styling changes and planned obsolescence than they do on research or pollution control. The point is that all of these new citizen-consumers, many modelling themselves on the national crusader Ralph Nader, are beginning to understand the vast private power to apply new technology and to influence national decisions that is wielded by corporations, and which is largely outside normal political control.

It is well to note at this point the massive expenditures of industry in influencing and often corrupting our culture, our national priorities, and the citizen-consumers. Dr. Carl Kaysen of Princeton has called our industry-dominated mass media, "The great teachers of our society . . . far more pervasive in their reach and far more persistent in their influence than school or church." The cost of all advertising in the United States is estimated at some $18 billion annually, and the cost of public relations activities another $2 billion annually. This constant barrage of information, whether to sell products, to "educate" consumers on the benefits of the free enterprise system, to influence legislation, to lobby for appropriations for pet projects such as military hardware or supersonic transport planes, or to push for approval of new drugs or pesticides, has now quite overwhelmed the pitiful efforts of un-organized citizens to register and communicate their disapproval. And this is not to mention corporate power in electing candidates to Congress. Many corporations insist that their officers give personal donations to political parties and set up dozens of paper organizations to channel their donations to candidates so as to evade laws forbidding direct corporate contributions. The new cultural consumerism is the first vague stirrings of understanding that the political process is almost secondary today to this enormous influencing (often by deep psychological incursions capitalizing on personal fears and insecurity) of the individual's behavior via the commercial mass media.

Let us look at some recent examples of the unanticipated effects and growing regurgitation of all this mass media pollution. One of the oldest and best examples is the popularity among the young of MAD magazine, which spoof commercials. The emotional tyranny in the advertising of soaps, deodorants, and mouth washes, designed to generate fears of bad breath, body odor, and personal rejection, may have helped produce the healthy reaction of the defiantly human, gloriously unwashed, unshaven young people of today. Wouldn't it be wonderful to rediscover that we like each other anyway — without dousing ourselves with all those expensive chemicals! NBC's Laugh-In has touched this raw nerve in our psyches with its anti-commercials. As far back as 1937, Karen Horney described the intense psychological pressures on the individual caused by mass media advertising-induced "keeping up with the Joneses." In 1953 Marshall McLuhan's milestone study, *The Mechanical Bride* opened our eyes to the psychological subversion of our intellect and our traditional cultural values through advertising. Cars, for instance, were not sold as transportation — but magical icons to restore masculinity. Vast sums are spent by agencies in motivational research to discover more of our hidden weaknesses, in order to exploit them and sell more goods.

Today the ads become more virulent than ever, tempting us with instant happiness, over-indulgence, selfishness and easy answers. Sex is profaned to sell merchandise; and even Presidents are merchandised like soap! Cigarette ads still portray the unhealthy and unesthetic habit of smoking as youthful and virile, and some, such as those for Virginia Slims, capitalize on women's current uncertainty in their roles by telling them that they can find a new identity by smoking a cigarette. Drug companies spend millions to push their pills and patent remedies as instant solutions to life's normal measure of vexing situations. We are urged to take pills to wake up, to go to sleep, to reduce anxiety, to induce mind-changes, whenever we wish. And then we wonder why a generation which has grown up with this kind of constant "education" should be fascinated with drugs and use them for instant relief for all *their* emotional ills. Similarly endless commercials tempt our poorer citizens with a mouth-watering array of consumer goodies they can never afford, and then we are shocked at the looting of these items during civil disorders. Or take the average minority child who is urged "to go right to your store and be the first on your block to get" the latest burp-gun or walking doll. No mention is made that the child must first get the money from mother or dad! Or take the airlines' ads, "Come on down to Florida — pay later — You deserve the best," or the ones that more subtly tempt; their implication is clear, throw up your responsibilities, walk out on your job, lock up your apartment, escape and *"get into this world."* How many plodding conscientious citizens, managing on a skin-tight budget have been almost tried beyond endurance by this kind of titillation? How many others have decided that in the never-never land of credit cards and instant money thrift and even money itself isn't very important? All of these examples relate to our topsy-turvy priorities, and our industries which push more and more consumer gadgets or more travel in polluting cars or jets onto over-extended or surfeited consumers, without regard to the ominous, ecological consequences of waste, pollution, and the starvation of badly-needed public sector programs.

Another growing form of media pollution which is causing its own backlash is the recent spate of commercials from power companies, oil refiners, and other industries, which attempt to distort the pollution issue so that the public will be misled into thinking that all will be well if we leave it to business. Recent power industry ads for instance, charge that "A Few Conservationists are Pulling the Plug on America." This kind of mindless nonsequitur makes responsible public dialogue on what kinds of new power are needed and means to produce it all but impossible. The current spate of oil industry ads, whether it's Phillips 66 "clean air motor oil," Mobil's "detergent gasoline," or Standard Oil's recent series extolling their anti-pollution efforts, are all equally misleading. Then there are those infuriating ads showing a scene of rugged natural beauty, and claiming that you owe all this, not to the Almighty, but to the XYZ logging company or the ABC pulp mills for so graciously consenting to clean up their own mess! Or take the detergent manufacturers who buy millions of dollars worth of time and space in the mass media to extoll their cleaning products. They conveniently forget to mention that the housewife may be enjoying sparkling dishes at the expense of sparkling lakes and rivers. General Electric recently began a campaign to influence public discussion of the costs and benefits of nuclear power plants. All the benefits were mentioned — but none of the costs of thermal pollution or disposal of radio-active wastes. I'm sure that everyone has his own pet examples of this kind of media pollution. The cynicism and widening credibility gap that it produces further undermine public respect for all our institutions.

Cultural consumerism is the growing backlash to all of this massive and expensive propagandizing by corporations. The consumer is beginning to understand that "truth in advertising" should go a lot further than policing extravagant claims for a product or deceptive pricing. The consumer is now realizing the extent of psychological manipulation involved and that deceptive advertising can influence politics, public decision-making on pollution control, and even our national priorities. Consumers are also aware that our mass media communication channels are open only to those large powerful organizations who can afford to use them. Few citizens can afford *their* day in the court of public opinion when a page in a newspaper or magazine can cost some $9,000, or a minute on network TV $65,000.

What is needed now is a much wider awareness on the part of all of us of the enormous impact of much of our corporate information-dissemination and other technological activities and their destructive influence on many of our earliest traditional values of moderation in consumption of goods, thrift, and love of simplicity. We ecologists understand the need for a change in our cultural values, one that would incorporate many of these older values of thrift and simplicity as well as new values based on our ecological awareness. How will we implement our new understanding of the interdependence of man and nature, the need for an equilibrium economy, recycled production and consumption, quality of life rather than quantity of material possessions, except by supporting and widening the cultural consumerism I have been describing? How can we counter the extreme industry arguments against change? Many of these companies sound rather like the extreme ecology buffs. They say "Use our products — whether cars, beer cans, detergents or gasoline; or walk, go unwashed and generally go back into the trees." They never point out that there are many options to these extreme alternatives. For instance, nonpolluting minicars, better mass transit, biodegradable soap, recycling packaging and scrap metal, compacting or composting garbage, better energy conversion ratios in fuel and power consumption . . . the list is endless. A vigorous attack is needed on all corporate practices and advertising that prevent understanding and adoption of the necessary cultural change. Not on the corporations themselves: because Marxism is no answer; the Volga is as polluted as the Potomac. Let's try some heavy muscled thinking on how best to bring technology back under political control and how to make our overgrown institutions, whether corporations, government agencies, or voluntary organizations, more responsive to those they should serve — not dominate.

If we are to achieve a new era of ecological ethics and cultural values, we are going to need more and more of the kinds of citizens organizations I have described. The cultural consumerism movement, with its perceptive questioning of capitalism and how and what it produces, is one of the most creative forces in our society today. It is also profoundly conservative in the true Burkean sense of the term, because it often seeks to re-interpret and enforce existing statues, many of which, particularly in our regulatory agencies, have become eroded by the political power of modern corporations. This new movement is a kind of reverse market research — this time initiated by the consumer. As its power grows, it may become as vital a force in helping capitalism adapt to and survive new conditions as was the labor movement. The changes brought about by organized labor have been largely beneficial: apart from helping prevent a socialist takeover, labor also pushed for un-employment insurance and social security which helped iron out business cycles, and created the more stable economy we know today. And yet we must never forget that these changes were fought by business every inch of the way — even child labor laws were opposed by the capitalists of the day as "socialistic" and "ruining business"! So we must take the current howls and media barrages of today's corporations with a grain of salt. They, too, will find ways of re-cycling formerly wasted by-products, and probably end up with more profits than before. In fact many of them are now getting into the pollution control business, so they can make money off both ends — producing the polluting equipment and products, and then selling more equipment to control the same pollution!

We must remember that business tends to operate on narrow value-free economic criteria, which will always be at odds with the over-arching values of the public interest. Business because of its power over public opinion has been able to force these narrow, quantifiable, economic values onto society at large, which normally operates on the consensus of its members as to what constitutes "the good society." Or to paraphrase Oscar Wilde — it is possible to know the price of everything and the value of nothing. The prime example of this type of thinking is the imposition on our national decision-making and resource allocation process of that monster of economic ineptitude, the Gross National Product, which includes as a plus the cigarettes that are killing us and omits the minuses of social costs of cleaning up the mess that production makes — i.e., the pollution of the environment. This "Gross National Problem" is the first item that needs to be tackled, as our society at large begins the tough job of reasserting noneconomic values into the decision-making process. The GNP must be replaced by a "Total Social Accounting System" of *all* costs and benefits, as described by Dr. Daniel Bell. To regain our lost sense of priorities, citizens in the new cultural consumerism movement are going to have to intervene to correct socially harmful corporate decision-making *and* the government and public decision-making that business influences; by all the economic and legal means available. Let's make John Stuart Mill's prediction of an "equilibrium capitalism" come true, rather than Marx's prediction that capitalism will destroy itself! If there are enough of us, we still may avert disaster and turn our potentially creative enterprise system from a death-industrial complex to a life-industrial complex.

THE PRESS AND
GROUP ACTION

Eleanor O'Brien

In the battle for population limitation and the restoration of the environment the press is a key terrain. Less subject to pressure from government and special interests than that of any other great country in the world, the American press is extraordinarily hospitable to innovative views and to criticism of the practices and policies of whatever "establishment" happens to be in power. Our aim should be not to capture the press, but to use it intelligently, as the primary means of publicizing the work of our action groups and thereby attracting supporters to them. The secret here is to be interesting. In an age in which organizations of all kinds spend so much on publicity it is remarkable that so little of it meets this simple criterion.

Mrs. O'Brien gives us some down-to-earth advice on how to use the press — and by implication the other news media — to interest readers in our side of the story.

Eleanor O'Brien is Chairman of the Great Lakes Regional Council of Planned Parenthood/World Population and has long been active in the field of publicity and public relations.

When word of "Earth Day, 1970" began to appear in wire copy, editors around this country started to accumulate cartoon copy which would brighten editorial pages, balancing the messages of eco-disaster they would receive. Many of them reused a series of cartoon drawn by J. W. (Ding) Darling of the St. Louis *Post Dispatch.*

For most of his life Ding fought the good fight for conservation, a knight with a pen for a sword, battling nearly alone, the terrible destruction of our landscape. If you have had the opportunity to examine these cartoons in your local paper, you will note that many things he campaigned for have been accomplished. Ding dramatized the careless destruction of our wild flowers. Laws were passed to protect them. He depicted the wrath of the farmer whose meadow-land was littered with the remnants of a careless picnic. We now have public parks and camp sites.

Ding also showed us raw sewage pouring into our rivers, smoke smudging our skies. He drew those cartoons in the 1920's and those problems are still here. We can point to exceptions to illustrate that such conditions need not exist and then raise the question: What can the media do to change opinion, to change behavior?

Ding used his medium, and where change of behavior required no great sacrifice, change could happen. He did not succeed when the stakes were great.

There is a technique for motivating people to act differently than they are acting at a particular moment. Simply, we must supply enough information, facts, if you please, about our problem. If our presentation is carefully prepared, we will soon see a change in attitude about the problem, and with this change in attitude, there should follow a change in behavior.

Ding waged a one-man war. Because of his skillful drawing, he could give a great deal of information in a three-column sketch. If Ding had had additional reinforcement from other media, we might not have had to wait so long for his message to reach us.

I am suggesting that now is the appropriate time to use all media, magazines, newspapers, television, and radio to provide an intense educational thrust to alert our citizens to the eco-catastrophe that awaits us.

If we can remember two basics in teaching — reinforcement and repetition — we will find, not only a shift in public opinion toward concern for our environmental crisis, but more significantly, a change in behavior regarding ALL things connected with this crisis.

Let us examine ways in which we can approach the problem of getting our message across to the community. It will be the editorial staff of the paper which will make the decision as to the value of our information and how to present it. The editorial staff, when dealing with a complex subject, finds itself with a multiplicity of sources. The important sources for newspaper stories employ public relations or publicity people, professional or not, and on any given day, several releases may be received.

The newspaper is not going to run separate stories on one subject on the same day, so the usual technique is to combine the releases, taking a paragraph or so from each. This does not satisfy any of the several organizations concerned.

Obviously, if they have done their job well, they have supplied only information they think important for publication, and when only a fifth or a tenth of that information is published, they are unhappy and the medium is criticized.

A solution would be to combine several interested organizations or agencies into a single committee for publicity or public information purposes and thus permit the agencies themselves to decide what is the most important or urgent information to be supplied. If the urgent matter is a piece of pending state legislation, the committee could give that its priority and concentrate on furnishing the media with a point of view having behind it the strength and importance of the coalition committee.

An example of this is "Voices for Environment," a fledgling coalition group which is attempting to pull together all environmentalists in the Toledo area so there will be one common and united public image. This kind of "umbrella" covers the duck hunter as well as the chapter of ZPG.

Information from this group can be supplied to many different newspaper staff members, depending upon the size of the newspaper. By using this technique, variety, which is another way of reinforcement, can be helpful.

A typical large paper will have many specialists and several of them may be able to deal with aspects of the general concern. For instance, pollution or environment and population could involve the writers on science, medicine, urban affairs, education, religion, outdoors, business and financial affairs, and staff members in state and national capitals.

Top level management and government will make the hard decisions about pollution problems which can only be solved by money commitments. The women in your community will be the ones who buy the phosphate-less soap products, make the decisions to abandon floral toilet paper, take the birth control pills, and have the abortions. Your committee should be certain to establish a good relationship with the staff which handles news pertaining to women, and the staff should have such confidence in the value of the coalition that it would know that it could contact members for additional information to clarify and personalize wire copy.

The more complex the matter under consideration, the more

specialists will be involved and they should be contacted and informed of the point of view of the committee. If rapport between individual members of the committee and particular newspaper people can be established, this will be mutually beneficial. The conservation editor understands fish weirs, doe limits, management of wild turkey flocks. He will be responsive to information which will broaden his outlook. For the amateur who has a cause but has to learn the names and numbers of all the players, the outdoor editor can help him chart his political course. The writer is grateful for the contact who can give him immediate expertise in his field.

Most papers find space for a local columnist. He usually has his guaranteed position in his paper because of a facility with words. These columns have wide readership, and items that appear in them carry impact. The less obvious the connection, the more valuable the position. For example, an item on smoke pollution, population, or littering that appears in the sports editor's column reaches a public that would never read the item in a news column.

Generally editors believe that "standing heads" limit readership. The aim of all editors is to find a way for the reader to stop at every page. If you are interested in the items carried under the standing head, you will stop to read the items. If "Environment" means nothing to you, you will pass it by. If our purpose is to use the newspapers to educate, we must vary our approach to be certain that one way or another, the reader meets our message.

Assuming you have a public relations committee, it would be advisable to find a way to discuss your problems with the editor. This is particularly true if your paper is small, but local situations may differ. Find out who can get the paper to do things, and deal with him. There is never any harm in a courtesy call to the boss, particularly if your message is for the good of the whole community.

If you need a spokesman for your group, take a tip from the advertising companies. Instead of releasing the opinion of the well-known community leader who is on every committee, always talking about something, it might be better to have a local sports figure or union official make your comments. If an idol of the sports fans can sell cigarettes or soap, maybe he can sell anti-pollution too. Be certain you get the right one, and make sure he believes what he is saying. The conversion of Eddie Albert and Arthur Godfrey to the ecocrisis are examples which could be applied at the local level.

When you are dealing with the media, try to avoid fanaticism, no matter how right your cause and how deeply you are personally involved and committed. Newspapers are assaulted from all sides by advocates of all sorts, and it is refreshing to deal with an intelligent, persuasive purveyor of facts, rather than with someone who has hold of a cause and regards it as the only important issue in the editor's life. Controversy is always news, but reckless statements and over-concern make skeptics of newspapermen. They feel safer with facts.

Occasionally, the most valuable spot for your comments will be in the Letters to the Editor columns, a section of the paper with high readership. There are some simple rules to follow: Keep the letters short, keep them light, keep them rational.

Amateurs in the public relations field tend to be drawn to the drama of the "press conference" with electronic media coverage. There are moments when this is specifically indicated, and certainly your story on national news spots, or a documentary shown at prime time is invaluable in reaching millions of people. For local concerns, both television and the press should be used. Remember that a half hour of time on television is equal to four columns of type. There is another thing to remember — newsprint is just that — something in type that is recoverable, rereadable, able to be copied and circulated.

It is now that you find a way to plug into the political and community activists who understand thoroughly the value of placing a particularly pertinent news story, editorial, or column on the desk of a legislator the morning he is voting on a specific piece of legislation. If the legislator appears on television, he probably will watch that news program. If he has a large enough staff, he will have TV monitored, but this would not be a likely practice with local politicians concerned with local problems.

The social climate is in an extremely fluid state, and change is built into all our institutions that have any chance of survival. You may find your first contact with the media frustrating. The newspaper may take an editorial stand with which you do not agree. Do not despair. The news columns are always open, and newspaper readers can read your side. Don't cut the paper from your contacts. Opinions have been known to change, sometimes abruptly, even with editorial writers, and that job which you started to do to educate the legislature, industrialists, and consumers, could result in educating the newspapermen, too.

THE POLITICS
OF FERTILITY

Richard D. Lamm

*Group action, as we have seen, is both an educational tool and a major way of at-
tracting support for the population-environment movement, but its underlying
purpose is political, and a great part of its strategy is to use existing political
channels to achieve its ends. If progress on the political front is difficult, it is also
immensely rewarding: every enactment of a bill, every judicial decision or executive
order favorable to the movement is a solid victory and gives us an advanced base
from which to continue our struggle.*

*Richard D. Lamm, a member of the Colorado legislature who led the fight for
that state's liberalized abortion law — the first in the nation — gives us an insight
into the practicalities of political action and provides the kind of information
we need if we are to transform our aspirations into concrete results. Like
our other contributors with political experience, Mr. Lamm warns us not to
rely exclusively on the legislative process, but he goes beyond them in giving
us very specific advice as to how to use it for what it can accomplish for us.*

*Reelected last year to the Colorado legislature, Richard Lamm is a faculty
member of the College of Law of the University of Denver and President of the
Council on Population and Environment of Chicago.*

To what extent can population stability be achieved by legislative
means? An increasing number of people argue that even after birth
control and abortion make every child a wanted child some parents will
still want too many children to allow society to attain demographic
stability. Thus it would seem that new legislation is required to deal
with the population explosion; but before we consider what forms this
legislation might take, it would be well to recognize that social change
cannot be produced simply by enactment. Successful legislation demands
a climate of opinion that will support it.

This is especially true when dealing with human fertility. Historically, governments have not been successful in attempting to raise the birth rate, and it is questionable whether they would be any more successful in attempting to lower it. Some observers have gone so far as to suggest that laws governing family size would be more likely to bring down the government than the birth rate.

Nevertheless, any legal scholar will attest that as a final resort law can and will be invoked to prevent a society from destroying itself. Conceivably — but always as a final resort — legislation could be enacted to dictate how many children a couple could have; as a member of the Indian parliament once said to me "If the law says you can have only one wife, why can't it tell you that you can have only two children?"

Fortunately there is a wide variety of social controls other than laws to teach, persuade or compel people to conform to a particular set of values. Society has a wide variety of ways to impose "musts" or "must nots" — a raised eyebrow, withholding of approval, social ostracism, insults, etc. These other social controls are already being brought into play to help achieve small family size. One cannot go on a major college campus without recognizing that social pressures are toward fewer children and a social duty to "save the earth" from pollution and overpopulation.

If society is going to prevent government dictating family size, it must move now to activate the other methods of social controls, to make large families unacceptable, so that a future generation doesn't have to make them *illegal*.

This doesn't mean, however, that the legislative process can be ignored while we explore the effectiveness of other means of bringing about population stability. There is at the present time a wide variety of laws already on the books which reflect pro-natalist policies and must be removed from the law. Birth control, abortion, and sterilization are restricted in varying degrees by law and continue to force motherhood on a shocking number of women. Our tax structure continues to discriminate in favor of married people and to subsidize children through income tax deductions, and in some states a spouse who does not wish to have children violates the obligations of marriage.

There are increasing numbers of people who argue that we should adopt a system of "incentives" or "disincentives" toward small family size. Incentives toward small family size, as with any other incentives do operate on freedom of choice, but in a way which is both minimal and which has precedent within our system. We give "investment credits" for new equipment and "credits" for anti-pollution devices, and we may with equal logic give incentives for small family size. Some go beyond this logic and point out that as each child born in a society costs X number of dollars, that a couple ought to have the free choice between the child and the X dollars.

The Legislative Process

Whatever the legislative goal, there are certain realities of the political process which must be explored and understood by those proposing social change.

The ability to move society in a democracy imposes special burdens on those propounding the change. Democracy depends on the will of the governed, and this will is expressed at relatively short intervals in elections at which time those who promulgate policies have to defend their actions. Political scientists extoll the system of democratic change, pointing out that the voters may remove offending political figures in a "bloodless revolution" at the ballot box. New ideas are thus tested at relatively short intervals by voters who are presumed to know their own interests and express them by the ballot.

The system has, unquestionably, worked at least as well and probably better than any other form of governmental organization. Its success has probably been greatly enhanced by the system of universal free public education, which gives the populace the education necessary to make this system of enlightened self-interest work.

However, like many of our other institutions, the system must be re-thought and streamlined to survive in the twentieth century. Town meeting democracy is gone, replaced by a system which values public opinion rather than individual opinion. A U.S. Congressman who in the year 1900 represented 190,000 people, today represents close to 500,000, and individual thought and new ideas often have a hard time percolating to the top of the political process. A politician must almost by necessity count the number of letters he receives rather than analyze their contents, on the Gertrude Stein assumption that a voter is a voter is a voter.

Another factor severely testing the concept of democratic change, is the rate of change itself. Its acceleration puts severe strains on the adaptability of man and his institutions. There are many factors which account for this acceleration. The population explosion is one factor; there are others. In 1969 the United States spent 15 per cent of its national budget on Research and Development, supplementing the already large research and development budgets of private industry. These funds, private and public, support a cadre of scientists and technicians sometimes estimated (loosely but dramatically) as 90 per cent of all those who ever lived. In a few short years changes occur that formerly would have required centuries.

The speed of scientific and technological change, with consequent changes in life styles, standards of living, values, and mores, is at a minimum unsettling and frustrating. People feel that they have little or no control over their lives and the events around them. They react against change; conventional wisdom is yesterday's wisdom, not tomorrow's.

The policy maker in elective office is thus constantly faced with a classic dilemma — he sees the need for dynamic new policies but questions his political survivability if he proposes them. He is caught between what he knows necessary and what he thinks will be accepted politically. He attempts at the same time to keep his eyes to the horizon and his ears to the ground.

The dilemma is historic and has been faced by political figures throughout history. Al Smith, one of the world's most practical politicians, once said, "A politician can't be so far ahead of the band he can't hear the music." His value system, like that of most political figures, placed political survivability at the absolute top of his priorities, and however progressive his thinking, it was within the context of the next election.

It is altogether likely that within a democratic framework this will continue to be true. One may long for heroic political figures who are willing to take a long lead off the safe second base of political respectability. Yet even when one does display his own profile of courage he is seldom in a position to succeed in passing legislation solely by his own efforts. However heroic they may be, their success depends on a full majority of conventional politicians.

Given the limitations of the democratic system, those who advance controversial ideas must exercise a special understanding and a special wisdom about moving for change. One should first ascertain whether it could not come through the other strong force for social change — the courts. As was seen in *Brown v. Board of Education* (school desegregation) and *Griswold v. Connecticut* (birth control), it is often the courts which initiate change. The abortion repeal movement is a relevant example. Proponents of abortion law repeal are using both the courts and the legislatures to bring about the desired change. However, if the courts are not available, one *must* effect reforms through the legislature. Whether adding new proposals such as tax disincentives or attempting to repeal old laws such as those on abortion one must work within the limitations of the legislative process. Most standard lobbying techniques are applicable to the politics of fertility.

The essence of getting successful legislation passed consists of marshalling and, in some cases, manufacturing the necessary support for attainable goals. In dealing with matters such as abortion, sex education, birth control, and tax disincentives, it is extremely important to focus all sympathetic groups on an agreed and attainable goal. Inertia and opposition to all new legislation are so great that supporters must not themselves be divided. In Colorado the process of changing our 100-year old abortion law was greatly advanced by the agreement among people of various viewpoints that a law allowing abortion for reasons of mental and physical health, fetal deformity, rape, and incest would be worth while. Some viewed it as an end result, many as merely a first step, but all agreed it was worth supporting. Proponents of change, to the extent possible, should attempt to work out disagreements prior to the introduction of legislation and present as united a front as possible.

The legislator who will be chief sponsor of the legislation is extremely important both for what he is and what he seems. His image in the political community is important: the more respected the better. Ideally, he should have a good record at passing successful legislation and not have a reputation of introducing only controversial bills. The chief sponsor should also have the time, interest, and ability to learn the subject matter of the bill and be able to articulately defend his position. He must know how to explain his legislation and how to defend it from attack.

Both he and his supporters should understand the legislative process. They must know who the co-sponsors are to be, what committee the bill should be assigned to, who will testify at the hearings, what compromises are acceptable and necessary, what forces can best be brought to bear on the legislative process, and how one can get the Governor to sign the bill.

One of the main factors in the life or death of a particular piece of legislation is the legislative hearing. It is here that the legislative process is the most visible. The press and the public get their main impression of a proposal at this hearing and other legislators size up the support. The hearing should, if possible, be staged as a play. All supporting viewpoints should be represented, by as many responsible spokesmen as are available.

The abortion reform/repeal hearings around the country serve as a case in point. Those which were most successful were carefully tailored, with conservative spokesmen supporting what was once a radical idea: Baptist and Methodist churchmen rather than Unitarians; lawyers from conservative business law firms rather than the A.C.L.U.; Church women, A.A.U.W. and League of Women Voters members rather than feminists. Controversial legislation must be given as respectable an image as possible.

This image can also be enhanced by the press. A visit to the editorial department of all local newspapers by responsible spokesmen who explain in advance what they are trying to accomplish can negate criticism and often win editorial support.

Engendering public support and persuading supporters to write to legislators are also important. Ad hoc groups are often formed ("Colorado Citizens for . . .") which make a few voices sound like many. It is important to have people let their legislators know that they approve of the legislation. Supporters should attempt as far as possible to find out who a particular legislator listens to and see if they can get the support of that source.

Finally, if the bill fails to pass in the first legislative session, it is important to get the chief legislative supporters re-elected. Nothing scares politicians like defeat, and if the proponent of an idea is defeated, the issue suffers a sharp blow. If he is re-elected it shows that support of the idea does not mean defeat at the polls. The issue must stand the test of political survivability.

Population control which was yesterday a whisper, is today a cry and will tomorrow be a roar. It is imperative that society start a dialogue on what ethical and moral means can best bring man into balance with nature. It is hoped that means other than laws will bring the desired results, but those who advocate optimum population and environment must be sophisticated and knowledgeable in the legislative process. Population and environment are clearly political issues, and, ironically, policies toward clean air and a livable environment often are initiated in smoke-filled rooms. We must learn to do business in those rooms.

PART FOUR

THE LARGER CONTEXT

We have examined the overall situation in which we find ourselves, discussed some of the particularly human factors that complicate it, and considered strategies and tactics for resolving it. We have seen that there is no ready-made answer to the population-environment problem, that, rather, we must all get together to evolve one. The aim of this book has been to provide information and agenda for the dialogue and the action through which we will evolve our answer.

Still, something is missing. Call it motivation for the coming struggle. We have been warned often enough that unless we act — and act promptly — the earth will face total disaster, something not less real for being unimaginable; but as motivation fear is not enough: when it is not simply paralyzing it tends to produce spasmodic and ill-considered actions that end in hopelessness. For the long, slow haul that lies ahead we need something better than warnings of calamity.

Without minimizing our difficulties or resorting to the cloudy rhetoric of moral uplift, George Wald, scientist and humanist, provides the kind of motivation we need by reminding us of the unique dignity and importance of man and his planet in the cosmic scheme of things.

THE HUMAN ENTERPRISE

George Wald

Dr. Wald, a recipient in 1967 of the Nobel Price, is Higgins Professor of Biology at Harvard University.

We have come to a time of great decision not only for man but for much of life on the earth. We are in a period of great crisis, in fact, of many crises. John Platt has spoken of them as a "crisis of crises". They are all coming upon us at once, all coming to a head within the next fifteen to at most thirty years; and this, of course, faces us with multiple problems. We have very hard decisions to make.

The things we need to face and try to do are terrifying in their complexity and their difficulty. We need in fact a revolution. I use the word in its literal sense, a turn-about. We here in America, living in a democracy, still hope that we can *vote* ourselves that revolution; but vote it or not, that revolution must come if we are to survive.

Nor can it be done piecemeal. Most of our problems are closely interrelated, so that we have to deal with them together, each one dependent upon the others. That calls for a tremendous effort that involves not only the people of this country but to a great degree of the globe. That means that we will have somehow to learn to move and work together; and that in turn calls for some sort of common acceptance of the questions that men have always tried to answer throughout their history: Whence they come, what kind of thing they are, and out of these realizations at least some hint of what is to become of us.

Those are the age-old questions. Men have always tried to answer them, and all the traditional religions try to answer them. Fortunately for us at this time one can find a kind of answer in the world view of science, an answer that presents an astonishingly unified view of the universe, the place of life in it, and the place of man in life. In that unified view I think we can find new sanctions for our beliefs in the sanctity of life and in the dignity of man, more credible and more reliable than any that the older traditions offered us.

What is that unified view? We know now that we live in a historical universe, one in which not only living creatures but stars and galaxies are born, come to maturity, grow old and die. That universe is made of four kinds of elementary particles: protons, neutrons, electrons, and photons, which are particles of radiation. If not the whole universe then surely large parts of it began in a kind of gas, a plasma, of such elementary particles, filling large sections of space. Here and there, quite by accident, within that plasma an eddy formed, a little special concentration of material, and this, though the ordinary forces of gravitation, began to pull in the stuff around it, to pull in the particles out of the space around it. So it grew, and the more that there was, the harder it pulled. It swept the material out of larger and larger sections of space and grew and grew, a condensing mass of elementary particles. As that mass condensed, as all such masses in condensation do, it heated up. When the temperature in the deep interior reached about five million degrees, something new began to happen.

That new thing was that one of these praticles, the protons — a proton is the nucleus of a hydrogen atom, so that one speaks of them as hydrogen — the protons began to join together, four protons condensing to make a nucleus of the atom helium, four protons, each approximately of mass 1, condensing to make a helium nucleus of mass approximately 4.

But in that transaction a little mass is lost; and that little bit of mass is converted into radiation, according to Einstein's famous formula, $E = mc^2$, in which E is the energy of that radiation, m is the little bit of mass, and c is a very big number, the speed of light, 186,000 miles a second, 3×10^{10} centimeters per second. Multiply even a little bit of mass by that big a number and you get an awful lot of energy. That energy beginning to be poured out in the deep interior of what had been a condensing mass of particles backs up the condensation, and this mass comes into an uneasy steady state, in which its further impulse to collapse through gravity is held back by the outpouring of energy inside. What I have just described, of course, is the birth of a star. Our own star, the sun, was born in that way about six billion years ago. It is just an ordinary run of the mill, middle-aged star. It has approximately another six billion years to run.

Stars live by this process. They live by the so-called "burning" of hydrogen to helium. Inevitably the time comes when every star begins to run out of hydrogen. With that, it begins to produce less energy; and with that it begins to collapse again. With that, it heats up again. When the temperature in the deep interior reaches about one hundred million degrees, something new begins to happen.

That is the "burning" of helium. Those helium nuclei of mass 4 begin to unite with one another. It's all simple arithmetic. Two helium nuclei condense: four and four make eight. That is beryllium 8, an atomic nucleus so unstable that it disintegrates within so small a fraction of a second that it has never been measured. Yet always at these enormous concentrations of matter and enormous temperatures there are a few beryllium atoms; and here and there a beryllium nucleus captures another helium nucleus. Eight and four make twelve, and what is twelve; *Carbon;* and that is where carbon comes from in our universe. And when you have got the carbon, that carbon 12 can capture another helium nucleus: twelve and four make sixteen, and what is sixteen? *Oxygen;* and that is where oxygen comes from. And when you have some carbon, that can do another thing. The carbon itself can begin to pick up protons, hydrogen nuclei. And carbon 12 plus two protons make fourteen, and what is fourteen? That is *Nitrogen.*

These processes produce a new enormous outpouring of energy in the deep interior of the star, enough energy not only to back up the further condensation but to puff it out to enormous size. It is now a red giant, a dying star, gigantic because it has been puffed up to enormous size, and red because it has cooled off somewhat in its outermost layers. A red giant, a dying star.

Those red giants are in a delicate condition. They are always distilling a lot of stuff off their surfaces into space. Every now and then a great streamer of material goes shooting off into space: a flare. Every now and then a whole star threatens to blow up: a nova. Every now and then it does blow up: a supernova. And in all these ways the stuff of which red giants are made is spewed out into space to become part of the huge masses of gases and dust that fill all space. It is sometimes estimated that as much as half the mass of our universe is in the form of gases and dust.

Then here and there in the gases and dust a new eddy forms, a new little knot of material, that once again by gravitation begins to pull in the stuff from all around it; and a new star is born.

But those later generation stars, unlike the first generation of stars made entirely of hydrogen and helium, contain the carbon and nitrogen and oxygen; and we know that our sun is such a later generation star, *because we are here* — because we, as all other living creatures we know, and I am sure, though that is another story, that must be true every-where that life occurs in the universe, because 99 percent of our living substance is made of just those elements I have been naming: hydrogen, carbon, nitrogen, and oxygen. It is a moving realization that stars must die before organisms may live.

Stars are at too high temperatures for the atomic nuclei to gather the electrons about themselves in orderly ways. That can happen only in the cooler places of the universe, on the planets. There, where the electrons can be brought into orderly ways around the atomic nuclei, those electrons can begin to interact with one another, and so become the first molecules.

Molecules are a great new thing in the universe, for until there are molecules nothing has a shape or size. We are still in the world of Heisenberg's Indeterminancy Principle. So long as one is in the world of elementary particles, even atoms, there are no shapes or sizes of even definable positions and motions. All those things come into the universe with the first molecules.

So molecules are a great thing. As soon as the earth was formed, some four and a half billion years ago, the molecules began to form. In the primitive atmosphere of the earth there were such molecules as hydrogen, ammonia, water and methane; and in the upper layers of the atmosphere, sparked by sunlight and electric discharges, those and other molecules began to interact to form that would eventually give rise to life, the so-called *organic* molecules, the molecules made of hydrogen, carbon, nitrogen and oxygen. Over the ages they were leached out of the atmosphere into the seas. About three billion years ago somewhere, sometime, or perhaps several times in several places, an aggregate of such molecules in the ocean reached a condition that a competent biologist, had he been present, would have been willing to concede to be alive.

Life, too, was a great new thing in our universe. I have heard life called disparagingly a disease of matter. No, it is no disease of matter. It is a *culmination* of matter. Give matter a chance, and give it that chance for long enough, and life appears inevitably. It is a culmination of matter, so far as we know the most complex state of organization that matter achieves in our universe.

And life, since it appeared on the earth, has transformed the whole environment. Even biologists still occasionally make the mistake of thinking that the environment is something given for life to fit itself into or perish; that it is the environment that plays the tune to which life must dance or die.

But it isn't that way at all. The early atmosphere of this planet in which those first organic molecules appeared that led to life, contained no oxygen gas, O_2, the stuff with which all animals and all higher plants respire. There was no oxygen gas in the early atmosphere of the planet. It was put into the atmosphere by living organisms, by plants in the process of photosynthesis; and it is now held in the atmosphere entirely by that process.

All the molecular oxygen gas in our atmosphere comes out of plants in the process of photosynthesis and goes into plants and animals in the process of cellular respiration, and so is completely renewed, about every two thousand years.

Two thousand years is just a moment in geological time. With carbon dioxide it is still more strange. All the carbon dioxide, not only in the atmosphere but dissolved in all the waters of the earth, goes into photosynthesis and comes out of respiration and so is completely renewed every three hundred years.

Life is a great thing on this planet. Two-thirds of the planet is covered with water; yet all the water on the earth goes in and out of living organisms and is completely renewed every two million years; and two million years is just a day in geological time. We have had men on the earth for that long.

The appearance of oxygen through the process of plant photosynthesis did another very strange thing for life on the earth. You see, the radiation from sunlight produced in the way I have described, by turning hydrogen into helium, contains short wave length ultraviolet components that are incompatible with the existence of life, that no life or even such large molecules as proteins or nucleic acids can tolerate. So long as that radiation poured onto the surface of the earth, life could not exist on the surface. It had to stay under water.

But there in the ocean photosynthesis began. About four-fifths of all the photosynthesis on the earth still occurs in the upper layers of the ocean. The photosynthesis poured oxygen into the atmosphere; and in the uppermost layers of the atmosphere, sparked by sunlight, some of the oxygen formed a little *ozone.* (Oxygen gas is O_2, ozone is O_3.) That little ozone absorbed and still absorbs those ultraviolet radiations out of sunlight that are incompatible with life. It is only because of that little ozone in our upper atmosphere that animals and plants were able to come our from under water and populate the earth and the air.

How much ozone? The whole story represents a delicacy, a sensitivity of control almost beyond belief. The only thing that lets us survive outside of water on the surface of the earth is that ozone; yet all the ozone in the upper atmosphere, if brought to 1 atmosphere pressure — ordinary air pressure at the surface of the earth — and zero degrees centigrade, would form a layer only three millimeters thick, about one eighth of an inch.

And so, particularly after the oxygen and the ozone had arrived, life flourished on the earth and populated every corner of the earth with a most extraordinary ingenuity — every corner. Every place where a little energy can be obtained that makes life possible, you find life there, fitting itself into the most extraordinary conditions.

About two million years ago, man appeared. Man too is a great new thing, man and his like, a great new thing in the universe. You see, you have to wait a long time, all those things have had to happen, and then at last — and I think, given enough time, inevitably — a creature appears who begins to know; a science-and art-making animal, who begins to cast back on this whole history, and begins for the first time to understand it.

You may have heard it said that a hen is only an egg's way of making another egg. In just the same sense a man is the atom's way of knowing about atoms. If you wish, a man is the star's way of knowing about stars — a great new thing.

But in his knowing, man also begins inevitably, as part of that knowing, going hand in hand with that knowing, to breed a technology. The technology isn't artificial; it is part of nature, since it is part of human nature. The technology comes along with that kind of knowing on the part of any such creature, wherever he arose.

I have heard the silly question asked, "Why is the earth about five billion years old?" — and the silly answer — a silly question always deserves a silly answer: Because it took that long to find that out. That is the way it is. Now we are coming to ask another curious question:

When you have come to the point of finding that out, can you go much further? Is such a development self-limiting?

I am sure that there is not only life in very many places in the universe, but there are also man-like creatures; not men, but similarly contemplative, technology-making creatures, in many other places in the universe. I see no reason offhand why many of them shouldn't be far ahead of us.

We are beginning to develop our technology very rapidly, and at an increasing pace. If that kind of thing is true for us, it might well be true for them. If they have had another thousand years — and a thousand years is nothing — why not a hundred thousand, a million years, why indeed not a billion years — where might they have reached by now?

Think of where we might reach in even another hundred years if we survive, if we manage well. One has to begin to ask, are there such highly superior technological civilizations elsewhere in the universe, or is there not only a time in which such a creature arrives, but a somewhat later time, perhaps not very much later, in which he departs? That problem now very much concerns us.

Because we have reached a point suddenly in which our very existence and continuance, not only as a civilization but as a species, is threatened by wholly new problems. One of the most important of those problems is overpopulation. It is entirely new. Darwin gave us the phrase, "the survival of the fittest"; and biologists, who like to measure all things, long ago began asking how we were to measure fitness. Long ago we decided that the measure of fitness would be reproductive success — that we would consider those lines of organism most fit that breed the largest number of offspring that themselves survive to sexual maturity and reproduce. I suppose that man is the first species on earth, animal or plant, to be threatened by his own reproductive success.

As everyone knows, by all present indications, unless we can bring something different to happen very quickly, the present world population of something over three and a half billion will have increased by the end of the century to perhaps double that number. Long before that we exepct famine in many parts of the world on an unprecedented scale. Yet those famines aren't the heart of the problem. If they were, one could even feel slightly optimistic, because in the last decade the world production of food has increased a little faster than the world population; but that isn't the heart of the problem.

The heart of the problem, as of all human problems, is one of *meaning*.

It would be altogether meaningless and bankrupt now to make of the human enterprise a simple exercise in production, an attempt to see how many people one could keep alive on the surface of the earth. Our problem isn't one of numbers, but of the *quality* of human lives. What we need to do is to produce that size of population in which human beings can most fulfill their potentialities.

From that point of view — some may disagree with me and quite properly — in my opinion we are already overpopulated, not just in such places as India, China, and Puerto Rico, but here and in Western Europe. With that overpopulation in our Western world there has been, I think, a signal deterioration in our culture all through the last century.

I think that though this period is kinder to the sciences than to the arts, the life of the individual scientist is nothing like it was. It has deteriorated enormously. I look back a century and envy those scientists who lived then — the way they lived, the way they made their science, the amount of science they succeeded in making, and its quality. All those things have gone badly downhill.

And then we have a closely related problem, also enormously threatening and important, and that is the way we are wasting all our remaining resources and polluting the surface of the earth — a terrible problem, and to an extraordinary degree an American problem.

We are the worst offenders — not *they, we.* We with six percent of the world's population are said to consume about forty percent of the world's irreplaceable resources, and to account for about fifty percent of the world's industrial pollution. It is we Americans who do those things not only to this country but to all the world.

And then there is a third gigantic problem. We have come into the nuclear age. I should like to say something about that, because what should have come to humankind as a promise of a new degree of freedom such as men on earth and life on earth had never experienced before, comes upon us instead as a threat, perhaps the most serious threat we now have to face.

Why do I say a promise? It is very simple. You see, there came a point for life on earth that was absolutely critical and revolutionary. (The big revolutions are the revolutions of nature. The big revolutions among men are the revolutions of science. Make no mistake about that. Darwin nursing his dyspepsia in a garden in Cambridge was a much greater revolutionary than Karl Marx. He changed our world.)

Life first arose on the earth out of that aggregation of organic molecules leached out of the atmosphere into the seas over ages of time. Having arisen, it lived on those molecules. That is a losing game, because just so many of those molecules had accumulated, and living organisms had begun to use and destroy them, just as we have almost finished by now using and destroying our accumulations of fossil fuels.

Eventually that process would have had to come to an end, and life would have come to an end. All of it would have had to begin again from the beginning. But before that happened something else took place: living organisms invented photosynthesis, by which using the energy of sunlight, they could begin to make their own organic molecules. That made them independent of their previous history, of the stores of organic molecules that had accumulated over previous ages on the earth.

Now with the coming of the nuclear age we have a similar opportunity, one of those things that happen only once in several billion years, if then. Because, you see, all life up until now has lived on sunlight, the plants directly, the animals by eating the plants.

Now we can begin to make our own sunlight. That process that the sun lives by, turning hydrogen into helium, is the same process that goes on in a hydrogen bomb. What a disgrace! Think of it! A nuclear reaction which could mean that we could shortly make our own sunlight, that we could make a new basis for life on the earth, that we could make our own energy — that reaction is turned mainly into a weapon that threatens our lives, that promises to become the biggest polluter of our environment, and that now threatens our existence and much of the rest of life on the earth.

It is a symptom of the illness of our society that people think of that as inevitable. Of course one makes a bomb as fast as one can. But there is nothing inevitable about it. That is just our present way of life. It is our western culture at work, our western culture with its beautiful Judeo-Christian ethic. It is our culture alone among the cultures of the earth that sees it that way, that has brought the technology of killing and destruction much further than any culture on the earth ever dreamed of doing before.

It was the Chinese who invented gunpowder. And what did they do with it? They used it for firecrackers. Poor people! All of us know, we are all being told, that the Chinese are crazy. They can't be trusted, they didn't know what to do with gunpowder as we did. But we have taught them.

And the space program: The next person who says to me that we can solve the population problem because we can now get to the moon, I think I will kick him. That is the wrong model, and if we follow it we will be in terrible trouble. That trip to the moon was an exercise in what you can do with lots of wealth and power. The scientific content was trivial and negligible. It was an exercise of power; and as for its technology, that is expected to be very useful in our future weaponry.

There is no inevitability about using all our technology for killing and destruction. We have just taken the wrong turn. So I should like to end with a parable — not a Biblical parable, a biological parable.

Some 200 million years ago we were in the Age of Reptiles. The dinosaurs were the lords of the earth. They looked very fine, those dinosaurs. They were big, the biggest land animals that have ever existed. They were well-armed: horns, teeth, claws. They were well protected: scales, armor plate. They looked awfully good, those dinosaurs.

And back in the shadows, hiding among the roots of the trees was a small, tender, defenseless group of animals. They were the first mammals. They had little to offer, but one thing. They had rather large brains for their size. The dinosaur had a very small brain for its size. The proportion of brains to brawn in a dinosaur was very low. The mammals were doing better in that regard.

And pretty soon there were no more dinosaurs. The Age of Reptiles had given way to the Age of Mammals.

And the mammals kept working on the beautiful brain. Two million years ago they gave rise to man.

Man, as I have been telling you, is a wonderful thing. A man, standing on his own two feet, with that wonderful brain — gentle, harming no one and nothing, altogether in control — a beautiful creature, something one could love. But put him in a car! Now he is making a roar and a stink through the streets. You hardly see the man. It's hard to love a man in a car. And the proportion of brains to brawn has again sunk very low. He has become a kind of medium sized dinosaur.

And dangerous. Cars kill more than 50,000 Americans per year. Please notice one says that cars kill those Americans, not men in cars; because we realize all too well that the man isn't altogether in control. While we weren't watching, we've become dinosaurs again. And cars are just the beginning of it. There are trucks and trains and planes and hydrogen bombs — the proportion of brains to brawn has sunk terribly low, and it is going down fast. And this time if we have an extinction it will be a do-it-yourself extinction. And this time there is no other creature to take over.

Mammals brought another thing into life on earth, infinitely precious. Mammals take care of their young. Dinosaurs laid their eggs and left them. That was the way it was with all the previous creatures: the fishes, the amphibia, the reptiles. Not mammals. Mammals carry their young inside them, and after they have given birth to them they nurse them for months more (that is where the word "mammal" comes from, the nursing); and after that they watch them play in the sun, and protect them, and feed them, and teach them the ways of life.

That is another of our problems. We are no longer taking good care of our young. We have introduced them into a world that offers them little that they want and threatens their very existence. We have become dinosaurs again, and that is our problem.

So what are we to do? Please realize where we are, because whatever we do now we have to try somehow to do as men and not as dinosaurs. The temptation is great to do those things as dinosaurs. That is true every way one turns now. There are traps besetting us now in every-thing we try to do.

Take the population problem, for example. We are being told from some quarters that the attempt to control population is an attempt to commit genocide, an attempt on the part of the well-to-do to limit the numbers of the poor, an attempt on the part of the well-to-do nations to limit the numbers in the underdeveloped nations. Yet the only hope of the poor and of the underdeveloped nations is to limit population.

So what is wrong? One has to couple that attempt to limit population with a genuine and effective taking care of all the people there are. To do the one without the other would be conscienceless. We need to limit population, but we need meanwhile to take care of people better than we do now, and most of all we need to take care of children, all children everywhere, very much better than we are doing.

So I have almost done, because it is that way with the pollution prob-lem, too. That, too, is beset with such traps, two of them rather obvious. One trap is to try to make of pollution, of our new concern with the environment, an issue that will distract people, mainly young people, from all the other problems that now properly concern them. The second trap is to turn pollution into a new dinosaur, to turn pollution into the new multi-billion dollar business. The only way to deal with pollution that really would mean anything is to stop it at its source; but that is difficult, and very strongly opposed by some powerful forces. The temptation is great to let the pollution go right on, but to superimpose on it a new multi-billion dollar business of anti-pollution; and in these days of conglomerates it would be the same business: one division would pollute, the other division would clean up; and both would make a lot of money.

So here we are at the crossroads. We have to make hard choices. We have not only to try to do, but to succeed in doing those fantastically difficult things, so difficult that if there were any alternative we would be well advised to avoid them. But there is no alternative. Those are the things that *must* be done, for us, and much more for our children. For it is they who must inherit a good earth, a decent place in which they can live their lives — they and their children, and their children's children.